Saint Michael the Archangel in Medieval English Legend

Richard F. Johnson

THE BOYDELL PRESS

First published 2005
The Boydell Press, Woodbridge

ISBN 1 84383 128 7

The Boydell Press is an imprint of Boydell & Brewer Ltd
PO Box 9, Woodbridge, Suffolk IP12 3DF, UK
and of Boydell & Brewer Inc.
668 Mt Hope Avenue, Rochester, NY 14620, USA
website: www.boydellandbrewer.com

A CIP catalogue record for this book is available
from the British Library

Library of Congress Cataloging-in-Publication Data
Johnson, Richard F. (Richard Freeman), 1961–
  Saint Michael the Archangel in medieval English legend / Richard F. Johnson.
    p. cm.
  Summary: "A study of the representations of St. Michael in the liturgy,
literature, and iconography of the period" – Provided by publisher.
  Includes bibliographical references and index.
  ISBN 1–84383–128–7 (alk. paper)
    1. Michael (Archangel) – Cult – England – History – To 1500.   2. England –
Religious life and customs.   3. Michael (Archangel) – Legends – History and
criticism.   4. Legends, Christian – England – History and criticism.   I. Title.
  BT968.M5J64 2005
  235'.3 – dc22   2004025427

This publication is printed on acid-free paper

Typeset by Pru Harrison, Hacheston, Suffolk
Printed in Great Britain by
Athenaeum Press Ltd., Gateshead, Tyne & Wear

Saint Michael the Archangel in Medieval English Legend

Although there exists a vast body of scholarly work on St Michael the Archangel, this book is the first comprehensive study of the genesis and diffusion of the legends of the archangel in medieval England. Part I of this study identifies and analyzes the concerns, conflicts, and roles with which St Michael is associated from scriptural and apocryphal literature through the homiletic literature of the medieval period. Part II begins with a discussion of the vernacular recensions of the popular account of the archangel's earthly interventions (BHL 5948). A close examination of the legendary accounts in Old English, Anglo-Norman, and Middle English of the archangel in his roles as guardian, intercessor, psychopomp, and warrior-angel follows. The Appendices contain the first English translation of the archangel's hagiographic foundation-myth (BHL 5948); an annotated bibliographic list and motif index of textual materials relating to the archangel; and an essay on the iconographic representations of the archangel in medieval England.

DR RICHARD F. JOHNSON is Assistant Professor of English at William Rainey Harper College. He is also Chair of the Humanities Department and Co-Coordinator of International Studies and Programs at the college.

Contents

Tables

For Silas, Ellie, Nate, and Blair

Acknowledgements

This work began some ten years ago as research toward the preparation of my doctoral dissertation. During that time and since, I have received much help from many quarters. The members of my dissertation committee, Professor Catherine A. Regan, Professor Barbara Newman, Professor William D. Paden, Jr., and Professor Thomas N. Hall, each deserve my hardy thanks for their steady guidance during those long years. I would especially like to honor the memory of my friend and advisor Professor Phillip Pulsiano. I must also extend a measure of personal gratitude to Professor Thomas Hall, Professor Charles D. Wright, Professor Raymond J. S. Grant, Dr. Christine Rauer, Dr. John Damon, and Dr. Timothy Graham for their enduring friendship and encouragement in my work. I wish to thank especially Professor Gordon Whatley for his unfailing encouragement of my work and his generous help on the translation of St. Michael's hagiographic dossier (*BHL* 5948) which appears as Appendix A. For permission to reprint the Monumenta Germaniae Historica edition of the "De apparitione Sancti Michaelis" by G. Waitz in Appendix A, I thank Wolfram Setz. For help over the years in resolving issues major and minor, I also thank Professor Sarah Keefer, the late Professor J. E. Cross, Professor Zbigniew Izydorczyk, Professor Thomas Head, Professor R. I. Page, Dr. Thomas Tipton, Dr. David Johnson, Dr. Mildred Budny, and Dr. John C. Arnold. And for her divine patience and genuine sympathy, I wholeheartedly thank Caroline Palmer, Commissioning Editor, Boydell & Brewer.

I would be remiss if I did not acknowledge my esteemed colleagues and co-chairs of the English Department at William Rainey Harper College, Kurt Neumann and Seema Kurup (and most recently Catherine Restovich), for creating a departmental environment conducive of this sort of scholarly endeavor and for their supreme indulgence of my scheduling needs. I would also like to thank Timothy Philbin of the Interlibrary Loan Department of Harper College for his uncanny and indefatigable skills at procuring many of the works I consulted, and William Pankey, Coordinator of Library Technologies, for his comments on and enthusiasm for my work on St. Michael. I should also thank my Honors students at Harper College for patiently and uncomplainingly reading portions of Part I of this work; your comments have made this text marginally more readable. And thanks to Patti, Janet, Diana, Judy, and even Keith for putting up with me and this obsession.

Finally, I owe the deepest debt to my wife Blair and our children, Silas, Elspeth, and Nathaniel, who have suffered patiently the demands this project has made on my time and energy. In some small measure of recompense, I dedicate this book to them.

Naturally these acknowledgements of gratitude and debt involve no reciprocal complicity in whatever errors or infelicities remain in the text. I alone assume the responsibility for any such indiscretions.

Harper College   R.F.J.
Feast of St. Michael the Archangel
29 September 2004

Abbreviations

AASS	[Bollandists] *Acta Sanctorum* (Brussels, 1643–)
AB	*Analecta Bollandiana*
AOT	H. F. D. Sparks, *The Apocryphal Old Testament*
APOT	R. H. Charles, *Apocrypha and Pseudepigrapha of the Old Testament*, 2 vols. [cited by volume and page]
ASE	*Anglo-Saxon England*
ASMMF	Phillip Pulsiano *et al.*, eds., *Anglo-Saxon Manuscripts in Microfiche Facsimile* (Binghamton, NY, 1994–) [cited by volume]
BHG	[Bollandists] *Bibliotheca Hagiographica Graeca*
BHL	[Bollandists] *Bibliotheca Hagiographica Latina, antiquae et mediae aetatis*, 2 vols. (Brussels, 1899–1901), with supplement by Henryk Fros (1986) [cited by number]
BHO	*Bibliotheca Hagiographica Orientalis*
BL	British Library
BM	Bibliothèque Municipale
BN	Bibliothèque Nationale de France (Paris)
CCCC	Cambridge, Corpus Christi College
CCSL	Corpus Christianorum, Series Latina
CSASE	Cambridge Studies in Anglo-Saxon England
Culte	O. Dobiache-Rojdestvensky, *Le Culte de Saint Michel et le Moyen Age Latin* (Paris, 1922)
EEMF	Early English Manuscripts in Facsimile (Copenhagen)
EETS	Early English Texts Society
ES	Extra Series
OS	Original Series
SS	Supplementary Series
Elliott, ANT	J. K. Elliott, *The Apocryphal New Testament*
HBS	Henry Bradshaw Society [cited by volume]
HE	Bede, *Historia Ecclesiastica*, ed. and trans. Colgrave and Mynors [cited by book and chapter]
James, ANT	M. R. James, *The Apocryphal New Testament*
JBL	*Journal of Biblical Literature*
JTS	*Journal of Theological Studies*
MÆ	*Medium Ævum*
MGH	*Monumenta Germaniae Historica*
SRL	*Scriptores Rerum Langobardicarum et Italicarum*
SRM	*Scriptores Rerum Merovingicarum*
MSM	J. Laporte *et al.*, eds., *Millénaire Monastique du Mont Saint-Michel*, 6 vols. [cited by volume and page]

N&Q   *Notes and Queries*
OTP   James H. Charlesworth, ed., *The Old Testament Pseudepigrapha*, 2 vols.
               [cited by volume and page]
PBA   *Proceedings of the British Academy*
PG   *Patrologia Graeca*
PL   *Patrologia Latina*
PMLA   *Proceedings of the Modern Language Association*
PO   *Patrologia Orientalis*
PRIA   *Proceedings of the Royal Irish Academy*
RB   *Revue Bénédictine*
RBMA   F. Stegmüller, ed., *Repertorium Biblicum Medii Aevi*, 11 vols. (Madrid,
               1950–) [cited by number]
RC   *Revue Celtique*
SASLC   *Sources of Anglo-Saxon Literary Culture*, Volume 1: *Abbo of Fleury, Abbo of
               Saint-Germain-des-Prés, and Acta Sanctorum*, ed. Frederick Biggs, Thomas
               D. Hill, Paul E. Szarmach, and E. Gordon Whatley (Kalamazoo, MI,
               2001)
SASLC: Trial   *Sources of Anglo-Saxon Literary Culture: A Trial Version*, ed. Frederick
               Biggs, Thomas D. Hill, and Paul E. Szarmach (Binghamton, 1990)
SPCK   Society for the Promotion of Christian Knowledge
SVTP   Studia in Veteris Testamenti Pseudepigrapha

Introduction

The cult and legends of St. Michael were widespread in the British Isles during the Middle Ages.[1] Veronica Ortenberg has suggested that the archangel "was probably the most popular of the great saints in England after St. Peter,"[2] while Owen Chadwick has remarked that in Wales St. Michael was second in popularity only to the Virgin Mary.[3] There is abundant textual and physical evidence that the cult of the archangel flourished in Ireland and Scotland as well.[4] Although the evidence of pre-Conquest church dedications is scant,[5] by the Reformation churches dedicated to the archangel in England alone numbered 611.[6] Thus, it is clear that by the end of the Middle Ages there was a well-developed insular cult of St. Michael. Despite this wealth of evidence, there has never been a detailed examination of the establishment of the cult of and the proliferation of the legends of St. Michael in medieval England.[7]

There have, however, been numerous book-length studies of the archangel and various aspects of the development of his cult, and Part I of this book is indebted to that body of work. In the late nineteenth century, E. Gothein argued in his ethnographic

---

1 For a detailed overview of Michael as saint and archangel, see Maria Grazia Mara, "Michele," in *Bibliotheca Sanctorum*, 12 vols. and index (Rome, 1961–70): 9, 410–46. See also my doctoral dissertation, "The Cult of Saint Michael the Archangel in Anglo-Saxon England" (Northwestern University, 1998). An excellent resource for the study of St. Michael is the six-volume series *MSM*. The third volume of this series is devoted entirely to the cult of the archangel, *Culte de Saint Michel et Pèlerinages au Mont*, ed. M. Baudot (Paris, 1971). Another general resource is the work of O. A. Dobias Rozdestvenskaia (Olga Dobiache-Rojdestvensky), *Kult sv. Michaila v latinskom Srednovekovi* (Petrograd, 1917). Unfortunately the work is only accessible to non-Russian readers in a poorly abridged French translation, *Culte*. Other studies of St. Michael are discussed in the course of this Introduction.

2 *The English Church and the Continent in the 10th and 11th Centuries* (Oxford, 1992): 108. For a general introduction to the cult in England, see H. P. R. Finberg, "The Archangel Michael in Britain," in *MSM*, 3, 459–69 and *Culte*, 18–28.

3 "The Evidence of Dedications in the Early History of the Welsh Church," in *Studies in Early British History*, ed. H. M. Chadwick *et al.* (Cambridge, 1959): 177.

4 For a general introduction to the cult of St. Michael in Ireland and Scotland, see Helen Roe, "Ireland and the Archangel Michael," and Monsignor David McRoberts, "The Cult of St. Michael in Scotland," in *MSM*, 3, 481–86 and 471–79 respectively.

5 W. Levison lists only three churches dedicated to the archangel before the ninth century (*England and the Continent in the Eighth Century* [Oxford, 1946]: 263).

6 Frances Arnold-Foster, *Studies in Church Dedications or England's Patron Saints*, vol. 3 (London, 1899): Appendix 1, 21.

7 Although Dorothy Rushing treats many of the legends of St. Michael in Old English in her dissertation, "The St. Michael Legends in Anglo-Saxon and Middle English" (University of Illinois-Urbana, 1949), she makes no attempt either to analyze the texts or to discuss the establishment, characteristics, and extent of the cult in early medieval England. For a brief description of this dissertation, see Phillip Pulsiano, *An Annotated Bibliography of North American Doctoral Dissertations on Old English Language and Literature* (East Lansing, MI, 1988): 22–23 (number 75). My doctoral dissertation, "The Cult of St. Michael the Archangel in Anglo-Saxon England" (Northwestern University, 1998), analyzes the development of and measures the extent of the archangel's cult in Anglo-Saxon England.

study of the archangel in German-speaking territories that St. Michael replaced the war-god Thor in the religious pantheon of the primitive Germans.[8] A few years later, the British Egyptologist E. A. W. Budge made available for the first time valuable information on the cult of the archangel in northern Africa in an edition and translation of several Coptic homilies on St. Michael.[9] In the last few years of the nineteenth century, Wilhelm Leuken first discussed the popular roots of devotion to the archangel in Judaism and early eastern Christian traditions.[10] And only a few years after Leuken, in the early decades of the twentieth century, the Russian historian Olga Dobias Rozdestvenskaia (Olga Dobiache-Rojdestvensky) published an analysis of the cult of St. Michael in the Latin Middle Ages.[11]

Over the past half-century, important works on Michaeline religious sites and iconography have continued to appear. Among these perhaps the most significant for a study of the development of the archangel's cult in the West have been the works of Wolfgang von Rinteln,[12] who first studied the cult of St. Michael in southern Italy, and J. P. Rohland,[13] who studied the representation of St. Michael as a healing figure in the biblical and extrabiblical literature of the second century BCE through the sixth century CE. The celebration of the millenary of the establishment of the Benedictine abbey of Mont-Saint-Michel witnessed the publication of a massive six-volume collection of essays devoted to various aspects of the archangel and his monastery.[14]

In recent decades, continental studies of St. Michael have been dominated by two Italian scholars, Carlo Carletti and Giorgio Otranto. Individually these two scholars have authored a number of articles relevant to the study of St. Michael and his cult in Italy.[15] Together they have edited several collections of essays on the archangel,[16] which have included articles on such topics as the archeology of the earliest western cultic site on the summit of Monte Gargano (Monte Sant'Angelo) on the southeastern coast of Italy,[17] the graffiti and runic inscriptions found on the walls of the grotto chapel at Gargano,[18] and the manuscript tradition of the Garganic foundation-myth (*BHL* 5948).[19]

[8] *Die Kulturenwicklung Süd-Italiens in Einzel-Darstellungen* (Breslau, 1886).
[9] *Saint Michael the Archangel: Three Encomiums* (London, 1894).
[10] *Michael: eine Darstellung und Vergleichung der judischen und der morgenländisch-christlichen Tradition von Erzengel Michael* (Göttingen, 1898).
[11] See note 1 above.
[12] *Kultgeographische Studien in der Italia byzantine*, Archiv für vergleichende Kulturwissenschaft 3 (Meisenheim am Glan, 1968).
[13] *Der Erzengel Michael. Arzt und Feldherr. Zwei Aspekte des vor- und frühbyzantinischen Michaelskultes* (Leiden, 1977).
[14] See note 1 above.
[15] For a full list of their respective articles, see the Bibliography at the end of this volume.
[16] See especially *Il Santuario di S. Michele sul Gargano dal VI al IX Secolo*, Contributo alla storia della Langobardia meridionale (Bari, 1980) and *Culto e Insediamenti Micaelici nell'Italia meridionale fra tarda antichità e medioevo* (Bari, 1994).
[17] Antonio Renzulli, "La construzione dell'ingresso monumentale longobardo e la modificazione di luoghi dell'*Apparitio*," and Marco Trotta, "I luoghi del 'Liber de Apparitione.' Il santuario di S. Michele dal V all'VIII secolo," in *Culto e Insediamenti*, 125–66 and 167–72 respectively.
[18] Antonio Quacquarelli, "Gli apocrifi nei riflessi di un graffito del Calvario e il 'Liber de Apparitione'," and Carlo Alberto Mastrelli, "Le iscrizioni runiche," in *Il Santuario di S. Michele*, 209–39 and 321–32 respectively; and Maria Giovanna Arcamore, "Una nuova iscrizione runica da Monte Sant'Angelo," in *Culto e Insediamenti*, 185–89.
[19] Vito Sivo, "Ricerche sulla tradizione manoscritta e sul testo dell'*Apparitio* latina," in *Culto e*

In North America, the recent work of three scholars merits attention. The doctoral dissertation of John Charles Arnold traces the diffusion of the archangel's cult in the West. Arnold's recent work has focused on the liturgical landscape of the Garganic site.[20] The art historian Glenn Peers has published a body of work on St. Michael, focusing on eastern representations of and devotional practices to the archangel.[21] And most recently, the work of Katherine Smith on Mont-Saint-Michel and its hagiographical corpus promises to yield interesting results.[22]

And yet, although there exists this vast body of work on St. Michael, there has never been a detailed analysis of the legends of St. Michael in medieval England, aside from one article in the Mont-Saint-Michel millenary volume mentioned above and a dissertation over fifty years ago.[23] The present volume focuses on the establishment and diffusion of the legends of St. Michael, archangel of the Lord and commander of the heavenly host, in medieval England.[24] The term "legend" (derived from the Latin *legenda*, meaning "things to be read") was first used by the early church to denote any work of edification, but particularly the accounts of the lives of the saints, which were often read as part of the liturgy. In the view of H. Delehaye, many of the legends of the saints reduced historical characters and events to a body of "types" or patterns and thus represented a Christian folklore which appealed particularly to the general public.[25] More recently, scholars such as Peter Brown, André Vauchez, Benedicta Ward, Thomas Heffernan, and Sherry Reames have demonstrated the far more complex historical interplay between the life of the church (both locally and universally), the diverse needs and expectations of the community of faith, the continually evolving constraints of the genre itself, and the imaginative skill of the "author(s)" in the production of the

Insediamenti, 95–106. The hagiographic text of the foundation myth, known as "De apparitione Sancti Michaelis," is listed under the rubric *Michael archangelus* (number 5948) in *BHL*: 868. The text is printed as "De apparitione Sancti Michaelis in Monte Gargano" in *MGH SRL*, ed. G. Waitz (Hanover, 1878): 541–43; and as "Apparitio S. Michaelis in Monte Gargano" in the Bollandists' *AASS*, Septembris VIII (Antwerp, 1643): 61–62.

20 "Ego sum Michael: The Origin and Diffusion of the Christian Cult of St. Michael the Archangel" (unpublished Ph.D. dissertation, University of Arkansas-Fayetteville, 1997) and "Arcadia becomes Jerusalem: Angelic Caverns and Shrine Conversion at Monte Gargano," *Speculum* 75 (2000): 567–88.

21 "Holy Man, Supplicant, and Donor: On Representations of the Miracle of Michael the Archangel at Chonae," *Mediaeval Studies* 59 (1997): 173–82, and "Hagiographic Models of Worship of Images of Angels," *Byzantion* 67 (1997): 407–40. See also his book, *Subtle Bodies: Representing Angels in Byzantium* (Berkeley, 2001).

22 Smith's work examines the archangel's hagiographic dossier from Mont-Saint-Michel. She has delivered two papers at the International Congress on Medieval Studies at Western Michigan University in sessions sponsored by PINNATUS The Society for the Study of Angelology: "The Dragon-Slayer and the Bishop: The Cult of St. Aubert at Mont-Saint-Michel" in May 2002, and "Mary or Michael? Saint-Switching, Gender, and Physicality in a Miracle Text from Mont-Saint-Michel" in May 2003.

23 See notes 2 and 7 above, respectively.

24 By the term "medieval," I denote three distinct periods of English history: the Anglo-Saxon, Anglo-Norman, and late medieval periods. Rather than assign inevitably contestable dates to these periods, I have chosen to organize my discussion of the texts from these periods according to the language groups associated with each period, namely Old English, Anglo-Norman, and Middle English.

25 See especially Delehaye's seminal work *Les légendes hagiographiques*, translated by Donald Atwater as *The Legends of the Saints* (New York, 1962).

legends of the saints. It is with this intricate interpretive matrix in mind that I use the term "legend" to refer to the full range of narratives about St. Michael.

As an asomatic being who does not participate in the earthly and temporal reality of humans, the archangel possesses a hagiographic dossier which is necessarily different than those of other saints. For example, the material relics which fed the cults of most medieval saints could not exist for St. Michael, though several monastic foundations, most notably Mont-Saint-Michel, claimed to possess the archangel's shield and sword. The source of the archangel's appeal, therefore, lay less in the efficacy of any alleged relics than in the graphic descriptions of his roles at the moment of death and at the end of time found in his legends. St. Michael is provided with a hagiographic *vita*-of-sorts in the Garganic foundation-myth, "De apparitione Sancti Michaelis" (*BHL* 5948) and the text fulfills the functions of what Thomas Heffernan calls "sacred biography."[26] In Heffernan's functional paradigm, the "De apparitione" text first establishes the worthiness of St. Michael for veneration by documenting his interventions on behalf of the Sipontans and his foundation of the grotto-chapel at Monte Gargano and then becomes the principal vehicle of the further diffusion of the archangel's cult.

Indeed, the organization of this book is built around an analysis of the development and dissemination of the legendary motifs associated with St. Michael in his "sacred biography," the "De apparitione" text. This book is divided into two parts followed by a collection of appendices. The two chapters of Part I focus on the "Genesis and Migration of the Legends." Chapter One, "Literary Origins of the Archangel's Legendary Roles," begins with a historical survey of the biblical and extra-biblical texts which served as the principal quarry for the development of the medieval legends of St. Michael. The chapter contextualizes the ensuing discussion of the migration of the cult by grounding it in its "literary" origins. Although the archangel is only mentioned five times in scripture, these references came to define his principal functions for Christians: to battle Satan, to be the advocate of God's chosen people, to rescue the souls of the faithful from the devil, and to lead the souls of the faithful to heaven. The elaboration of these roles in the apocryphal and pseudepigraphal texts only increased the popular appeal of the archangel. Chapter One surveys the literary origins of the concerns, conflicts, and roles with which St. Michael is consistently associated from scriptural and apocryphal literature through the legendary literature of the Middle Ages.

A review of the legends and hagiographic foundation-myths of St. Michael's cultic sites follows, since it was these texts which helped establish the legends in medieval England. Chapter Two, "The Archangel's Legendary History," charts the migration of the cult from its origins in the ancient Near East to the foundation of Mont-Saint-Michel. This chapter focuses on the three cultic centers of Michaeline devotion in western Asia Minor, Monte Gargano, and Mont-Saint-Michel. Based on an examination of the hagiographical foundation-myths of these cultic centers, it demonstrates that after a series of apparitions and earthly interventions each of the three great regional powers, Constantine's empire, the Lombards, and the Carolingians,

---

[26] According to Heffernan, "Sacred biography . . . refers to a narrative texts of the *vita* of a saint written by a member of a community of belief. The texts provides a documentary witness to the process of sanctification for the community and in doing so becomes itself a part of the sacred tradition it serves to document" (*Sacred Biography*, 16). See Appendix A for the text and translation of *BHL* 5948.

appropriated St. Michael, commander of the heavenly host in battle, as the patron saint of its imperial ambition. Finally, this chapter demonstrates that the hagiographical accounts of St. Michael's legendary apparitions at the three cultic centers had a significant impact on the characterization of the archangel in the medieval English legends examined in Part II.

Taken together, then, the two chapters in Part I explore the literary origins of St. Michael's traditional roles and the historical genesis of his hagiographic dossier. The literary origins of St. Michael's medieval legendary roles can be found in the representations of the archangel in biblical and extra-biblical literature. The development of the archangel's roles in this literature as guardian, intercessor, psychopomp (conveyor of souls), and warrior-angel served as the principal quarry for medieval English writers in their representations of St. Michael.

These representations are the subject of Part II of this study and provide the organizational rationale for the second half of the book. Chapter Three, "Vernacular Versions of the Hagiographic Foundation-Myth," explores the many vernacular recensions of the popular account of the archangel's earthly interventions atop the steep cliffs of the Garganic peninsula in southeastern Italy. The sheer number of the versions suggests an abiding interest in the archangel's military prowess, his efficacy as an intercessor, and his mercy as a psychopomp. The next two chapters examine the legendary accounts of the archangel in these roles.

Chapter Four, "The Archangel as Guardian and Psychopomp," examines the vast store of early English legendary representations of St. Michael in these roles from the Venerable Bede to *Piers Plowman*. The idea that each individual has a guardian spirit watching over him was a familiar notion to the early English. It is not surprising that, given St. Michael's association with the conveyance of the soul of the Virgin Mary to paradise, the archangel should be the psychopomp of preference. As the texts in this chapter indicate, the medieval English embraced the archangel in this role. Perhaps one of St. Michael's most compelling roles, however, is that at Judgment. Chapter Five, "The Archangel and Judgment," explores the English legends of St. Michael's involvement in the individual, post-mortem judgment and the Final Judgment. As the chapters in Part II demonstrate, St. Michael is widely represented in the prose literature of the Anglo-Saxon, Anglo-Norman, and Middle English eras. In these texts, the archangel is represented performing all four of the offices assigned him by Christian tradition.

The book is completed with four appendices. Appendix A reprints and translates the Waitz edition of the archangel's hagiographic foundation myth at Monte Gargano (*BHL* 5948).[27] Appendix B, "The Michael Inventory," is an annotated bibliographical list of textual material mentioning St. Michael the archangel in his various roles in sacred history. This inventory is followed by a "Motif Index" in Appendix C. The Motif Index contains much of the same information as Appendix B but is organized according to St. Michael's roles (as opposed to the texts). Neither Appendix B nor C is comprehensive; instead, they are meant to serve as a useful source list of material on St. Michael. Appendix D is a brief guide to the extant iconographic representations of St. Michael in medieval England.

---

[27] G. Waitz, ed., "Liber de Apparitione Sancti Michaelis in Monte Gargano," *MGH SRL* (Hanover, 1878): 541–43.

Part I

Genesis and Migration of the Legends

I

Literary Origins of the Archangel's
Legendary Roles

> Hear Michael speaking! I am he who stands in the sight of God
> every hour. As the Lord lives, in whose sight I stand, I do not stop
> one day or one night praying incessantly for the human race, and I
> indeed pray for those who are on the earth; but they do not cease
> committing iniquity and fornications, and they do not do any
> good while they are placed on earth; and you have consumed in
> vanity the time in which you ought to have repented.[1]
>
> The Apocalypse of Paul (*Visio Pauli*)

St. Michael the archangel appears by name in scripture only five times: three times in
the Old Testament (Daniel 10:13, 21 and 12:1) and twice in the New Testament (Revelation 12:7–9 and the Epistle of Jude 9). Despite this relative paucity of references to the
archangel in canonical literature, there exists a vast store of legendary material from the
Middle Ages concerning the archangel's roles in the unfolding of human history. In this
chapter, I explore the literary origins of St. Michael's medieval legendary roles by
examining the representations of the archangel in biblical and extra-biblical literature.
The development of the archangel's roles in this literature as healer and guardian,
intercessor, psychopomp, and warrior-angel accounts for his popular appeal in early
medieval England. Indeed, the representations of the archangel in the literature
reviewed in this chapter can be seen as having served as the principal quarry for early
medieval English writers in their representations of St. Michael the archangel.

Many of the texts of the biblical era, though by no means all, which refer to St.
Michael fall under the genre of "apocalypse" in their form, character, and/or content.[2]
Often conveying a message of the imminent end of the world, apocalyptic literature is
fundamentally concerned with the relation between man's life, individually and

---

[1] Elliott, *ANT*, 638.

[2] For a comprehensive discussion of the genre and an exhaustive survey of all biblical and
extra-biblical texts which might be classified as "apocalypses," see the series of articles published in
Apocalypse: The Morphology of a Genre, *Semeia* 14 (1979). In his Introduction to this volume, J. J.
Collins defines "apocalypse" as "a genre of revelatory literature with a narrative framework, in
which a revelation is mediated by an otherworldly being to a human recipient, disclosing a transcen-
dent reality which is both temporal, insofar as it envisages eschatological salvation, and spatial,
insofar as it involves another, supernatural world" (9). For a slightly more recent, though not
substantially different, consideration of the issue, see *Apocalypticism in the Mediterranean World and the
Near East*, ed. David Hellholm (Tübingen, 1982).

collectively, in history and the future promise of the heavenly realm. The implicit conflict of the apocalyptic impulse is played out in what Bernard McGinn has called "the triple eschatological pattern of [present] crisis – [imminent] judgment – [future] vindication."[3] In this tripartite paradigm, it is the hope for the vindication of salvation, the transcendence of death, that provides the believer with the strength to endure the present crisis. In the context of this eschatological drama St. Michael commands a significant presence in the literature of the Old and New Testament eras.

St. Michael's roles in this drama exemplify what the biblical scholar P. G. Davis has called "a triple pattern of mediation."[4] The archangel's character operates on both the temporal and the spatial planes. On the temporal plane, the archangel bridges the gulf between the discernible history of man's life on earth and the future promise of God's eternity. As a psychopomp, he facilitates the transition from this life to the next, and as a healer and commander of the angelic host, he guarantees the physical and spiritual safety of the faithful. On the spatial plane, St. Michael serves as an intermediary between this world and the heavenly realm, conveying man's prayers before the Lord. Overlaying these two aspects of St. Michael's character, however, is the third dimension of his three-fold pattern of mediation: his extra-temporal and extra-spatial role at Judgment, both the individual judgment at death and the Final Judgment at the end of time. In the literature of the biblical era, St. Michael's popular appeal lies primarily in his ability to act as a powerful advocate before the Lord on behalf of humankind, as an ambassador-of-sorts to the heavenly court.

Although St. Michael's character and roles appear nearly fully developed in early Hebrew literature (especially 1 Enoch and Daniel), there is a significant shift of emphasis between the literatures of the Old Testament and those of the New Testament. In the biblical and extra-biblical literature of the Old Testament, St. Michael strides across the world stage in the past, present, and future. His intercessory powers span the three periods of human time, and his efficacy extends into the eternity of God's time. In the canonical books of the New Testament, however, St. Michael virtually withdraws from the stage of the present. Instead, Christ is proclaimed the sole mediator, "whose saving accomplishments . . . embrace past, present, and future," on behalf of Christians in the New Testament.[5] St. Michael's appearance in Revelation 12:7–9 underscores his withdrawal from the present, while emphasizing his dual roles in the past and future: expelling the fallen angels at the beginning of time and defeating the forces of evil at the end of time. Although the three-fold paradigm of mediation does not extend to the extra-canonical books of the New Testament era and later, I believe it will become clear that St. Michael's efficacy returns to the present in much of this literature.

Since St. Michael's persona developed in the Jewish apocalyptic tradition, there is a degree of continuity between the representations of St. Michael in the Old and New

---

3 "Early Apocalypticism: the Ongoing Debate," in *The Apocalypse in English Renaissance Thought and Literature*, eds. C. A. Patrides and Joseph Wittreich (Ithaca, New York, 1984): 9.
4 "Divine Agents, Mediators, and New Testament Christology," *JTS* n.s. 45 (1994): 479–503. Although Davis's argument refers to Christ's "triple pattern of mediation," I have adapted the concept in the following paragraphs to underscore the significance of St. Michael's roles in salvation history.
5 *Ibid.*, 488.

Testaments, especially in the extra-biblical literatures of these periods. In this literature, we will see St. Michael become increasingly distinguished from the other named
angels in a range of roles from angel prince of the Israelites to the "Angel of Righteousness" who will command the heavenly host in the final battle against evil. By charting
the development of St. Michael's roles in the canonical and non-canonical literatures of
the Old and New Testaments, this chapter documents the literary origins of the
concerns, conflicts, and roles with which St. Michael is consistently associated from
scriptural and apocryphal literature through the legendary literature of the medieval
period.

St. Michael in Judaic literature

The earliest work that provides a glimpse of the full range of St. Michael's roles is
the extra-biblical Ethiopic Book of Enoch the Prophet, or 1 Enoch (*RBMA* 78, 16).[6] It is
generally agreed that 1 Enoch is a composite of five independent books.[7] The references to St. Michael occur within the first two books, the Book of Watchers (chapters
1–36) and the Book of Parables (chapters 37–71).

The author of the Book of Watchers, which is dated to the third century BCE or
possibly earlier, introduces the text as "The words of the blessing of Enoch according to
which he blessed the chosen and righteous who must be present on the day of distress
(which is appointed) for the removal of all the wicked and impious" (1:1). The Book of
Watchers is further characterized as "a holy vision in the heavens which the angels
showed to me" (1:2). The remainder of the Book of Watchers constitutes a parable that
Enoch relates as a prophecy of coming judgment. The narrative of the Book of
Watchers is thus set in the context of a cataclysmic judgment in which God will come
with "ten thousand holy ones to execute judgment upon them and to destroy the
impious" (1:9).

In connection with the events of Judgment, St. Michael and the angels Gabriel,
Suriel, and Uriel intercede on behalf of mankind (1 Enoch 9:3–11).[8] St. Michael alone
is responsible for binding Semyaza, leader of the fallen angels, until Judgment when he
and his followers will be shut in the abyss of fire for all eternity (1 Enoch 10:11–16). St.
Michael is also charged in the Book of Watchers with the preservation and protection
of the range of seven mountains covered with precious stones and fragrant trees where
the throne of the Eternal King will be established at Judgment (24:1–6). The throne of
Judgment will be placed before the Tree of Life on the seventh mountain. St. Michael
tells Enoch that at Judgment the fruit of the Tree of Life will be given to the righteous,

---

[6] A recent edition and translation of the Ethiopic text is by Michael A. Knibb, *The Ethiopic Book of
Enoch*, 2 vols. (Oxford, 1978). I have used the translation in *AOT*, 169–319, which is based on Knibb.
The text also appears in *OTP* 1, 5–89; and Matthew Black, ed., *The Book of Enoch or 1 Enoch: A New
English Edition*, SVTP 7 (Leiden, 1985).

[7] For a discussion of the various textual traditions of 1 Enoch, see Knibb's introduction to the text
(*Ethiopic Book of Enoch*, vol. 2, 1–47).

[8] The earliest reference to the intercession of angels on behalf of mankind, however, occurs in the
Book of Zechariah (1:12–13). The book consists of two parts, chapters 1–8 and chapters 9–14. The
first part, in which the reference to the intercession of an angel occurs, has been dated with some
precision to the early reign of Darius the Great (522–485 BCE).

and by it they will gain eternal life (25:4–7).[9] St. Michael is set over this holy place to protect and preserve it until Judgment. In the Book of Watchers, then, St. Michael's roles are primarily protective and intercessory. St. Michael is set over the best part of humankind (20:5), assigned the destruction of the evil angels and their leader (10: 11–16), and charged with the care of the site of Judgment (24: 1–6).[10]

Although in this and other early apocalyptic texts St. Michael acts as one of a group of mythic heroes, his specific tasks in this text (overseeing the best part of mankind and binding Semyaza until Judgment) foreshadow the importance of his later and more singular roles as psychopomp and warrior angel. Indeed, St. Michael's roles at Judgment are greatly expanded in the Book of Parables, or Similitudes (1 Enoch 37–71).[11] Although one editor has claimed that "there is no convincing proof that it ever existed before the fifteenth century CE,"[12] most scholars agree that the Book of Parables was written much earlier (proposed dates range from the end of the first century BCE to the end of the third century CE).[13]

In the Book of Parables, St. Michael's actions as a hero on the cosmological stage are limited to his roles at Judgment. The Book of Parables consists of three parables, each of which concerns one aspect of the events at Judgment. In the first parable (chapters 38–44), Enoch is escorted to the end of heaven, where he has a vision of the "dwelling of the righteous and the resting-places of the holy" (39:4), and of the multitude which stand before the Lord (40). Surrounding the Lord stand four figures, the angels Michael, Raphael, Gabriel, and Phanuel.[14] St. Michael is designated the "merciful and long-suffering" (40:9) and his "voice blesses the Lord for ever and ever" (40:5).

The second parable (chapters 45–57) concerns "those who deny the name of the dwelling of the holy ones and of the Lord of Spirits" (45:1) and their lot on the day of Judgment. On that day, St. Michael, with his lieutenants Gabriel, Raphael, and Phanuel,[15] will throw the hosts of Azazel into the furnace of burning fire as vengeance for the iniquity they practiced on earth (54:6).

---

9   St. Michael's promise of the fruit of the Tree of Life has suggested to one critic that 1 Enoch influenced the Apocalypse of Moses, in which a similar promise occurs (Esther Casier Quinn, *The Quest of Seth for the Oil of Life* [Chicago, 1962]: 28–29).

10 St. Michael is also said to rule over humankind in two late apocrypha: the Apocalypse of Moses 32:6 (*OTP* 2, 287) and the Latin A version of Christ's Descent into Hell 19:1 (Elliott, *ANT*, 192). See also Appendix B.

11 *AOT*, 221–56.

12 *Ibid.*, 174.

13 For an overview of the debate, see D. W. Suter, "Weighed in the Balance: The Similitudes of Enoch in Recent Discussion," *Religious Studies Review* 7 (1981): 217–21. See also Sparks' discussion of this issue (174–75).

14 The earliest list of the names of seven holy angels appears in the Book of Watchers (1 Enoch 20:2–7): Uriel, Raphael, Raguel, Michael, Saragael, Gabriel, and Remiel. The fact that the lists of the principal angels in the Book of Watchers and the Book of Parables differ underscores the separate authorship of the two works.

15 Another first century CE text which identifies four principal angels as angels of Judgment is Book 2 (lines 215–19) of the Sibylline Oracles (John J. Collins, "The Sibylline Oracles" in *OTP* 1, 350):
> Michael, Gabriel, Raphael, and Uriel,
> who know what evils anyone did previously,
> lead all the souls of men from the murky dark
> to judgment, to the tribunal of the great
> immortal God.

In the third parable (chapters 58–69), which concerns the righteous and the chosen, St. Michael reveals to Enoch that on the day of Judgment two monsters, one male, one female, will be separated from each other. In this parable, God promises Noah that St. Michael, who is in charge of the waters,[16] will be the one to judge the angels who debauched themselves with women. St. Michael explains that this judgment will serve as a testimony to kings, for the waters will "serve for the healing of the bodies of the kings, and for the lust of their bodies" (67:13). After the deluge, the waters will become the "fire which burns for ever," presumably a reference to the fire of Judgment.

In a scene which underscores the archangel's compassion and advocacy for humankind, St. Michael laments with Raphael the severity of the judgment of the fallen angels, especially as their fate is unlikely to change the ways of men already intent on evil (68). In the context of the judgment of the fallen angels, St. Michael is also said to be in charge of the secret oath of creation, Akae (69:15), which he reveals to the angel Kesbeel.[17] The Book of Parables closes with St. Michael showing Enoch "all the secrets of mercy and the secrets of righteousness" (71:3). It is with the knowledge of these secrets and many others that Enoch comes to be called the "Son of Man."

It is clear that the author of the Book of Parables was familiar with the earlier Enoch books, principally the Book of Watchers. Although St. Michael's roles are similar in character (he is charged with the removal of the leader of the evil angels in both), in the Parables St. Michael's stature is second only to that of Enoch, the Son of Man. In these Parables, the Son of Man is the primary figure of divine consolation for the audience of this text. His authority guarantees the righteous safe passage through the trials of judgment, which are imposed by St. Michael and his fellow angels. Although the two judgments Enoch views in the second and third parable are past (of the fallen angels) and future (at the end of time) respectively, the revealed knowledge of their place and function entails a profound significance for the present. Just as these visions of judgment and the secrets of mercy and righteousness prepare Enoch for his transformation into the Son of Man, the narrative assures the righteous reader of his destiny in the heavenly realm. Unlike the general judgment of humanity in the Book of Watchers, the judgment of the Book of Parables is more individual. Although the term "righteous" in the Book of Parables could refer to a community, as it clearly does in the Book of Watchers, its overtones of moral selectivity suggest an individual judgment. St. Michael's role in this paradigm of individual judgment is two-fold. He serves as the agent of both revealed knowledge and judgment, functioning on both the temporal and spatial axes of the apocalyptic narrative. Furthermore, by revealing the secrets of mercy and righteousness, St. Michael mitigates the audience's fear of individual judgment.

In Judaic literature, the next significant development in St. Michael's persona occurs

---

[16] In the early Christian church of Egypt and the countries along the Nile, St. Michael was often invoked to ensure the regular occurrence of natural phenomena, in particular those associated with water. There are early prayers to St. Michael beseeching him to guarantee rainfall and the flooding of the Nile. For homiletic references to St. Michael's association with water, see the "Mysteries of St. John the Apostle and Virgin," in E. A. W. Budge, *Coptic Apocrypha in the Dialect of Upper Egypt* (London, 1913): 233–57; and the "Encomium by Eustathius, Bishop of Trake," in E. A. W. Budge, *Saint Michael the Archangel: Three Encomiums* (London, 1894): 74*–108*.

[17] For a brief discussion of this oath, see M. E. Stone, "Lists of Revealed Things in the Apocalyptic Literature," in *Magnalia Dei: The Mighty Acts of God*, eds. F. M. Cross, Werner E. Lemke, and Patrick D. Miller, Jr. (Garden City, NY, 1976): 414–52 at 429.

in the apocalyptic narrative of the second half of the book of Daniel (7–12) and in his role as the "guardian angel" of the Jews.[18] The only canonical book of the Hebrew Bible to mention the archangel and the sole example of apocalyptic literature in the Hebrew Bible, Daniel is written partly in Hebrew and partly in Aramaic.[19] Although many attempts have been made to explain the composite structure of Daniel, the essential unity of the work has been generally accepted. The work falls neatly into two parts: chapters 1–6 and chapters 7–12. In the first part, the court tales, the figure of Daniel is introduced as a young Jew exiled to the court of the Babylonian King Nebuchadnezzar. In contrast to the court tales, the narrative of the second section is primarily in the first person and is apocalyptic in tone. The narrative of the second half falls into four units and includes revelations to Daniel, a legendary figure of the past associated with wisdom in Ezekiel 28:3 and righteousness in Ezekiel 14:13–14 and 19–20; three visions (Daniel 7, 8, and 10–12) which are each interpreted by an angel; and a prophetic prayer (Daniel 9). All three references to St. Michael the archangel occur in the context of Daniel's third vision (chapters 10–12) and depict him as the principal guardian angel of the Israelites.

This third vision fits neatly into the three-part eschatological pattern of present crisis, imminent judgment, and future vindication. In this vision, an angel in the likeness of a man appears to Daniel[20] and tells him that although he has been fighting with the protecting angel of the Persian empire, he has with the aid of St. Michael been able to free himself for a short time to reveal to Daniel the fate of the Israelites (Daniel 10:13–14, 21):

> 13 However, the prince of the Persian kingdom opposed me for twenty-one days; now Michael has come to my aid, after I was detained there with the kings of Persia.
> 14 So I have come to make you understand what is to befall your people in the days to come, for there is yet a vision for those days. . . .
> 21 No one is helping me against them except your prince, Michael. However, I will tell you what is recorded in the book of truth.

Set in the context of this prophecy (10:14 and 21), chapter 11 narrates the account of the angel's revelation to Daniel. The revelation comprises an account of the history and fate of the Seleucid empire, recounted in terms of an *ex eventu* prophecy, up to the death of Antiochus IV Epiphanes (163 BCE).[21] Antiochus's persecution of the Jews

---

18 For a different perspective on St. Michael in the Book of Daniel than what follows, see Lewis O. Anderson, "The Michael Figure in the Book of Daniel" (unpublished Th.D. thesis, Andrews University, 1997).

19 The literature on Daniel as an apocalypse is vast. For a treatment of Daniel within the apocalyptic paradigm described above, see John J. Collins, "The Jewish Apocalypses," *Semeia* 14 (1979): 30–31. Two other excellent commentaries and studies are John J. Collins, *The Apocalyptic Vision of the Book of Daniel* (Missoula, MT, 1977), and André Lacocque, *The Book of Daniel* (Atlanta, 1979).

20 It is possible that this angel is Gabriel, who appeared to Daniel earlier in the form of a man and helped him interpret his first two visions (Daniel 8:15–26 and 9:20–27).

21 Although the stories of Daniel in the Babylonian court and his apocalyptic visions are set in the Babylonian and Persian periods (sixth to fourth centuries BCE), the Book of Daniel is thought to have been written, or at least compiled in its final form, at a later date. As the circumstances of Antiochus's death are incorrectly "prophesied," it has generally been accepted that the book was written before his death, probably around 164 BCE, at the height of his persecution of the Jews (167–163 BCE). In the context of *ex eventu* prophecy such backdating served to augment the authority of the revelation and its disguised historical prophecy.

(11:36–44) is represented as the present crisis which the faithful must endure to achieve final vindication. The person of Antiochus is depicted as an eschatological enemy, the prophecy of whose death introduces the themes of coming judgment and final vindication.

Chapter 12 sets the events of the present persecution and crisis in the context of a larger war between the forces of God and the powers of evil. In the apocalyptic time of distress following the death of the final tyrant, the angel tells Daniel, St. Michael will assist his people.

> 1 At that time, the great prince, Michael, who stands beside the sons of your people, will appear. It will be a time of trouble, the like of which has never been since the nation came into being. At that time, your people will be rescued, all who are found inscribed in the book.

In this apocalyptic vision of judgment and destruction, the dead will rise to meet their final fate and the wise men will shine as radiantly as the sky. Thus, according to the revelation, the final reward of the faithful for enduring the persecution will be resurrection and the ultimate defeat of death.

It should not be surprising that St. Michael, the great prince, appears as a significant player in this tripartite drama of doom and judgment. St. Michael's roles in this drama, however, are more sharply focused than in 1 Enoch. In that text, St. Michael was set over the best part of mankind and watched over the site of Judgment. In Daniel, the archangel's guardianship centers on a specific people, the Jews, among whom he is considered a "great prince." No longer is he solely the curator of the site of Judgment; at Judgment St. Michael will effect a resurrection of all the people "who are found inscribed in the book" (12:1). Thus, in Daniel, the future vindication of the promise of resurrection by the hand of St. Michael is intended to fortify the text's immediate audience in its present trial, namely, the persecutions of Antiochus IV Epiphanes. The forces of evil will be overcome by the forces of good, among whose ranks the St. Michael the archangel stands as a powerful martial hero.

Although singled out as a mythic hero who will raise the dead at the end of time, in the middle of the second century BCE St. Michael is first and foremost represented as a guardian angel, a protecting angel associated with a specific people, the Jews (Daniel 10:13 and 12:1).[22] The notion of angels as guardians, though not as permanent companions, seems to have arisen out of their larger role as the emissaries of Yahweh. On many occasions in the Old Testament, Yahweh intervenes in human history

---

[22] The doctrine of "guardian angels" arose out of the development of Israelite angelology in the Post-Exilic period (post-538 BCE). After the Babylonian exile, Jewish angelology developed rapidly into an elaborate system of belief. The triumph of monotheism translated into the increasing tendency to describe the transcendence of Yahweh. All divine commerce with this world was consigned to supernatural agents acting on Yahweh's behalf. These developments naturally led to the multiplication of the ranks of angels, the class of beings responsible for this commerce. At this stage, angels were charged with all manner of duties: maintaining the proper order and function of the natural world; undertaking specific missions as messengers; keeping a strict record of human activity; and ensuring the protection of nations and, ultimately, individuals. For a detailed discussion of the various forms and stages of the development of Hebrew angelology, see the article under the entry "Angels and Angelology" in the *Encyclopedia Judaica*, vol. 1 (New York, 1971): cols. 957–77.

through the ministry of angels.[23] In each instance, however, the angel of the Lord is not a permanent guardian. The angel disappears after he has accomplished the specific mission upon which the Lord sent him. It is not until the Book of Daniel that the development of the notion of a lasting relationship between an angel and his charge, whether a nation or an individual, seems to have appeared (aside from two references in Psalms 30:8 and 91:11 where an angel of the Lord is said to watch over those who fear Him). The designation of St. Michael as a "great prince" of the Israelites in Daniel 12:1 suggests a permanent relationship.[24]

The nature of the permanent relationship between St. Michael and the Israelites is made explicit in the cosmology of the War Scroll, a unique text found among the scrolls in the Qumran caves. Although the War Scroll was not known to medieval writers, it is important in the development of St. Michael's legendary character because it depicts his elevation to the stature of a cosmic hero. The War Scroll narrates the cosmic conflict between the forces of the Sons of Light, under the command of St. Michael, and the forces of the Sons of Darkness, led by Belial.[25] Although there is some debate as to the dating of various segments of the narrative of the War Scroll, most scholars agree that the conception of the battle between the forces of Light and Darkness has affinities with the eschatological reviews of history in Daniel and 1 Enoch (partial copies of which were also found in the Qumran caves), and therefore can be dated with some certainty to the second century BCE.[26]

Despite its affinity with Daniel, however, the War Scroll differs in two significant respects.[27] In Daniel, St. Michael is a "prince" among other princes. He is associated with the people of Israel just as the other angelic princes are associated with the people of Persia and Greece. Although there is no question of his military superiority and his

---

[23] For example, Yahweh dispatches an angel to lead the Israelites from Egypt to the promised land and to destroy their enemies along the way (Exodus 23:20 and Numbers 20:16). In the time of Joshua, an angel of the Lord rebukes the nation of Israel for breaking His covenant (Judges 2:11). In II Kings 19:35, the Lord delivers the people of Israel from the threat of the Assyrians by sending an angel to strike down 185,000 of the Assyrian camp, forcing King Sennacherib to retreat.

[24] Such a permanent relationship is also hinted at in a later work, the Ascension of Isaiah. Although this work shows definite signs of Christian editing, its origins are clearly Jewish. In the Slavonic and Latin recensions of this text, St. Michael is identified as the "more glorious angel" who possesses the book of the deeds of the sons of Israel, suggesting his role as both protector and judge of the Israelites. The Slavonic text has been edited by A. N. Popov, *Opisanie rukopisei i katalog knig tserkovnoi pechati biblioteki A. I. Khludova* (Moscow, 1872): 414–19. The Latin text has been translated by R. H. Charles, *The Ascension of Isaiah* (London, 1900). A modern translation appears in *AOT*, 775–812.

[25] The text has been edited by Yigal Yadin, *The Scroll of the War of the Sons of Light against the Sons of Darkness* (Oxford, 1962).

[26] Based on an analysis of columns 2–7 of the Scroll, Yadin dates the copying of the Scroll to the "second half of the first century BCE or . . . the first half of the first century CE" (243) and the composition to sometime during the Roman period (246). Focusing his attention primarily on columns 2–9, P. R. Davies argues for a complicated history of composition and interpolation beginning in the Maccabean era and culminating in the Roman period (*1 QM, The War Scroll from Qumran* [Rome, 1977]). John J. Collins ("The Mythology of Holy War in Daniel and the War Scroll," *Vetus Testamentum* 25 [1975]: 596–612 at 610–11) and other scholars consider the framework of the cosmic battle the oldest section of the work, dating from the second century BCE (see L. Rost, "Zum Buch der Kriege der Söhne des Lichts gegen die Söhne der Finsternis," *Theologische Literaturzeitung* 80 [1955]: 206; and P. von der Osten-Sacken, *Gott und Belial* [Göttingen, 1969]).

[27] For a detailed analysis of these affinities, see John J. Collins, "The Mythology of Holy War in Daniel," *Vetus Testamentum* 25 (1975): 596–612.

final victory, St. Michael is merely a guardian, a mythic hero who fights on behalf of a chosen people. In the War Scroll, however, St. Michael is elevated to the status of a leader. No longer are there any ethnic associations with his guardianship; St. Michael is the leader and protector of all that is good. Thus, St. Michael has been promoted to supreme commander and has acquired a stature of greater cosmic scope than he had in Daniel.

The second difference is that while in Daniel there is little doubt as to the outcome of the battle between the prince of the Israelites and the prince of their enemies, in the War Scroll the forces of the Sons of Light and the Sons of Darkness seem equally matched and prevail alternately over one another. It is only when God intervenes on behalf of the Sons of Light that final victory is assured their forces. Although the certainty of the archangel's single-handed victory has diminished, the final outcome of the struggle raises the authority of St. Michael over the other angels and ensures the dominion of Israel over all other nations (17:7). Furthermore, unlike the conflict in Daniel, which is imminent, the battles of the Sons of Light and Darkness are entirely in the future. It is significant that, despite the differences in their representations of St. Michael, in each of the three texts, Daniel, 1 Enoch, and the War Scroll, St. Michael acts in the past, present, and future, a pattern which repeats itself in many Jewish texts. Thus, for the historical evolution of his character, St. Michael's elevation to the stature of a cosmic hero would resonate not only with an "apocalyptic community"[28] such as that at Qumran, but also with the authors of a vast body of literature over the next two centuries.

The final text to be considered in this survey of the evolution of St. Michael's character in Judaic literature is the Testament of Abraham (*RBMA* 84), a text written in the early Christian era, but not known in the Middle Ages.[29] In Jewish texts of the early Christian era, St. Michael becomes more closely associated with individuals as a powerful guardian and intercessor, and psychopomp.[30] This process is most fully realized in the Testament of Abraham, in which St. Michael is closely associated with the life and death of the patriarch. Although not strictly a "testament,"[31] the Testament of Abraham describes a heavenly journey in which Abraham views a scene of judgment,

---

[28] Based on an analysis of many of the texts found in the caves, F. M. Cross has characterized Qumran as a community whose eschatological expectations present an opportunity to study the communal setting of apocalyptic thought (*The Ancient Library of Qumran*, revised edition [Garden City, NY, 1961]: 76–78).

[29] *AOT*, 393–421. While there is much debate over the dating of the text (first half of the first century CE to sometime in the second century CE), most scholars agree that the text is essentially Jewish in character but reflects a degree of Christian influence. M. R. James prints two Greek recensions in *The Testament of Abraham* (Cambridge, 1892). Included in James' volume is an appendix with extracts translated from the Arabic version of the Testaments of Abraham, Isaac, and Jacob by W. E. Barnes. The text also appears with an Introduction in *OTP* 1, 871–902.

[30] For texts which specifically mention St. Michael in these roles, see Appendices B and C.

[31] Testaments are valedictory addresses by a father to his son(s) or a leader to his people, in which the speaker, facing death, typically exhorts his audience to live righteously and occasionally reveals a vision of the future. Although God instructs Abraham, through his intermediary St. Michael, to put his affairs in order, no final testament is made. Furthermore, the Testament of Abraham is not in the form of an address; the narrative is primarily in the third person. For a discussion of this genre, see especially A. B. Kolenkow, "The Genre Testament and the Testament of Abraham," in *Studies on the Testament of Abraham*, ed. G. W. E. Nickelsburg (Missoula, MT, 1976): 139–52.

and it therefore shares an affinity with the apocalypses.[32] The significance of the Testament of Abraham for a consideration of the development of St. Michael's character in Judaic literature lies in the prominence of the archangel's roles in the narrative and the centrality of the heavenly journey episode.[33]

The central feature of the Testament of Abraham is the patriarch's view of the individual judgment of the good and evil souls. Indeed, the primary purpose of the work seems to have been to describe the judgment scene. Abraham's reluctance to die provides the author the occasion to present both the tour of the earth and the scene of judgment. The author's intention is to reconcile ordinary mortals to the idea that although death is inevitable it need not be feared.[34] Good works, repentance, and compassion can mitigate the various trials of the judgment at death. The author also implies that intercessory prayer can be effective, and St. Michael's role is significant in this regard. As the synopsis of the text indicates, St. Michael's stature as a superhuman actor on the cosmic stage makes him a powerful ally in fulfilling Abraham's desire to aid the soul whose deeds are equally balanced between good and evil. The success of this intercession leads Abraham to repent his severe punishment of the sinners destroyed during his tour of the earth. The patriarch and St. Michael then implore God to restore the sinners to life, and it is done. What John J. Collins has called the "apocalyptic cure"[35] (in this text, the mitigation of the fear of death) is largely effected by means of these intercessions. Thus, St. Michael plays a significant role in the implementation of the "cure," and thereby in fulfilling the author's objective.

The author of the Testament of Abraham depicts St. Michael in a variety of functions. He is a messenger, charged with bearing the news of Abraham's death to the patriarch and his family. He is a guide, taking Abraham on his tour of the world and judgment. He is a psychopomp, charged with conveying Abraham's soul to heaven. The multiplicity of his roles in the Testament of Abraham underscores the fact that he is closely associated with Abraham and deeply concerned with his well-being.[36] The choice of St. Michael, however, is significant in another regard; it suggests that the archangel's stature as a cosmic hero capable of interceding with God and mitigating judgment was well-established in the first century CE

The Jewish apocalypses discussed above have each featured St. Michael prominently. In this literature, St. Michael has acted in the past, present, and future in three

---

[32] The heavenly journey episode (chapters 10–15 in Sparks' edition) of the Testament of Abraham has been classified as an apocalypse by John J. Collins, "The Jewish Apocalypses," *Semeia* 14 (1979): 42. See also Collins' discussion of the Testament of Abraham in his *The Apocalyptic Imagination* (New York, 1984): 201–204; and G. W. E. Nickelsburg, "Eschatology in the Testament of Abraham: A Study of the Judgment Scenes in the Two Recensions," in *Studies on the Testament of Abraham*, ed. G. W. E. Nickelsburg (Missoula, MT, 1976): 23–64.

[33] For a summary of St. Michael's roles in this text, see Appendix B. The Testament of Abraham is a text full of curious angel lore. For example, St. Michael appears to be afraid of riding a horse (2:16–19); his tears turn into precious stones (3:12); and St. Michael asks God how he as an incorporeal being is supposed to feast with Abraham (4:18–22).

[34] It is important to note, however, that the Testament of Abraham envisions an individual judgment at death and does not concern itself with a general judgment of all humanity in the future.

[35] *Apocalyptic Imagination*, 204.

[36] St. Michael's close association with Abraham is first suggested in a Late Hebrew version of the Testament of Naphtali (*APOT* 2, 361–63 at 8:4 and 9:1,5), and continued in the Testaments of Isaac and Jacob (*AOT*, 423–464). On these texts, see also Appendix B.

essential roles. The archangel is primarily a guardian angel who possesses great intercessory powers which he employs on behalf of God's faithful (Book of Watchers,
Daniel, War Scroll, Testament of Abraham). St. Michael's second important role is an
extension of his role as guardian of the faithful. As psychopomp, St. Michael protects
the souls of the faithful as he conveys them to heaven (Book of Watchers, Book of Parables, Testament of Abraham). The archangel's third role in the Jewish apocalypses
concerns the fate of humanity at judgment, both individual and general (Book of
Watchers, Book of Parables, Testament of Abraham). As St. Michael's character developed under the impulse of Jewish apocalypticism, there is a degree of continuity
between the representations of St. Michael in the literatures of the Old and New Testament. In both, St. Michael is principally a guardian and intercessor, and a psychopomp.
In the biblical and extra-biblical literature of the New Testament, however, these roles
will be greatly expanded, both in number and authority.

St. Michael in Early Christian Literature

In the canonical literature of the New Testament, St. Michael undergoes a significant transformation. Whereas in the Jewish texts St. Michael's roles in human history
unfold in the past, present, and future, his activities in the canonical literature of the
New Testament era are limited to the past and future. Although his capacity to act in
the present is usurped in the new dispensation by the resurrected Christ, St. Michael
retains his authority as the *archistrategos*, the commander-in-chief of the angelic host, in
the canonical works of the New Testament era. In this capacity, St. Michael is seen
striving valiantly in the past and the future to safeguard humankind in his appearance
in the book of Revelation 12:7–9. In other New Testament works, St. Michael's
conflicts in the past and future are understood to have an immediate significance for
the present. Thus, in many of the early Christian texts he is frequently associated with a
venerable figure of the past (such as Moses in the Epistle of Jude 9), whose ordeal
suggests a lesson or a course of action for the present. The archangel's roles in other
texts suggest an expectation of the future, as in the Shepherd of Hermas. In these texts,
he is often associated with a figure whose premonitions or visions of the future also
have an impact on the present.

The extra-canonical literature of the New Testament, however, reflects a renewed
interest in St. Michael's potential to act in the present. In the Apocalypse of Paul, for
example, St. Michael is reintroduced in his role as a powerful intercessor on behalf of
humankind, a role first developed in many Jewish apocalyptic texts. The theme of the
archangel's intercession will become a significant aspect of St. Michael's persona in the
legendary literature of the Middle Ages. Not all of the extra-canonical texts of the New
Testament in which St. Michael appears are apocalypses, however; some of the most
significant texts for the development of St. Michael's character in the literature of the
Middle Ages are those narratives associated with the life and death of the Virgin Mary.
In these Marian narratives, St. Michael is principally charged with the protection and
conveyance of Mary's soul to heaven. Of all the texts of the early Christian era (first
through sixth centuries), however, the earliest and most important for the development
of St. Michael's legendary character in the Middle Ages is the Book of Revelation, the
first Christian text in which St. Michael is restricted to acting only in the past and future.

Generally thought to have been written sometime in the last decade of the first century CE by its self-proclaimed author, John of Patmos (1:1, 4, and 9; 22:8), the Book of Revelation features a mythologized account of St. Michael's role in the expulsion from heaven of Satan and the rebellious angels (12:7–9). Although ostensibly episto-lary in form, Revelation falls within the genre of "apocalypse," and indeed is often called the "Apocalypse of John."[37] As an apocalypse, the revelation is mediated by Jesus Christ (1:12–16), and various other holy and angelic characters (e.g., 1:1; 5:5; 7:13; 10:1, 9, 11; 17:1, 7; 19:9, 21:9). Although Revelation does not contain two impor-tant features of traditional "apocalypses," pseudonymity and historical review,[38] the visions of the book fulfill the apocalyptic expectation of the three-fold drama of present crisis, imminent judgment, and future vindication.

It has long been recognized that the Book of Revelation is a composite of elements from various ancient Near Eastern "combat myths."[39] In the context of the "combat myth," Adela Yarbro Collins has pointed out the centrality of chapter 12 to the overall structure of the book of Revelation. Not only does chapter 12 introduce the second cycle of visions, but it also "makes explicit for the first time that the combat myth is the conceptual framework which underlies the book as a whole."[40] Collins argues that elements of the pattern of the combat myth, which govern the structure of each cycle of visions in the book, are present in their fullest form in chapter 12:

a. Threat (12:3–4)
b. Salvation (12:5–6)
c. Combat-Victory (12:7–9)
d. Victory Shout (12:10–12)[41]

Collins concludes that chapter 12 serves as a paradigm for the book of Revelation as a whole. St. Michael's role in the unfolding of this "combat" paradigm will be significant for the later development of his legendary roles in salvation history.

It should not be surprising that St. Michael appears in the context of the heavenly contest between the forces of good and evil described in chapter 12. In this vision, a pregnant woman, "clothed with the sun, and the moon under her feet, and on her head a crown of twelve stars" (12:1), is threatened by "a great red dragon, having seven heads, and ten horns, and on his heads seven diadems" (12:3) that "when she should be delivered, he might devour her son." (12:4).[42] The woman bears a male child, "one

---

[37] For a full discussion of the issues surrounding the designation of Revelation as an "apocalypse," see John J. Collins, "Pseudonymity, Historical Review, and the Genre of the Revelation of John," *Catholic Biblical Quarterly* 39 (1977): 329–43; Adela Yarbro Collins, "Early Christian Apocalypses," *Semeia* 14 (1979): 70–72; and David Hellholm, "The Problem of Apocalyptic Genre and the Apocalypse of John," *The Society of Biblical Literature Seminar Papers*, ed. Kent H. Richards (Missoula, MT, 1982).

[38] For a discussion of these two features, see the essays by John J. Collins and A. Y. Collins in the previous note.

[39] For a thorough discussion of these myths and their influence on Revelation, see A. Y. Collins, *The Combat Myth in the Book of Revelation* (Missoula, MT, 1976), especially chapter 2 (57–101). See also Frank M. Cross Jr., *Canaanite Myth and Hebrew Epic: Essays in the History of the Religion of Israel* (Cambridge, MA, 1973) for a consideration of specifically Canaanite manifestations of these myths.

[40] A. Y. Collins, *Combat Myth*, 231.

[41] *Ibid.*, 232.

[42] All quotations of the New Testament are from the Douay-Rheims version, *The Holy Bible translated from the Latin Vulgate* (Rockford, IL, 1989).

who was to rule all nations with an iron rod" (12:5); and he is immediately taken up to God. In fear, the woman flees into the wilderness to escape the wrath of the dragon (12:6).

In a narrative shift which Collins believes "suggests that the account of the battle in heaven (12:7–9) was originally distinct from the story of the woman and the dragon," the story of St. Michael's struggle in heaven is introduced:[43]

> 7 And there was a great battle in heaven, Michael and his angels fought with the dragon, and the dragon fought and his angels. 8 And they prevailed not, neither was their place found any more in heaven. 9 And that great dragon was cast out, that old serpent, who is called the devil, and Satan, who seduceth the whole world; and he was cast unto the earth and his angels were thrown down with him.

The narrative of the woman and the dragon continues in verses 13–17. Cast down to earth, the dragon persecutes the "woman who brought forth the man child" (12:13) but is unable to capture her. Thwarted in his efforts to kill the woman and her child, the dragon makes "war with the rest of her seed, who keep the commandments of God, and have the testimony of Jesus Christ" (12:17).

In the larger scheme of the development of St. Michael's character, the account of St. Michael's contest in heaven serves as an apocalyptic flashback. It underscores the eschatological parallels of St. Michael's struggle with Satan at the beginning of time and his battle with Antichrist at the end of time. In Revelation 12:9, the adversary of the vision is named Satan and is identified with the dragon. As Collins has pointed out, it is Satan's epithet, "he who seduceth the whole world," that links the battle between St. Michael and Satan to their primordial battle at the beginning of time.[44] The narrative of the heavenly battle in Revelation 12:7–9, however, also encompasses a future dimension. By their association with the dragon, the adversaries and their wars on the faithful of the second cycle of visions,[45] especially the early association of the beast (11:7, 13:11) with Antichrist, hint at the final eschatological battle in which St. Michael and the angelic host will defeat the forces of evil. Thus, St. Michael's authority in Revelation arises directly out of his stature as the cosmic hero *par excellence*, the military hero whose success in battle straddles time.

St. Michael's efficacy, however, is restricted to the past and the future. In the redactional commentary on the battle in heaven (12:10–12), St. Michael's victory and expulsion of the evil angels is ascribed to Christ. In the new dispensation, it is Christ alone who can act in the present on behalf of humankind. Despite the implicit circumscription of St. Michael's activities in Revelation, his mythic stature as a heavenly combatant resonates in many works of the early Christian era. The Book of Revelation is unique, however, among these texts in that St. Michael's roles in the apocalypse

---

[43] *Ibid.*, 102.

[44] *Ibid.*, 232. In the use of his Jewish source for the heavenly battle, the Christian redactor of chapter 12 found the character of St. Michael fully developed as a hero of cosmic stature. The motif of Satan's expulsion from heaven occurs commonly in many Jewish and early Christian apocalypses, and St. Michael features in several, suggesting that the account of the archangel's battle in heaven was widely known and needed little elaboration. For a description of this motif, see Appendix C.

[45] These are the beast from the sea and its war on the saints (13:1–10); the beast from the earth, the false prophet, and his war of deception on the people (13:11–18); and the persecution of the saints by the harlot (17:1–6).

encompass both the past and the future. In other texts of this period, St. Michael's roles are restricted to either the past (Epistle of Jude) or the future (the Shepherd of Hermas).

The author of the canonical Epistle of Jude describes himself as "Jude, the servant of Jesus Christ and brother of James." This "James" is possibly the brother of the Lord described as the head of the Christian community of Jerusalem (Galatians 1:19, 2:9 and 1 Corinthians 15:7). The author of the epistle, then, may be the Jude, "brother of the Lord," mentioned in Matthew 13:55 and Mark 6:3. In his epistle, Jude warns against the immoral instructions of false teachers and the licentious behavior they practice. In urging his audience to "contend earnestly for the faith once delivered to the saints" (3), Jude vividly depicts the manner in which the Lord judges the disobedient. He reminds them of the destruction of the unbelieving Israelites in the wilderness, the fate of the rebellious angels, and the annihilation of Sodom and Gomorrah. To illustrate a model of restraint worthy of emulation, Jude refers to a Jewish apocryphal tradition in which St. Michael refrains from judging Satan harshly. According to the tradition, at Moses's death Satan contends that Moses is not worthy of burial as he was a murderer.[46] Although provoked to anger by Satan's charge, St. Michael "durst not bring against him the judgment of railing speech, but said, 'The Lord rebuke thee.' " (9).[47] The tradition of St. Michael in Jewish literature as a psychopomp, charged with the care of the dead, is an extensive one.[48] The significant aspect of the Epistle of Jude for the study of St. Michael's character is that it is representative of a body of literature in which St. Michael's roles are limited to the past.

By the middle of the first century CE, it is clear that St. Michael was widely recognized as a powerful advocate for the faithful in his role as guardian and conveyor of the dead. In these early texts, however, we have seen that St. Michael's powers are eclipsed by those of the risen Christ. Associated with venerable figures of the past, specifically Moses, St. Michael's authority is primarily restricted to the past. Nonetheless, the archangel's actions imply a lesson for the present. In the context of the Epistle of Jude, Moses was worthy of the archangel's protection as he lived a moral life, one which did

---

[46] It is thought that the particular manifestation of the tradition found in the Epistle of Jude, however, is borrowed from a lost apocryphon known as "The Assumption of Moses" (M. R. James, *The Lost Apocrypha of the Old Testament* [London, 1920]: 42–51; and most recently, Johannes Tromp, *The Assumption of Moses: A Critical Edition with Commentary*, SVTP 10 [Leiden, 1993]). Although an apocryphon exists by that name, the scene of St. Michael's dispute with Satan is not found there (*AOT*, 601–16; R. H. Charles, *The Assumption of Moses*; and *APOT* 2, 409–24). Charles was of the opinion that the text known as the "Assumption of Moses" was in fact a Hebrew "Testament" of Moses, written between 7 and 29 CE, which originally circulated separately from the "Assumption" proper. A Greek version, of which only fragments survive, of the entire work appeared later in the first century CE, suggesting to Charles that the two works were ultimately joined together (*APOT* 2, 407–409). In his introduction to the "Assumption of Moses," H. F. D. Sparks points out that, in his Acts of the Council of Nicaea, Gelasius of Cyzicus attributes several quotes to an "Assumption of Moses" (*AOT*, 602). Two of the three quotes attributed to the Assumption text concern St. Michael's contention with Satan over the body of Moses. In both St. Michael explains the manner in which the world came about: " 'In the Book of the Assumption of Moses', Gelasius writes, 'Michael the archangel, disputing with the Devil, says, for from his Holy Spirit we all were created. And again he says, From God's presence went forth his Spirit, and the world came into being' " (qtd. in *AOT*, 602).

[47] Based on its use of Jewish apocryphal tradition and the nature of the errors denounced, the Epistle of Jude is generally dated to about the year 80 CE or slightly later.

[48] On St. Michael as a psychopomp in Jewish texts, see Appendix C.

not abide the false teachings of immoral teachers. In the Christian dispensation, Christ is the supreme protector of the faithful, and it is He who will secure for the faithful soul everlasting life. Other texts of the New Testament era in which St. Michael plays a role suggest an expectation of future life.

In much of the literature of the New Testament era, St. Michael's responsibility for the protection of the Israelites has been transferred to that of the Christians. Perhaps the earliest evidence of this transference is found in the Shepherd of Hermas (*RBMA* 287).[49] Immensely popular during the second, third, and fourth centuries, the Shepherd of Hermas is thought to have been written sometime during the reign of either the Emperor Hadrian (117–138 CE) or his successor Antoninus Pius (138–161 CE). In the Eighth Similitude of Book Three of the Shepherd of Hermas, the nature of sin and penitence are treated allegorically.[50] The Shepherd shows the narrator a large willow tree from which an Angel of the Lord has pruned and distributed many branches to the people standing in the shade of the tree. In the context of the allegory, the tree is the Law of the Lord and the people who are gathered in its shade are those who have heard and believed the proclamation of the Law. The Angel of the Lord is St. Michael, who governs these people as it was he who gave them the Law. The conditions of the branches represent the various degrees to which the individual bearers kept the Law. Those who kept the Law faithfully are rewarded with crowns. Those who strayed from the Law are given the opportunity to repent. The planting of the branches of the sinful and St. Michael's care of the allegorical garden represents the hope of repentance: should their branches live and bloom, they will join the blessed in the tower. Although St. Michael's direct responsibility seems mostly to extend to the faithful, by turning the sinful over to the Shepherd for instruction in penitence, he indirectly provides for the possibility of their eventual redemption.

The allegory in the Shepherd of Hermas, then, reflects the hope and fear of the eschatological crisis at the end of time. In the text, St. Michael acts with authority in the context of future events. Once again, however, his actions imply a lesson for the present: sinners repent, for the end is near, and the Lord's punishment will be dreadful. While belief in Christ in the present guarantees individual redemption, it will be St. Michael who, in the context of the events at the end of time, will fight to protect the souls of the righteous.

Thus, in the literature of the New Testament era, St. Michael's roles are principally as a guardian and powerful intercessor, and a conveyor of souls to heaven. The representation of St. Michael in these roles became the foundation upon which the development of the archangel's legendary character was built in the Middle Ages. Principal among the extra-canonical texts that are especially significant for the development of St. Michael's legendary persona in the Middle Ages are the Apocalypse of Paul, the Gospel of Nicodemus, and the group of texts associated with the Life and Death of the

---

[49] Although the title of the vision is simply "The Shepherd," I will follow convention and cite the text as "The Shepherd of Hermas." The Shepherd of Hermas is translated in volume 1 of the *Ante-Nicene Christian Library*, eds. A. Roberts and J. Donaldson (Grand Rapids, 1950–52): 319–435. More recently, the text has been translated with a commentary by Graydon F. Snyder, "The Shepherd of Hermas," in *Apostolic Fathers*, vol. 6, ed. R. M. Grant (Camden, N.J., 1968). A. Y. Collins discusses the text in the context of the genre "apocalypse" in her article, "Early Christian Apocalypse," *Semeia* 14 (1979): 63–64, 74–75.

[50] For a summary of St. Michael's role in this text, see Appendix B.

Virgin Mary. Although St. Michael's roles remain largely the same in the extra-canonical literature of the New Testament, he is no longer excluded from the realm of the present. Thus, in much of the extra-canonical literature, the significance of his actions bears directly on the present.

The Greek Apocalypse of Paul and its Latin derivative, the *Visio Sancti Pauli*, are the most important extra-canonical texts for the development of St. Michael's legendary roles in the Middle Ages (*RBMA* 275–76). In the various recensions of this text, St. Michael's authority as a powerful intercessor is reinstated. Widely known in its Latin form in the Middle Ages, the *Visio Sancti Pauli* was largely responsible for the transmission of St. Michael's legendary role as intercessor. Thought to have been written originally in Greek sometime during the late fourth or early fifth century CE,[51] recensions of the Apocalypse exist in Latin, Coptic, Syriac, Old English, and other languages. As the first versions of the work were long and often difficult to follow, many shorter recensions of the text were created. Of these shorter recensions, the fourth became the most widely known in the Middle Ages, particularly in Anglo-Saxon and late medieval England.[52] In fact one critic, Theodore Silverstein, has argued that redaction IV had a "special currency in England (perhaps even its origin there.)."[53] The narrative of the Apocalypse is an elaboration of the reference in 2 Corinthians 12:3 to Paul's being "caught up to the third heaven." In the Apocalypse, Paul witnesses the death and judgment of the righteous and the wicked, and visits Paradise and Hell. Although St. Michael figures prominently at various points of the Apocalypse, his concern for and care of Christians, especially sinful ones, is most striking in a scene in which the archangel and Paul intercede on behalf of sinners (§§ 43–44).[54]

Acknowledging his role as chief intercessor for the human race, St. Michael first reproaches the sinners for their belated remorse. Then the archangel, Paul, the sinners, and all the angels raise their voices to beseech the Lord to have pity on the sinners. Sensitive to the mercy of St. Michael and Paul, the Son of God grants their intercession. In addition to being the definitive representation of St. Michael as chief intercessor, the

---

[51] The textual history of the Apocalypse of Paul is reviewed and the long Latin text is translated in Elliott, *ANT*, 616–44. The principal works on the Latin tradition of this apocryphon are Theodore Silverstein, *Visio Sancti Pauli*, Studies and Documents 4 (London, 1935), and "The Vision of St. Paul: New Links and Patterns in the Western Tradition," *Archives d'histoire doctrinale et littéraire du moyen âge* 26 (1959): 199–248. C. Tischendorf published an early Greek version in *Apocalypses Apocryphæ* (Leipzig, 1866): 34–60, and argued for a late fourth-century date in *Theologische Studien and Kritiken* 24 (1851): 439–42. Silverstein, however, argues for a fifth-century date in "The Date of the 'Apocalypse of Paul,'" *Mediæval Studies* 24 (1962): 335–48. A. Y. Collins discusses the text in the context of the genre "apocalypse" in her article, "Early Christian Apocalypses," *Semeia* 14 (1979): 85–86.

[52] For a thorough consideration of the various traditions of this apocryphon, see M. R. James, *Apocrypha Anecdota*, vol. 1 (Cambridge, 1897): 1–42 especially 4–7; and the two works by Theodore Silverstein listed in the previous note.

[53] Theodore Silverstein, "The Vision of St. Paul," *Archives d'histoire doctrinale et littéraire du moyen âge* 26 (1959): 199–248 at 212. Charles Wright, however, argues for an Irish origin in "Some Evidence for an Irish Origin of Redaction IV of the *Visio Pauli*," *Manuscripta* 34 (1990): 34–44.

[54] For a summary of St. Michael's role in this text, see Appendix B. The Coptic Apocalypse of Paul begins with chapter 16 of the Long Latin recension and expands the narrative frequently. One such expansion concerns St. Michael. Paul is shown the Archêerousa [sic] Lake and is told that therein St. Michael washes the souls of sinners who repent their sins. The cleansed soul is then allowed to join the good souls as if he had never committed any sin (Budge, *Miscellaneous Coptic Texts in the Dialect of Upper Egypt* [London, 1915]: 1051).

Apocalypse of Paul is responsible for the transmission of some of St. Michael's lesser known roles, principally as guarantor or rain and by extension agriculture.[55]

Harking back to his primary role in 1 Enoch 20:5, St. Michael is set over all humankind as a powerful intercessor in the Latin A version of Christ's Descent into Hell.[56] Usually associated with the Gospel of Nicodemus (*RBMA* 179, 4–27), the Descent into Hell tells the story of Christ's harrowing of hell. St. Michael is featured in the Oil of Mercy exemplum, which is introduced in the narrative just after Christ has descended into Hell and John the Baptist has described Christ's baptism in the river Jordan. Adam then asks Seth to tell the story of his journey to the gates of Paradise where he sought the oil of the Tree of Mercy so that he might anoint the body of his ailing father. Seth describes how he arrived at the gates and began praying that the Lord might pity him and his father. St. Michael appeared to him, and said, "I am sent to you by the Lord for I am set over the human race."[57] Although St. Michael denies Seth the oil for his father, the archangel promises Seth that after 5,500 years have passed, the Son of God will raise, baptize, and anoint Adam with the Oil of Mercy.[58]

As an intercessor on behalf of humankind, St. Michael plays a prominent role in the extra-canonical literature of the New Testament. St. Michael is featured with the Virgin Mary in two intercession scenes that are thought to have had an influence on similar representations in medieval legends of the archangel. The first text is the apocryphal text known as the Apocalypse of the Holy Mother (*RBMA* 273), a text which W. Wright argues was composed in Greek in the second half of the fourth century.[59] In the Apocalypse, Mary is praying on the Mount of Olives, and invokes the archangel Gabriel that he might descend and teach her "concerning the chastisements and concerning things in heaven and on the earth and under the earth."[60] As she prays, St. Michael appears, in Gabriel's place, with the angelic host. St. Michael salutes the Virgin who in turn hails St. Michael by a series of epithets which reflect his stature in heaven. After these opening salutations, Mary asks St. Michael to show her the punishments of the sinful in Hades. St. Michael commands the angels to open Hades, and the archangel escorts the Virgin on a tour of the punishments. The principal significance of this apocryphon for the study of St. Michael in medieval England is his role in the intercession scene for the damned.

Shown the punishment of many different sinners, Mary is moved to intercede only on behalf of the Christians chastised for performing the work of the devil and squandering the time of their repentance (§ 25). She prays that St. Michael might place her in the presence of the Lord. Once before the Lord, Mary begs that she might be chastised

---

[55] For St. Michael's association with water and agriculture, see Appendix C.

[56] Translations of the principal Greek and Latin recensions of the Gospel of Nicodemus are found in Elliott, *ANT*, 169–204. The Latin A text of Christ's Descent into Hell appears on pages 190–98.

[57] Elliott, *ANT*, 192.

[58] The Oil of Mercy exemplum is also found in two closely related Old Testament apocrypha: the Life of Adam and Eve (30–44) and the Apocalypse of Moses (5–14). The passages are printed on facing pages in *OTP* 2, 270–77.

[59] W. Wright, *Contributions to the Apocryphal Literature of the New Testament* (London, 1865): 7. M. R. James, however, has also published a Greek text and assigns it provisionally to the ninth century in *Apocrypha Anecdota*, vol. 1 (Cambridge, 1893): 109–26. James summarizes the text in *ANT*, 563. It is translated in full by R. Rutherford in *Ante-Nicene Christian Library*, vol. 9, ed. A. Menzies (Edinburgh, 1897): 167–74.

[60] *Ibid.*, 169.

for the Christians. The Lord asks how He can have mercy on them when they did not even have mercy on their own brothers. To press her plea, Mary marshals the support of St. Michael, Moses, John, and Paul. Together they all beseech the Lord to have mercy on the Christian sinners. Hearing their prayers, the Lord relents, but castigates the sinners for their forgetfulness before granting them some rest "on the day of Pentecost to glorify the Father and the Son and the Holy Spirit."[61]

Although M. R. James derides the Apocalypse of the Holy Mother as a late and derivative compilation of earlier texts,[62] St. Michael's role in its principal episode, the intercession for the damned, speaks to the powerful currency of the popular belief in the efficacy of St. Michael's intercessory powers, a belief which is widely reflected in medieval literature. Aside from St. Michael's role in the intercession scene, however, Mary's epithets for St. Michael reflect the scope of his duties in heaven, at least as they were conceived in the popular imagination of the ninth century. Mary designates him "commander-in-chief, the minister of the invisible Father," and the "associate of [her] Son." The "most dread of the six-winged," St. Michael "rules through all things and [is] worthy to stand beside the throne of the Lord"; in fact he is "first of all unto the throne of God." In a reference to his eschatological roles, Mary speaks of St. Michael as the one who is "about to sound the trumpet and awaken those who have been asleep for ages," an association hinted at in the apocryphal Apocalypse of St. John the Theologian.[63]

The second text in which St. Michael is represented as a powerful intercessor is a Syriac fragment of an Assumption narrative known as the "Obsequies of the Holy Virgin" (*BHO* 6), a text which is thought to have some connections to a Gaelic version of the Assumption of Mary.[64] The text is significant because it contains an intercession scene reminiscent of those in the Apocalypse of Paul and the Apocalypse of the Holy Mother. In the "Obsequies," St. Michael witnesses the torment of lost souls in the company of the Lord, the apostles, and the Virgin Mary. St. Michael addresses the lost souls, telling them how the angels intercede for all of the Lord's creation day and night. The fragment ends as the archangel is explaining how the angel who is set over the waters intercedes for the proper regulation of water.[65] Although St. Michael's reply in the Syriac account is incomplete, it is likely that the archangel would have continued by outlining the activities of a series of angels, each set over the regulation of a particular natural element. His reply would have ended with a description of his own principal activity: the continual intercession before the Lord on behalf of humankind. There

---

[61] *Ibid.*, 174. A. Y. Collins discusses the text in the context of the genre "apocalypse" in "Early Christian Apocalypses," *Semeia* 14 (1979): 91–92.

[62] James, *Apocrypha Anecdota*, vol. 1, 111–13.

[63] The Greek text is printed in C. Tischendorf, *Apocalypses Apocryphae* (Leipzig, 1866: repr. Hildesheim, 1966): 70–94. The text is translated in *Ante-Nicene Fathers*, vol. 8, eds. A. Roberts and J. Donaldson (New York, 1903): 582–86. For St. Michael's association with blowing horns/trumpets at judgment, see Appendix C.

[64] The text of the "Obsequies" is printed in W. Wright, *Contributions*, 42–51. St. John D. Seymour first noted the similarities of several episodes in both the "Obsequies" and the Gaelic Assumption text ("Irish Versions of the *Transitus Mariae*," *JTS* 23 [1921]: 36–43 at 39–40). In his edition of the Gaelic Assumption text, Charles Donahue explores in greater detail these similarities and posits an intermediary text O and its derivatives O_1 and O_2 which gave the Irish version its distinctive character (*The Testament of Mary* [New York, 1942]: 11–27, especially his diagram at 25).

[65] For references to St. Michael and the regulation of natural phenomena, see Appendix C.

exists a precedent for this reconstruction of St. Michael's reply in the Apocalypse of Paul. In that apocryphon St. Michael declares, "I do not stop one day or one night praying incessantly for the human race." It is significant that the intercession scene in the Apocalypse of Paul also ends with the granting of a respite ("a night and a day of refreshment forever").

The significance of the successful intercessions from the Apocalypse of Paul, Christ's Descent into Hell, the Apocalypse of the Holy Mother, and the Obsequies of the Holy Virgin will resonate in much of the legendary literature of the Middle Ages. Although St. Michael is recognized as a powerful intercessor in Jewish apocalyptic texts, especially the Testament of Abraham, his role as intercessor is usurped by the risen Christ in the literature of the New Testament era. With these scenes, however, St. Michael's role as a powerful intercessor gains renewed salience. The efficacy of St. Michael's actions on behalf of humankind is restored to the present. And, thus, once again, the archangel's authority spans the three ages of man's time and extends into the eternity of God's time.

The final role in which St. Michael's efficacy is restored to the present is that of psychopomp.[66] Perhaps St. Michael's most important charge in this capacity is the body and soul of the Virgin Mary, according to a legend found in a group of apocryphal works concerning the death and assumption of the Virgin. These works first began to circulate in the fourth century. Texts exist in Coptic, Greek, Latin, Syriac, Arabic, and many medieval vernaculars including Old English. M. R. James, who translated many of the texts, was of the opinion that "the legend was first elaborated, if it did not originate, in Egypt."[67] The texts of the Assumption apocrypha fall into two principal forms. In the Coptic form, Jesus appears to Mary before the Apostles have left on their missionary work and informs her of her imminent death and assumption. In the form found in the Greek, Latin, and Syriac texts, it is an angel who appears to Mary and informs her of her death after the Apostles have dispersed. In this form, Mary requests that the Apostles be with her at her death, and they are transported on clouds to her side. Although the Latin forms of the Assumption apocrypha had the greatest impact on the development of the tradition in medieval England, St. Michael also plays a prominent role as a psychopomp in the Coptic texts.

The principal Coptic text of the Assumption in which St. Michael appears is the Bohairic account of the Falling Asleep of Mary attributed to Evodius, Archbishop of Rome.[68] On her deathbed, Mary, afraid of the trials of the next world, is comforted by Jesus. Jesus and the apostles withdraw from Mary's chamber to allow Death to approach her. Sitting on a stone outside Mary's chamber, Jesus appeals to Death not to frighten his mother. When Death appears to Mary, her soul, white as snow, leaps into the bosom of her son. Jesus wraps the soul in fine linens and passes it into the protection of St. Michael, who bears it on his wings of light until Jesus appoints a place for her holy body.[69]

---

[66] For St. Michael's role as psychopomp in New Testament apocrypha, see Appendix C.

[67] James translates or summarizes the principal Coptic, Greek, and Latin versions of the Assumption apocrypha (ANT, 194–227 at 194).

[68] The Bohairic text is printed and translated in Forbes Robinson, *Coptic Apocryphal Gospels* (Cambridge, 1896): 44–67 and 66–89. The text has most recently been summarized by Elliott, ANT, 695–97.

[69] Robinson, *Coptic Apocryphal Gospels*, 60. The Virgin's soul is also passed into the keeping of St. Michael in a Syriac fragment printed in Wright, *Contributions*, 14.

The principal Latin account of the Assumption is the narrative of Melito, Bishop of Sardis, commonly known as the Gospel of Pseudo-Melito (*RBMA* 164), and widely known in medieval England. This text exists in two versions, designated "Transitus Mariae B" and "Transitus Mariae B²" by their respective editors.[70] Although the essential outline of the two narratives is the same, there are several significant anomalies which concern the roles of the archangels Michael and Gabriel in connection with the conveyance of the Virgin Mary's body and soul.[71] The anomalies, which are the principal focus of the ensuing discussion, are summarized in Table 1 below.

According to all the legends, at Mary's death, Christ entrusts her soul to the care of the archangel Michael. In Transitus B¹, however, Mary's soul is indeed consigned to St. Michael, the "chief of paradise and prince of the Jewish people," presumably for conveyance to heaven, but the archangel Gabriel is introduced to accompany them.[72] Although St. Michael also receives Mary's soul (once again the conveyance of her soul to heaven is assumed) and is designated "protector of paradise and prince of the Hebrew people" in all the manuscripts of B², there is no mention of Gabriel.[73]

After Mary's soul has been conveyed to paradise, Christ orders the apostles to bury her body in a new sepulcher which they will find on the east side of the city and to wait there until the third day when He will return. In chapter 16 of both texts, Christ returns. In the text of Tischendorf's principal manuscript of B¹, the Savior commands St. Michael to retrieve Mary's soul from heaven. Having done so, the archangel removes the stone from before the sepulcher in which Mary's body has lain for three days.[74] In an intriguing anomaly, the archangel Gabriel is introduced to roll away the stone in a manuscript variant Tischendorf designates as "MB."[75] Although this particular anomaly is not found in the principal manuscript of B², it does reappear in several variants of that text.[76] In the principal manuscript of B², however, it is St. Michael who presents the soul of Mary before the Lord, and there is no mention of the stone or the archangel Gabriel. Once the stone has been removed, Christ addresses Mary's body, which rises and leaves the sepulcher. Bowing before the Lord, Mary's body praises and

---

70 The two versions of the Gospel of Pseudo-Melito are printed as "Transitus Mariae B" in Tischendorf, *Apocalypses Apocryphae*, 124–36, and as "Transitus Mariae B" in M. Haibach-Reinisch, *Ein neuer "Transitus Mariae" des Pseudo-Melito* (Rome, 1962): 63–87. Tischendorf's B text is translated in James, *ANT*, 209–16, and Elliott, *ANT*, 708–14. The B text has not yet been translated. Tischendorf's Latin B has been designated B to distinguish it from Haibach-Reinisch's manuscripts of B.

71 These anomalies are acknowledged in the textual notes of both the Tischendorf and Haibach-Reinisch editions of the texts. These anomalies in the Latin texts are significant as they reappear in several Anglo-Saxon translations of the Assumption apocrypha, and in at least one case, provide a significant clue as to the ultimate source of a later medieval text (on which, see below, 76–78).

72 Tischendorf, 130: Et haec dicens dominus tradidit animam sanctae Mariae Michaeli, qui erat præpositus paradisi et princeps gentis Iudæorum; et Gabriel ibat cum illis.

73 Haibach-Reinisch, 76: Tunc Salvator commendavit animam sanctae Mariae Michaeli archangelo, custos paradisi et princeps gentis Hebræorum.

74 On the reason for the removal of Mary's soul from heaven, the text is ambiguous. It is to be presumed that Mary's soul is brought away from heaven to witness the conveyance of her body to heaven. Tischendorf, 135: Et [Salvator] iussit Michaeli archangelo ut animam sanctae Mariae deferret. Et ecce Michaeli archangelus revolvit lapidem ab ostio monumenti.

75 *Ibid.*, notes for chapter 16: Et ecce repente Gabriel archangelus revolvit lapidem ab ostio monumenti.

76 For a full list of these variants, see the textual notes for chapter 16 in Haibach-Reinisch (85).

Table 1. Summary of St. Michael's roles in the Latin Transitus Mariae B tradition

Transitus Mariae B[1]	Transitus Mariae B[2]
Chapter 8 St. Michael receives Mary's soul from Christ. Gabriel accompanies St. Michael and Mary's soul to heaven.	*Chapter 8* St. Michael receives Mary's soul from Christ. There is no mention of Gabriel.
Chapter 16 St. Michael retrieves Mary's soul from heaven, and rolls the stone away from before the sepulcher in which her earthly body lies. *MB variants:* St. Michael brings Mary's soul from heaven, but Gabriel is introduced to roll away the stone from before the sepulcher.	*Chapter 16:* St. Michael returns with Mary's soul. There is no mention of either the stone or the archangel Gabriel. *Variants:* 1. Gabriel is commanded to remove the stone from before the sepulcher, and St. Michael presents the soul of Mary before the Lord. (Haibach-Reinisch manuscripts: T, F, O[1], O[2], and V) 2. St. Michael and Gabriel together present the soul of Mary before the Lord. There is no mention of the stone. (Manuscripts: P[2], P[3]) 3. St. Michael is commanded to bring Mary's soul from heaven, and Gabriel is commanded to remove the stone from before the sepulcher. (Manuscripts: P[1], D, P[4])
Chapter 17 Mary's risen body is entrusted to the angelic host for conveyance to heaven.	*Chapter 17* St. Michael receives Mary's body and conveys it to heaven, accompanied by the angelic host.

glorifies Him. In Chapter 17 of B[1] and its variants, Christ kisses the risen body of the Virgin, and it is given over to the angels who convey her to heaven.[77] In B[2] and its variants, Christ also kisses the risen body, but it is entrusted to St. Michael, who conveys it to heaven in the company of the angelic host.[78]

In the literature of the early Christian era, then, St. Michael first loses and then regains some of the authority he possessed in the Jewish apocalypses. St. Michael's roles in the present are given over to the risen Christ, whose death is the means by which individual redemption is guaranteed, in the canonical literature of the New Testament era. The archangel regains much of his authority in the present, however, in the extra-canonical literature of the New Testament era. In the extra-canonical texts, St. Michael is reinstated to his former role as intercessor and advocate for humankind. It is in the Assumption apocrypha, however, that St. Michael's character achieves its fullest representation. In these texts, St. Michael serves as the Virgin Mary's guardian and

---

77 Tischendorf, 135: Et osculans eam dominus recessit, et tradidit animam eius angelis ut deferrent eam in paradisum.
78 Haibach-Reinisch, 86: Elevans eam Dominus osculatus est eam, tradidit eam Michaëli archangelo, et elevata est coram Domino in nube cum angelis.

guide, as the protector of her soul after the earthly death of her body, and as a powerful co-intercessor on behalf of the sinful in Hades. Furthermore, St. Michael's participation in the intercession scenes with St. Paul and the Virgin Mary is significant in the development of the archangel's legendary persona during the Middle Ages.

Summary

In the literatures of the Old and New Testament eras, the broad parameters of St. Michael's authority remain roughly the same. The archangel is a guardian angel of the Lord's people and a powerful intercessor on their behalf. At the death of one of God's people, St. Michael, the supreme psychopomp, guarantees the safe passage of the soul to heaven. In the literature of the New Testament, however, St. Michael's roles take on a new, larger significance, one in keeping with the new dispensation heralded by the New Testament. St. Michael's old contention with Satan, described in Revelation 12:7–9, becomes a preview of an eschatological battle between the forces of good and evil. Although restricted to acting in the past and the future, St. Michael remains a powerful advocate before the Lord on behalf of the faithful in the canonical works of the New Testament era. Restored to his previous authority in the extra-canonical literature of the New Testament era, however, St. Michael gains stature as a mythic hero whose actions straddle human time; his efficacy is restored to the past, present, and future. In his capacity as psychopomp, St. Michael is closely associated with the Virgin Mary, conveying her body to heaven and reuniting it with her soul for all eternity. As commander of the angelic host, St. Michael accompanies Christ on his descent to hell, and guides the holy ones of the Old Testament into paradise. The themes of St. Michael's intercession and his protection of the souls of the faithful at death become a significant aspect of St. Michael's legendary persona in the early Middle Ages, and especially in Anglo-Saxon and late medieval England.

Based largely on the archangel's roles in the scriptural and apocryphal literature of the Old and New Testament eras reviewed in this chapter, Judeo-Christian tradition in the West has assigned St. Michael four offices. The first is to do battle against Satan and his minions, as in Revelation 12:7–9. The second is to be the untiring champion of God's chosen people, namely the Jews in the Old Testament and the Christians in the New. The third office is to protect the souls of the faithful from the influence of the devil, especially at the moment of death. And the fourth office is to call away men's souls from their earthly life and bring them to judgment, as is suggested by the offertory chant of the Mass of the Dead: "Signifer sanctus Michael representet eas in lucem sanctam quam olim Abrahae promisisti et semini ejus" (May St. Michael, the standard-bearer, conduct them into the holy light, which you promised of old to Abraham and his seed).

The characterization of the archangel's roles in the literatures of the Old and New Testaments sets the stage for the genesis and migration of the archangel's cult in the late antique era and the early Middle Ages. Indeed, it is against the backdrop of the literatures of the Old and New Testament eras that the legends of the St. Michael the archangel first gripped the imagination of the Christian faithful in the communities of the Near East.

2

The Archangel's Legendary History

> And an angel of the Lord descended at certain times into the pond;
> and the water was moved. And he that went down first into the
> pond after the motion of the water, was made whole, of whatso-
> ever infirmity he lay under.
>
> John 5:4

Although there is no indication that the angel who agitated the water of the pool of
Bethesda was the archangel Michael, the story does suggest an early recognition of
angelic agency in healing waters. In the early Christian era, angels were widely venerated for their healing powers all across western Asia Minor. The size and influence of
the Jewish community in the region suggests that the devotion to angels may have in
some part developed out of Jewish angelology, itself a product of foreign influences.[1] In
several of his Epistles, St. Paul is particularly concerned with and preaches against the
worship of angels.[2] In his most polemical attack on the practice, the Apostle condemns
the Colossians for worshipping angels (Colossians 2:18).[3] In the fourth century, the
Council of Laodicea (ca. 360 CE) reiterated St. Paul's aversion to the worship of angels
and expressly prohibited the practice.[4] Writing some fifty years after the Council,
however, Theodoret, in his commentary on the Epistle to the Colossians, stated that
the "disease" against which St. Paul inveighed "long remained in Phrygia and Pisidia,"
adding that "even to the present time oratories of the holy Michael may be seen among
them and their neighbors."[5]

---

1 For an introduction to Jewish doctrines of angelology, see the entry "Angels and Angelology" in the
   Encyclopedia Judaica, vol. 1 (New York, 1971): cols. 957–77; also W. Heidt, *Angelology of the Old Testament* (Washington, D.C., 1949). For a discussion of the development and elaboration of the doctrine
   of archangels, see G. H. Dix, "The Seven Archangels and the Seven Spirits: A Study in the Origin,
   Development, and Messianic Associations of the Two Themes," *JTS* 28 (1927): 233–50. For the
   definitive discussion of St. Michael's roles in the context of Jewish angelology, see W. Leuken,
   Michael (Göttingen, 1898), especially chapter 2.
2 For a discussion of angels in the writings of the apostle Paul, see Lloyd Gaston, "Angels and Gentiles
   in Early Judaism and in Paul," *Studies in Religion* 11 (1982): 65–75.
3 J. B. Lightfoot, *Saint Paul's Epistle to the Colossians and to Philemon* (New York, 1900).
4 Lightfoot translates Canon 35 of the Council of Laodicea as follows: "It is not right for Christians to
   abandon the church of God and go away and invoke angels and hold conventicles; for these things
   are forbidden" (*ibid.*, 68).
5 Lightfoot quotes from Theodoret's commentary (68). A Latin translation of the original Greek text
   appears in *PG* 82, col. 614: Qui legem defendebant, eos etiam ad angelos colendos inducebant,
   dicentes legem fuisse per eos datam. Mansit autem per diu hoc vitium in Phrygia et Pisidia. Proinde

Thus, the earliest manifestations of a Michaeline cult are to be sought in the ancient Near East. In an effort to chart the migration of St. Michael's cult from East to West, this chapter focuses on three geographic centers of Michaeline devotion: western Asia Minor, southern Italy, and northern Gaul. Special attention is devoted to Italy since the foundation legend of the cultic center at Monte Gargano had a significant impact on medieval devotions to St. Michael. In at least two of these regions (the Near East and Italy) the archangel expropriated an existing cultic site and assumed some of the healing characteristics associated with the site. After a series of apparitions and earthly interventions, each of the three great regional powers, Constantine's empire, the Lombards, and the Carolingians, adapted and adopted St. Michael, Commander of the Heavenly Host in battle, as the patron saint of its imperial ambition. Since the legendary apparitions and interventions are attested in hagiographic texts, however, this chapter demonstrates that the narratives are constructed around roles traditionally associated with the archangel in the scriptural and apocryphal literature reviewed in the previous chapter. Finally, this chapter makes clear that the hagiographical accounts of St. Michael's legendary appearances enriched the inherited tradition of representation with new associations which were to have a significant impact on the characterization of St. Michael in medieval English legend.

Ancient Near East

In Eastern Christendom, St. Michael was almost exclusively associated with the healing powers of fountains and springs.[6] The most famous legend of St. Michael in the ancient Near East is that of his appearance at Chonae (present-day Khonas, Turkey). The legend, which exists in three Greek versions, a Latin recension, and an Ethiopian version, is actually a conflated account of two legendary interventions, one associated with a miraculous spring at Chairotopa (present-day Ceretapa, Turkey) and the other with the preservation of a shrine at Chonae.[7]

synodus, quae convenit apud Laodiceam Phrygiae, lege prohibuit, ne precarentur angelos. Et in hodiernum usque diem oratorium sancti Michaelis apud illos illorumque finitimos videre est.

6 For a discussion of the Eastern sources of the cult, see Victor Saxer, "Jalons pour servir à l'histoire du culte de l'archange Saint Michel en orient jusqu'à l'iconoclasme," *Noscere Sancta: Miscellanea in memoria di Agostino Amore* (Rome, 1985): 357–426; A. Baumstark, *Comparative Liturgy* (London, 1958): 137; and P. du Bourgnet, "Origines lointaines d'images de Saint Michel," in *MSM*, 3, 37–38. On veneration of angels in the East, see Glenn Peers, "Hagiographical Models of Worship of Images and Angels," *Byzantion* 67 (1997): 407–40, and *Subtle Bodies: Representing Angels in Byzantium* (Berkeley, 2001).

7 The oldest Greek text (*BHG* 1282) is attributed to the hermit Archippos and has been published by Max Bonnet, *Narratio de miraculo a Michaele archangelo Chonis patrato* (Paris, 1890); and F. Nau and J. Bousquet, "Miracle de S. Michel à Colosses," *PO* 4 (1907): 547–62. The second recension (*BHG* 1283) is attributed to Sissinius and has been printed in *AASS*, Septembris VIII: 14–47. The third Greek text (*BHG* 1284) is attributed to Simeon Metaphrastes and has been printed by M. Bonnet as "Narratio de miraculo a Michaele archangelo Chonio patrato," *AB* 8 (1889): 308–16. Only the prologue to the eleventh-century Latin recension (*BHL* 5947) has been published, "Miraculum Chonis Patratum, Inteprete Leone Mon. Montis Athomos," has been printed in *AB* 9 (1890): 202–203. The Ethiopian version (*BHO* 759) has been published by J. Bachmann, *Aethiopische Lesestücke* (Leipzig, 1893): 20–23.

In the Greek versions of the legend,[8] the apostles John and Philip, passing through the village of Chairotopa, announce that Michael the archangel will soon manifest his power in that place. Shortly after the departure of the apostles, a spring begins to flow in the vicinity of the village. The miraculous healing powers of the water become famous in the region, drawing throngs of visitors seeking cures for their ailments. One such visitor is a pagan man from Laodicea who brings his daughter, mute since birth, to the spring. The waters of the spring cure the girl of her illness, and the father builds a chapel dedicated to St. Michael near the spring.

The narrative of the legend continues some ninety years later with the establishment of a hermit named Archippos in the chapel sanctuary of St. Michael. Resentful of the healing power of the archangel's spring and sanctuary, however, the local heathen population now threaten to destroy them. By digging a series of canals, the heathen divert two rivers toward the shrine to inundate it. The hermit Archippos prays to St. Michael for the preservation of the spring and shrine. With thunder and lightning, the archangel causes a massive earthquake to open a deep chasm in the ground. The diverted waters of the two rivers funnel into the chasm, and the sanctuary and spring are preserved.

As Leuken has pointed out, the Greek text is a composite one which describes the origins of two distinct natural phenomena (the source of a spring and the funneling together of two rivers) as if they occurred at the same location. Leuken argues that the spring was in fact at Chairotopa as the various recensions of the legend suggest, but that the funneling of the rivers must have occurred at Chonae, which derived its name from the Greek word for "funnel" (*chone*).[9] Although Chonae is only mentioned in the title and the conclusion of the Greek recensions, Victor Saxer agrees with Leuken, and suggests that an analysis of the various recensions reflects the rise of Chonae, and its eventual supersedure of Chairotopa, as an important pilgrimage site.[10] While several critics have argued that the composition of the legend most likely dates from the sixth or seventh century, Saxer has shown that the legend must have first begun to circulate sometime in the second half of the fifth century, a time when "Chonae was universally known and recognized as the sanctuary *par excellence* of St. Michael."[11]

St. Michael was also associated with miraculous water at the ancient sites of Germia (Yürme, Turkey),[12] where fish inhabited the healing pool. Perhaps his most famous sanctuary in the ancient Near East, however, was the Michaelion built by the Emperor Constantine at Chalcedon on the site of an earlier temple known as Sosthenion. The site has a rich pagan history which is relevant to Constantine's appropriation of the

---

8 Bonnet, *Narratio de miraculo* (Paris, 1890). For a discussion of this legendary intervention, see Glenn Peers, "Holy Man, Supplicant, and Donor: On Representations of the Miracle of Archangel Michael at Chonae," *Mediaeval Studies* 59 (1997): 173–82.

9 *Michael*, 74, esp. n. 2.

10 "Jalons," 389–91.

11 *Ibid.*, 389: Chonè était universellement connue et reconnue comme le sanctuaire par excellence de saint Michel. In contrast, Bonnet argues that the text cannot be older than the ninth century. Saxer reviews the various dates assigned the recensions ("Jalons," 384–91 at 389).

12 Cyril Mango, "The Pilgrimage Centre of St. Michael at Germia," *Jahrbuch der österreichischen Byzantinistik* 36 (1986): 119–24. Mango has also suggested that the site, most likely a cult site of the goddess Cybele, came to be associated with St. Michael because of his similarity to the Great Mother's son, Attis ("St. Michael and Attis," *Deltion tês Christiankês Archaiologikês Hetaireia* 12 [1984–86]: 39–62 at 55).

site. According to the story told by John Malalas in the sixth century, the Argonauts were attacked at the Bosphorus by a force under the command of a local chieftain named Amycus while they were navigating their way to the Black Sea in search of the Golden Fleece.[13] The Argonauts sought refuge in a secluded cove, where they had a vision of a man with wings like an eagle. The figure prophesied their victory over Amycus, and the grateful Argonauts built a temple in which they set up a statue of the apparition. They called the site "Sosthenion" because they had been saved there. The legend continues that when Constantine visited the temple he recognized the statue as "an angel in the habit of a monk."[14] The identity of the angel was revealed to him in a dream (presumably by St. Michael), and Constantine built the Michaelion in honor of the archangel. The site became famous for miraculous healings and even apparitions of the archangel.

Several years after the foundation of the Michaelion, during his campaign against Licinius, Constantine allegedly had a series of visions in which his victory over his rival was declared. In the brief campaign, Constantine defeated his rival's forces at Byzantium, forcing Licinius to withdraw across the Bosphorus. In September 324, Constantine led his army into battle at Chrysopolis, not far from the Michaelion of Chalcedon. Constantine defeated Licinius and united under his control the eastern and western portions of the empire. Eusebius of Caesarea brings his *Historia ecclesiastica* to an end with the account of Constantine's defeat of Licinius. By ending his account of the development of the church in this way, Eusebius placed the unification of the empire in the larger context of the workings of Providence in the earthly sphere, suggesting that the empire and its emperor were the earthly parallel of the heavenly kingdom.[15]

In his official account of the Emperor's life, the *Vita Constantini*, however, Eusebius further elaborates on the significance of Licinius's defeat.[16] After his victory, Constantine commissioned a painting of himself and his sons standing on top of a serpent pierced by a weapon. The painting was displayed to the public in front of the Emperor's palace. The iconographic representation of Constantine's victory over Licinius is clearly a visual reworking of the mythic battle of Revelation 12:7–9. Thus, Constantine associated himself with St. Michael, the commander of the celestial host, as he had previously associated himself with other supernatural beings, such as Sol Invictus and Apollo.[17]

By the fourteenth century, Constantine's appropriation of and identification with Michaeline iconography had become fully integrated in the legendary account of the founding of the Michaelion. In his *Ecclesiastica Historia*, Nicephorus Callistus conflates the accounts of Constantine's vision of the angel that resembled a monk and his defeat of Licinius.[18] Nicephorus begins with the account of the Argonauts' fight against

[13] John Malalas, *Chronographia*, Book iv, PG 97: 157–60.
[14] *Ibid.*, col. 159: angeli speciem, in habitu monachi Christiani. In an intriguing and plausible argument, Cyril Mango suggests the statue was a figure of Attis ("St. Michael and Attis," 60–61).
[15] Eusebius, *The History of the Church from Christ to Constantine*, Book 10, chapters 7.1–9.7, trans. G. A. Williamson (New York, 1984): 408–14.
[16] Eusebius, *De Vita Constantini*, Book III, chapter 3, PG 20: col. 1058.
[17] Barbara Saylor Rodgers, "Constantine's Pagan Vision," *Byzantion* 50 (1980): 259–78. For a discussion of St. Michael's resemblance to Apollo, see G. F. Hill, "Apollo and St. Michael: Some Analogies," *Journal of Hellenic Studies* 36 (1916): 134–62.
[18] Nicephorus Callistus, *Ecclesiastica Historia*, Book VII, chapter 50, PG 145: 1327–32. See also Günter

Amycus and the establishment of the Sosthenion, following the lines of John Malalas's narrative. When he recounts the episode of Constantine's vision, however, Nicephorus reports the apparition's words in direct speech: "I am, says he, Michael, the chief of the military power of the Lord Sabaoth, protector of the faith of Christians; who as to a faithful and dear minister gave you while you fought against the impious tyrants the armies which aided you."[19] According to Nicephorus, then, there is no question that it was St. Michael who appeared to Constantine at the Sosthenion. Instead of revealing to him the identity of the angel-monk, however, St. Michael informed Constantine that his defeat of the "impious tyrants," the forces of Licinius, was a result of the aid with which the archangel had provided him.

With the defeat of Licinius and the unification of the eastern and western portions of the empire under Constantine, St. Michael's cult began its westward migration in the fourth and fifth centuries.[20] Following the path of many Greek heroes, popular devotion to St. Michael landed on the Greek-speaking soil of the ancient Garganic peninsula on the southwestern coast of Italy. Known in ancient times as Daunia, the promontory had provided safe haven for heroes such as Diomedes, who sought refuge there from the vengeance of Aphrodite after Troy.[21] According to Strabo, the Greek historian and geographer, Diomedes founded two cities, Canusium and Argyrippa, on this ancient peninsula.[22] The attribution is echoed by Virgil, who calls Diomedes "victor Gargani" for establishing the city of Argyrippa.[23] Strabo also remarks that on this same promontory, on a "hill by the name of Drium, are to be seen two hero-temples: one, to Calchas, on the very summit, where those who consult the oracle sacrifice to his shade a black ram and sleep in the hide, and the other, to Podaleirius, down near the base of the hill ... and from it flows a stream which is a cure-all for diseases of animals."[24] The burial places of Calchas, the soothsayer who foretold that the Greeks would fight unsuccessfully for nine years at Troy before taking the city in the tenth (Iliad, Book II, lines 324–332), and Podaleirius, one of the sons of Aesculapius the healer, had a long association with healing. Although he does not name the healing god's son, the Greek tragedian Lycophron describes Podaleirius's burial place as the site of great portents:

and to men sleeping in sheepskins on his tomb he shall declare in dreams his unerring message for all. And healer of diseases shall he be called by the Daunians,

Gentz, Die Kirchen Geschichte des Nicephorus Callistus Xanthapulus und ihre Quellen, ed. Friedhelm Winkelmann, Texte und Untersuchungen 98 (Berlin, 1966).

19 Ibid., col. 1330: Ego, inquit, sic sum Michael magister militiae Domini Sabaoth virtuum, Christianorum fidei tutor; qui tibi contra impios tyrannos belligeranti, fideli et dilecto illius ministro, auxiliaria arma contul.

20 For a discussion of the early cult in the West, see Culte (6–28); also M. Baudot, "St. Michel dans la liturgie chrétienne" and "Origine du culte de St. Michel," in MSM, 3 (23–7 and 15–22, respectively).

21 The legend of Diomedes' flight to Daunia was not known to Homer, who has him land in Argos (Odyssey, Book III, lines 181–82). The hero's arrival in Daunia is described in a poetic fragment once attributed to the poet Mimnermus but now thought to be spurious (Mimnermus, Fragment 22, in Iambi et Elegi Graeci, ed. M. L. West [Oxford, 1992]: 91, n. 22).

22 Strabo, Geography, Book VI, chapter 3.9, ed. Horace Leonard Jones, vol. 3 (Cambridge, MA, 1967): 129.

23 Virgil, Aeneid: Book XI, ed. K. W. Gransden (Cambridge, 1991): 46.

24 Strabo, Geography, 131.

when they wash the sick with the waters of Althaenus and invoke the son of Epius [Aesculapius] to their aid, that he may come gracious unto men and flocks.[25]

Considering the long tradition of worship and healing at the site, it is not surprising that the earliest and greatest center of St. Michaeline devotion in the West from the fourth century was a remote cavern on the summit of a hill on the ancient Garganic promontory.

Monte Gargano

Possibly as early as the turn of the eighth century, an Anglo-Saxon pilgrim named Leofwini climbed to the grotto chapel of St. Michael on the summit of Monte Gargano in Apulia, southern Italy. Perhaps wishing to secure the protection of the archangel for his journey to the Holy Land, the pilgrim carved (or had carved) his name in runes on a pillar of what is now gallery B of the sanctuary.[26] A well-known pilgrimage site in its own right, Monte Gargano was also a favored resting-place on the route to the ports of southeastern Italy where pilgrims gained sea-passage to the Holy Land.[27] If the dating of the inscription can be accepted (and the question is far from settled), then Leofwini was the first Anglo-Saxon name to appear among the many inscriptions carved on the walls of the grotto chapel.[28] The inscriptions consist mostly of personal names, presumably those of pilgrims, representing a wide variety of European nationalities.

[25] Lycophron, *Alexandra*, lines 1047–55, in *Callimachus, Lycophron, Aratus*, ed. G. R. Mair (Cambridge, MA, 1940): 406–409.

[26] On the basis of a linguistic analysis of the spelling of the name, Maria Giovanna Arcamore argues that the Leofwini runes were probably carved in the decades immediately before or after the year 700 ("Una nuova iscrizione runica da Monte Sant'Angelo," in *Culto e Insediamenti Micaelici nell'Italia meridionale fra tarda antichità e medioevo*, Atti del Convegno Internazionale Monte Sant'Angelo 18–21 novembre 1992, eds. C. Carletti and G. Otranto [Bari, 1994]: 185–89 at 188). René Derolez and Ute Schwab, however, take issue with Arcamore's onomastic analysis of the inscription, suggesting that the date is far from certain ("More Runes at Monte Sant'Angelo," *Nytt om Runer* 9 [1994]: 18–19). In an earlier article, Derolez and Schwab date the Garganic runes generally "between the late seventh and the middle of the ninth century" ("The Runic Inscriptions of Monte S. Angelo (Gargano)," *Mededelingen van de Koninklijke Academie voor Wetenschappen, Letteren en Schone Kunsten van België: Academiae Analecta*, Klasse der Letteren 45 [1983]: 95–130 at 113). In his book, *Runes: An Introduction*, R. W. V. Elliott agrees with Derolez and Schwab's dating of the runes (2nd ed. [New York, 1989]: 58). See also Klaus Düwel, "Die Runenarbeit am Seminar für deutsche Philologie (Arbeitsstelle: Germanische Altertumskunde), Göttingen," *Nytt om Runer* 10 (1995/1996): 9, and U. Schwab, "More Anglo-Saxon Runic Graffiti in Roman Catacombs," *Old English Newsletter* 37.1 (2003): 36–39. I would like to thank Professor Raymond I. Page generally for sharing with me his considerable expertise in runic matters and specifically for bringing to my attention the complex issues involved in the dating of the Garganic inscriptions. For a discussion of the archeological evidence of building phases at the grotto chapel, see Marco Trotta, "I luoghi del Liber de Apparitione. Il santuario di S. Michele dal V all' VIII secolo," in *Culto e Insediamenti*, 125–66.

[27] For a cogent discussion of Monte Gargano as a pilgrimage site, see Armando Petrucci, "Aspetti del culto e del pellegrinaggio di S. Michele sul Monte Gargano," in *Pellegrinaggi e culto dei santi in Europa fino alla prima crociata*, Atti del IV Convegno di Studi (Todi, 1963): 147–80.

[28] For an overview of the various graffiti, see C. Carletti, "Iscrizioni murali," in *Il Santuario di S. Michele sul Gargano dal VI al IX secolo. Contributo alla storia della Langobardia meridionale*, Atti del convegno tenuto a Monte Sant'Angelo il 9–10 dicembre 1978, eds. C. Carletti and G. Otranto (Bari, 1980).

Whatever the true dating of the Leofwini runes may be, it is clear that some time between the late seventh and mid-ninth centuries, a total of five English names were carved on the walls and pillars of the archangel's sanctuary. The names "wigfus" (A), "herræd" (C), and "hereberehct" (D) are inscribed in runes.[29] A fifth inscription, "eadrhidsaxso v<ir> h<onestus>," is carved in Roman letters on a different wall of the sanctuary.[30] Although the dating of these inscriptions is problematic, the possibility that these inscriptions all date from the first half of the accepted time-frame (i.e., the late seventh to the late eighth century) is corroborated by a group of English names scratched in runes and Roman letters in a fresco of St. Luke in the Cimitero di Commodilla in Rome. These carvings are securely dated to a period from the late seventh century to ca. 800 CE.[31] The common occurrence of English runes at Rome and Monte Gargano suggests a heavy pattern of Anglo-Saxon pilgrimage to Italian religious sites. Moreover, the Garganic runes strongly suggest the conclusion that devotions to St. Michael were known in Anglo-Saxon England from at least the early eighth century, and that it had become customary for Anglo-Saxons to travel to Monte Gargano either on pilgrimage to the Holy Land or to the chapel grotto of the archangel itself by this date.

The foundation-myth of Monte Gargano is contained in the hagiographical text, "De apparitione Sancti Michaelis" (*BHL* 5948).[32] The text as it exists now is clearly a composite text. One of its editors, G. Waitz, has assigned the composition of this final version of the text to the late ninth century, but this is contradicted by J. E. Cross, who has pointed out that the legend appears in homiliaries and legendaries of the early and mid-ninth century and must therefore be earlier.[33] Giorgio Otranto has argued that the composition of the final version belongs to the second half of the eighth century or early ninth century.[34] The author of the anonymous final version mentions the existence of an earlier text at the time of his redaction.[35] Studies of the final text have posited an original composition of the sixth century.[36]

---

[29] Derolez and Schwab, "The Runic Inscriptions of Monte S. Angelo," 113–18. See also R. I. Page, "English Runes Imported into the Continent," in *Runische Schriftkultur in kontinental-skandinavischer und -angelsächsischer Wechselbeziehung*, ed. Klaus Düwel (Berlin and New York, 1994): 181–82.

[30] Carletti, "Iscrizioni murali," no. 56.

[31] Carletti first published these carvings in "I graffiti sull'affresco di s. Luca nel Cimitero di Commodilla: Addenda et corrigenda," *Rendiconti della Pontificia Academia Romana di Archeologia* 57 (1984–85): 129–43. Derolez discusses their significance in "Anglo-Saxons in Rome," *Nytt om Runer* 2 (1987): 14–15.

[32] The text edited by G. Waitz, "De apparitione Sancti Michaelis," *MGH SRL*: 541–43, is the standard edition. I have reprinted and translated this text as Appendix A. The text also appears in *AASS*, Septembris VIII, 61–62. For an analysis of the sacred landscape of Gargano and the rhetorical techniques of the text, see John C. Arnold, "Arcadia Becomes Jerusalem: Angelic Caverns and Shrine Conversions at Monte Gargano," *Speculum* 75 (2000): 567–88.

[33] Waitz, 540; and Cross, "An Unrecorded Tradition of St. Michael in Old English Texts," *N&Q* n.s. 28 (1981): 12, n. 4.

[34] G. Otranto, "Per una metodologia della ricerca storico-agiografica, il santuario micaelico del Gargano tra Bizantini e Langobardi," *Vetera Christianorum* 25 (1988): 381–405 at 383.

[35] See Appendix A, section 1: hanc mortalibus hoc modo cognitam libellus in eadem ecclesia positus indicat.

[36] For textual analysis of the "De apparitione" text, see Antonio Quacquarelli, "Gli apocrifi nei riflessi di un graffito del calvario e il 'Liber de Apparitione,' " in *Il Santuario*, 209–39; and G. Otranto, "Il 'Liber de Apparitione,' il santuario di san Michele sul Gargano e i Longobardi del Ducato di Benevento," in *Santuari e politica nel mondo antico* (Milan, 1983): 210–45. For a discussion of the

The foundation-myth consists of three apparitions. The central and oldest element of the legend is most likely the story of St. Michael's apparition to the bishop of Siponto.[37] According to the legend, Garganus, a wealthy man of Siponto who owned a large herd of cattle, became enraged with a bull that had strayed from his herd. When he found the bull at the mouth of a cave, he shot it with a poisoned arrow which reversed its trajectory in mid-flight and killed him. Hearing of this mysterious event, the archbishop instructed the local citizens to fast for three days. During the course of the fast, St. Michael appeared to the bishop and revealed to him the significance of the event.

At this point in the hagiographical account, the narrative of Garganus and the bull is interrupted, and the account of St. Michael's military intervention on behalf of the Christians of Siponto is taken up.[38] According to this part of the legend, the Sipontans and their neighbors, the Beneventans, were besieged by the pagan Neapolitans. In despair, the Sipontans turned to their bishop for help. The bishop instructed them to perform a three-day fast and to pray for protection from St. Michael. The archangel appeared to this bishop and assured him of their victory over the pagans. The Neapolitans were defeated and as a sign of his aid in their victory, St. Michael left the mark of his footprints in the stone of the cave where Garganus had been killed.

After the description of the archangel's military intervention, the hagiographical narrative returns to the scene of the grotto and gives an account of his third apparition.[39] The Sipontans, in great doubt and fear as to whether they dare enter the grotto, consulted their bishop again. A third time, St. Michael appeared to the bishop and told him that there was no need to consecrate the grotto chapel since he had already done so. St. Michael instructed the bishop to enter the chapel first and conduct mass. In the cavern, he discovered an altar, covered with a red cloth. The bishop then appointed priests and psalm-singers to conduct daily services in the grotto-chapel. The account of the "discovery" of the grotto-chapel ends with a description of the clear and sweet water which seeped from the ceiling stone beyond the altar. When drunk from the glass vessel suspended by a silver chain near the source, the dripping water heals all manner of infirmities. The hagiographic account of St. Michael's three apparitions on Monte Gargano ends with St. Paul's observation on the function of angels (Hebrews 1:14): "For angels are ministering spirits and sent to minister for them who will receive the inheritance of salvation."

The archangel's three successive apparitions in the "De apparitione" text appear to have nothing in common and suggest at least three layers of narrative accretion. The first appearance follows on the heels of the story of Garganus and his bull, and is linked closely with Siponto and its anonymous bishop. Given the legendary traditions of healing on the Garganic peninsula, it seems likely that the story of St. Michael's apparition was appended to an earlier legend of the eponymous Garganus and his wayward bull. St. Michael's third appearance closely resembles the first and may in fact have been part of that narrative. The "discovery" of the grotto-chapel and its consecration

---

manuscript history of the "Liber de Apparitione," see Vito Sivo, "Ricerche sulla tradizione manoscritta e sul testo dell'*Apparitio* latina," in *Culto e insediamenti*, 95–106.

[37] See Appendix A, section 2.

[38] See Appendix A, section 3.

[39] See Appendix A, sections 4–6.

are clumsily interrupted by the account of the archangel's military intervention. Thus, the first two narrative layers would have included the legend of Garganus and the account of the establishment of St. Michael's church on the summit of Monte Gargano.

Several factors complicate efforts to assign a date to these two early narrative layers. The first is the existence of two *vitae* of Laurence, Bishop of Siponto.[40] Both texts assert that this Laurence was the bishop of Siponto to whom the archangel appeared on three occasions. Despite earlier attempts to date the composition of the texts to the sixth century, it is generally accepted now that the texts could not have been written before the eleventh century.[41] The second complication is that one manuscript of the *Liber Pontificalis* indicates that the grotto-chapel of the archangel was discovered during the pontificate of Gelasius I (492–496).[42] The first editor of the *Liber Pontificalis*, L. Duchesne, has pointed out, however, that the passage is a later interpolation, likely the work of a scribe familiar with one or both of the versions of the *Vita Laurentii*.[43]

The archangel's second apparition seems to allude to a historically attested dispute between the Sipontan-Beneventans and their traditional rivals, the Neapolitans. In his *Geography*, the first-century Greek geographer and historian Strabo describes Naples' Greek roots and the lingering Greek culture of the city in his day.[44] This Greek flavor was to dissipate, however, in the course of the Germanic invasions of the fifth and sixth centuries, during which Naples accommodated first Odoacer and then Theoderic. In 535, Justinian I sent his general Belisarius against the Ostrogothic forces in a brutal campaign to re-establish Byzantine control of Italy. For her allegiances to the Ostrogoths, Naples suffered terribly during the campaign of reconquest and was finally defeated in 536.[45] Although the city was to remain under Byzantine administration for several centuries, it was largely cut off from other Byzantine holdings in Italy and became a lonely outpost on the frontier of the Eastern empire.

With the Lombard invasion of the north in 568, southern Italy became contested territory once again. In 571, only three years after they gained control of northern Italy, the Lombards established a southern duchy in the city of Benevento. At the crossroads of the Via Appia and the Via Appia-Traiana, Benevento became a strategic Lombard outpost on the route to the Adriatic ports of Bari and Brindisi. The Lombards of Benevento were virtually autonomous of their northern neighbors and moved against

---

[40] Both the *Vita Maior* (end of the eleventh century) and the *Vita Minor* (first half of the eleventh century) are printed in *AASS*, Februarius II, 57–60 and 60–62, respectively. The *Vita Minor* is also printed by Waitz immediately following the "De apparitione Sancti Michaelis" text, *MGH SRL*, 543–45.

[41] Armando Petrucci has argued that the *Vita Laurentii* (presumably the *Vita Minor*) was written near the end of the sixth century ("Origine e diffusione del culto di San-Michele nell'Italia medievale," in *MSM*, 3, 339–52 at 342). Elsewhere Petrucci has argued that the *vitae* contain anti-Gothic sentiments which date the texts to a period shortly after the Gothic wars ("Aspetti del culto e del pellegrinaggio di S. Michele sul Monte Gargano," in *Pellegrinaggi e culto dei santi in Europa fina alla prima crociata*, Atti del IV Convegno di Studi [Todi, 1963]: 147–80). A. Campione offers the accepted argument for a later dating ("Storia e santità nelle due *Vitae* di Lorenzo vescovo di Siponto," *Vetera Christianorum* 29 [1992]: 169–213).

[42] *Liber Pontificalis*, 255: Huias temporibus inventa est aecclesia sancti angeli in monte gargano.

[43] *Ibid.*

[44] Strabo, *Geography*, Book V, chapter 4.7, ed. Horace Leonard Jones, vol. 2 (Cambridge, MA, 1940): 449–51.

[45] For a discussion of Naples' fate during the Byzantine reconquest, see E. A. Thompson, *Romans and Barbarians* (Madison, WI, 1982).

all vestiges of Byzantine control in southern Italy, plundering churches and monasteries, even attacking Monte Cassino in 580.[46] These rampages not only rid the region of Byzantine influence but also drastically reduced the population. In his *Historia Langobardorum*, Paul the Deacon claims that in the late seventh century, the Duke of Benevento let some Bulgarians settle on land vacated by the Byzantines.[47]

Thus, by the middle of the seventh century, the stage was set for the confrontation between the Byzantine city of Naples and the Lombard holdings of Benevento-Siponto. In 647, Grimoald acceded to the duchy of Benevento. Three years later, in 650, the Duke led a force against Byzantine Neapolitan troops who were marching on Siponto, intending to sack the Garganic "oraculum" of St. Michael.[48] The Byzantines were defeated, and the sanctuary preserved. Some critics have suggested that it is to this historical confrontation that the "Liber de Apparitione" refers.[49]

Whatever the actual historical occasion of this confrontation may have been, it is clear that the legendary account of the "Liber de Apparitione" was a composite narrative which first associated St. Michael with the ancient healing traditions of the Garganic site and then with a mythic military intervention. St. Michael's military authority clearly appealed to the Lombards, who essentially adopted the archangel as a "patron saint." The Lombard's first contact with the archangel came as a result of Grimoald's protection of the Garganic site. According to G. P. Bognetti, the primary motivation to adopt the cult of St. Michael was a purely political strategy to reconcile Arians and Catholics.[50] While Bognetti's argument is sound, it overlooks the possibility that the appropriation of the cult was also a political ploy to transform an essentially eastern, and more precisely Byzantine Greek, cult characterized by miraculous healings into an enterprise of nationalist expansion. Grimoald, defender of the Garganic site, became king of the Lombards in 662 and spread the cult to the northern portions of the realm. In an effort to rid southern Lombardy of the vestiges of paganism, Saint Barbatus, bishop of Benevento, received control of the diocese of Siponto from Duke Rumoald I (671–687) and adopted the warrior archangel as patron of his campaign. Cunipert (679–700) had an image of the archangel stamped on imperial coins, implying the archangel's patronage of the monarchy. The adoption of the cult of the archangel by the Lombard monarchs guaranteed the diffusion of the cult northward in the seventh and eighth centuries. This migration is attested by a series of church dedications. In Pavia, the capital of the Lombard "regnum," San Michele

46 Paul the Deacon, *Historia Langobardorum*, Book II, chapter 32, *MGH SRL*, 90–91. The text of the *Historia Langobardorum* also appears in *PL* 95, entitled "De Gestis Langobardorum," cols. 433–672. (Book II, chapter 32 is at col. 502.) The *Historia* is also available in translation by W. D. Foulke, *The History of the Langobards* (Philadelphia, 1907). For the history of Monte Cassino, see Herbert Bloch, *Monte Casino in the Middle Ages* (1986): I, 1–13.

47 Book V, chapter 29, *MGH SRL*, 154; or "De Gestis Langobardorum," Book V, chapter 29, *PL* 95, cols. 609–10.

48 Book IV, chapter 46, *MGH SRL*, 135: Qui dum esset vir belicosissimus, et ubique insignis, venientibus eo tempore Grecis, ut oraculum sancti Michaelis archangeli in monte Gargano situm depraedarentur, Grimoaldus super eos cum exercitu veniens, ultima eos caede prostravit.

49 G. P. Bognetti, "I *Loca Sanctorum* e la storia della Chiesa nel regno dei Longobardi," in *L'Età Longobarda*, vol. 3 (Milan, 1967): 334–35. G. Otranto reiterates the opinion of Bognetti in "Il 'Liber de apparitione,' il santuario di san Michele sul Gargano e i Longobardi del Ducato di Benevento," in *Santuari e politica nel mondo antico* (Milan, 1983): 225.

50 *Ibid.*

Maggiore was dedicated in the seventh century. In 702, the abbey of Lucedio in Vercelli was placed under the patronage of St. Michael. Churches to St. Michael were dedicated in Brescia and Lucca in 720 and 795 respectively. Thus, although the defeat of the Lombards by the Carolingians would transform the political landscape of Europe, the diffusion of the cult of St. Michael was secure. Already in the sixth century the cult had spread from Italy to Merovingian Gaul, establishing a foothold in what would become the southern territory of the Carolingian empire.[51]

Mont-Saint-Michel

Built first as a small chapel on the forbidding slope of a rocky promontory jutting into the sea off the coast of Normandy, Mont-Saint-Michel became St. Michael's most famous sanctuary in the West. Throughout the Middle Ages, throngs of pilgrims converged on the isolated island.[52]

The foundation myth of Mont-Saint-Michel corresponds in many details to that of Monte Gargano, suggesting a degree of influence, if not direct appropriation. The legend is contained in a text known as the "Revelatio ecclesiae sancti Michaelis."[53] According to the legend, St. Michael appeared to St. Aubert, bishop of Avranches, during the reign of Childebert III, and commanded him to build a sanctuary in the archangel's honor on the rocky slope of a "place called Tomba by the local inhabitants," some six miles from Avranches.[54] Although the text itself does not specify a date, the vision has traditionally been assigned to the year 709 by various editors.[55] The bishop, however, was confused about the exact intended location of the church and did not act on the vision.[56] St. Michael appeared to the bishop a second time, telling him that he would find a bull on the spot where he was to construct the church. The bishop also had doubts about the size of the church, and the archangel appeared to him a third time. St. Michael told Aubert that the church should be built according to the dimensions marked out by the bull's hoofprints (section 6). The bishop set about gathering a group of workers to construct the archangel's church, but there were two massive

---

[51] For a discussion of the establishment and diffusion of Eastern devotions in Gaul, see E. Ewig, "Die Verehrung orientalischer Heiliger im spätrömischen Gallien und im Merovingerreich," in *Spätantikes und fränkisches Gallien: Gesammelte Schriften*, vol. 2, ed. Hartmut Atsma (Munich, 1979): 393–410. See also Philip Rousseau, "The Spiritual Authority of the 'Monk-Bishop': Eastern Elements in some Western hagiography of the Fourth and Fifth Centuries," *JTS* n.s. 23.2 (1971): 380–419.

[52] For an overview of pilgrimages to Mont-Saint-Michel during the Middle Ages, see E. R. Labande, "Les pèlerinages au Mont-Saint-Michel pendant le Moyen âge," in *MSM*, 3, 237–50.

[53] The text is listed as "Apparitio in Monte Tumba" (number 5951b) in *BHL*. The text is printed in *AASS*, Septembris VIII, 76–78. For a discussion of the ancient sources of the text, which appears in Avranches BM, MS 211, fols. 180–89, see J. Hourlier, "Les sources écrites de l'histoire montoise antérieure à 966," in *MSM*, 2, 121–32, who dates the composition of the "original" text to the middle of the ninth century (128).

[54] *AASS*, 76: Hic igitur locus Tumba vocitatur ab incolis.

[55] The edition which appears in *AASS* is based on that of Mabillon, who assigns the date to 708. More recently, however, Owen Chadwick has suggested that this vision is the event recorded in the tenth-century *Annales Cambriæ* under the year 718 as "Consecratio Michaelis archangeli" ("The Evidence of Dedications in the Early History of the Welsh Church," in *Studies in Early British History*, ed. N. Chadwick [Cambridge, 1954]: 184).

[56] The narrative of the three visions appears in section 5 of the "Apparitio" text (*AASS*, 77).

boulders on the site which no human could possibly have moved. St. Michael appeared to a man named Baino of a nearby village, commanding him to go to the site of the church and move the rocks. Incredibly, Baino moved the rocks as if they had been weightless, and construction of the church proceeded. Once the church was finished, St. Aubert sent for some relics from the archangel's church on Monte Gargano. He received a piece of the red altar-cloth which St. Michael had spread over the altar there and a piece of the marble on which the archangel had left his footprints (sections 7 and 8). The traditional date of the dedication of this original church on Mont Tombe is October 16 (xvii kal. Nov.), a date which appears in many sacramentaries and martyrologies (section 10).

Two miracles chronicled in the anonymous "Revelatio" merit attention here since they link St. Michael to a tradition of healing. The first miracle is the healing of a woman from the village of Asteriacus who had been blind all her life, but was cured at the newly dedicated church on Mont Tombe (section 9). The second miracle is the discovery of water on the island (section 11). Since the rock on which the church was built was surrounded by the sea, there was no visible source of fresh water. On St. Michael's suggestion, a rock near the church was broken open and from it came a stream of water which provided more than enough water for every need on the island.

There are striking similarities between the foundation myth of Monte Gargano and that of Mont Tombe. Both sites are physically isolated and feature rough terrain, precipitous slopes, and massive rock formations. Both myths involve a series of three apparitions to a local bishop. Similarly, a bull marks the spot on which the future church is to be built in each legend. Although Mont Tombe does not have a long history as a cultic healing site, the miracle of the restoration of the blind woman's sight suggests a link with the miraculous cures of Monte Gargano. Finally, the discovery of water plays an important role in each legend. These resemblances suggest that the legendary account of the founding of Mont Tombe is derived in large part from that of Monte Gargano. This conclusion is strengthened by the inclusion in the Mont Tombe legend of St. Aubert's mission to Monte Gargano to gain "relics" (a piece of the red cloth adorning the Garganic altar and a piece of the marble with the archangel's footprints), a mission whose existence acknowledges the debt.

The evolution of Michaeline devotions in the Carolingian empire followed the broad patterns established by the Lombards. With the defeat of the Lombards and the Frankish conquest of northern Italy in 773–774, the archangel was destined to become part of the Carolingian imperial mythology. Although there is evidence that St. Michael had been liturgically venerated in Merovingian Gaul since the sixth century, the archangel became the official protector and patron of the new ruling dynasty, the Carolingians, under Charlemagne, who became king of the Franks in 768.

Perhaps the first suggestion of St. Michael's future importance to the Carolingian empire came in the form of a letter from an Anglo-Saxon scholar and courtier named Cathwulf.[57] In 775, the year after Charlemagne became "king of the Lombards," Cathwulf urged him to institute a feast in honor of the Trinity, the angels, and all the saints. The Anglo-Saxon specifically mentioned masses in honor of St. Michael and St.

---

[57] The letter is printed in MGH, Epistolae Karolini Aevi, vol. II, ed. Ernst Dümmler (Berlin, 1884): 501–504. For a full discussion of Cathwulf and his letter, see Joanna Story, "Cathwulf, Kingship, and the Royal Abbey of Saint-Denis," Speculum 74 (1999): 1–21.

Peter and suggested that if Charlemagne were to institute such a feast, he would rule for eternity with the angels and archangels.[58]

As part of the campaign begun by his father, Pepin III, to unify the Frankish liturgy, Charlemagne asked Paul the Deacon, who was returning to Monte Cassino in 783, to request from Pope Hadrian I (772–795) a copy of the Gregorian sacramentary.[59] Sometime between the years 784 and 791, Hadrian sent Charlemagne a copy of the papal sacramentary. This sacramentary, known as the *Hadrianum*, and its Supplement were to become the basis of the Carolingian liturgical reforms.[60] Charlemagne outlined his conception of the renewal of Carolingian society based on a unified and Romanized liturgy and a well-educated clergy in the *Admonitio Generalis* of 789. In the *Admonitio* and succeeding councils, Charlemagne prohibited the veneration of unknown angels and legislated a general observance of St. Michael's feast day for September 29 in the Frankish realm.[61]

Although it is now thought that Alcuin was not responsible for the authorship of the Supplement, it is known that Charlemagne asked him to compose a variety of liturgical forms. Perhaps the most famous of these for the study of Michaeline devotions in Carolingian Gaul is Alcuin's "Sequentia de Sancto Michaele," in which he commemorates the archangel as the commander of the celestial host, an intercessor before the Lord, and vanquisher of the dragon at the end of time.[62]

For the feast of October 16, which celebrates the dedication of the church of the archangel on Mont Tombe, Charlemagne had composed the following preface in the Gallican Supplement of the *Hadrianum*: "It is proper . . . that on this day we proclaim the merits of St. Michael the archangel. For however much we are to venerate all the angels who stand in the presence of your Majesty, it is proper that in this celestial order the warrior (angel) deserves the first rank."[63]

The *laudes regiae* of the Carolingian era confirm St. Michael's primacy. Although the two oldest formularies in which the *laudes* are included date from 783–787, they are known to have been in use earlier.[64] According to the *Liber Pontificalis*, the *laudes* were sung to Charlemagne in 774 when the monarch visited Pope Hadrian in Rome at Easter.[65] At Charlemagne's coronation as Emperor in 800, the *laudes* were also sung. As militant acclamations of the victorious Christ and His representatives on earth, the *laudes* "invoke the conquering God – Christ the victor, ruler, and commander – and

[58] Dümmler, 504.

[59] For the account of Charlemagne's request and the subsequent development of the papal sacramentary, I have relied on Cyrille Vogel's remarks on "Gregorian Sacramentaries," in *Medieval Liturgy: An Introduction to the Sources*, revised and translated by William G. Story and Niels Krogh Rasmussen (Washington, D.C., 1986): 79–92.

[60] For a discussion of the development, contents, and various manuscripts of the *Hadrianum* and Supplement, see C. Vogel, *ibid.*, 85–92.

[61] The text of the Admonitio has been published in *MGH, SRL, Capitularia* 1, Capl. 22, ed. A. Boretius (Berlin, 1886): 52–62.

[62] *MGH, Poetae Latini Aevi Carolini*, 1 (Weimar, 1951): 348.

[63] Quoted from a proper of the Diocese of Coutances in René Ringot, *Saint Michael: Très Glorieux Prince des Archanges* (Arras, 1951): 157.

[64] The definitive study of the *laudes regiae* is that of Ernst H. Kantorowicz, *Laudes Regiae: A Study in Liturgical Acclamations and Medieval Ruler Worship* (Berkeley, 1958). For a discussion of the date and place of origin of the Carolingian *laudes*, see Kantorowicz, 53–56.

[65] *Liber Pontificalis*, vol. 1, ed. L. Duchesne (Paris, 1886): 498.

acclaim in him, with him, or through him *his imperial or royal vicars on earth* along with all the other powers conquering, ruling, commanding, and safeguarding the order of this present world: the pope and the bishops, the ruler's house, the clergy, the princes, the judges, and the army."[66]

The significance of the Carolingian *laudes* for the present study lies in the distribution of saints and apostles, those accorded to the pope and those to Charlemagne, in the *laudes regiae*.[67] Although the pope is acclaimed first, he is grouped with the apostles. Charlemagne is acclaimed second, but receives the first group of saints: Mary and the three archangels, Michael, Gabriel, and Raphael. Thus, the Carolingian *laudes regiae* invert the traditional order of saints and apostles found in the Litany of the Saints and thereby seem to inflate the importance of the king by associating him with the saints who are among the "first rank" of the celestial hierarchy.[68] Furthermore, Charlemagne is once again associated with St. Michael, first among the archangels and second only to the Virgin Mary in intercessory power.

St. Michael presided over the Carolingian era as the patron saint of its social, cultural, and imperial ambitions; Charlemagne ordered an image of the archangel depicted on the imperial standards with the inscription, "Patron and Prince of the Empire of the Gauls" (Patronus et Princeps Imperii Galliarum). Even more than for the Lombards, the archangel represented for the Carolingians the spiritual embodiment of their empire, their civilization. As Olga Dobiache-Rojdestvensky has explained, the Carolingian fascination with St. Michael the archangel was "a religious image, – superhuman, but linked to terrestrial interests, – eternal, immaterial, but incorporated in a dramatic myth, in which the struggle and the triumph, the past and the future are joined."[69]

In the foundation myth of Mont-Saint-Michel, St. Michael is not associated with healing. Although Mont Tombe is thought to have been the site of earlier pagan cults, the archangel superseded these not so much as a healer but as a founder of churches. He was a builder first of structures and later of empires. The legacy of Monte Gargano represented by the piece of the altar-cloth and the marble was appropriated by the new foundation myth to symbolize a transference of cultic power. Mont Tombe, its small chapel, and later Mont-Saint-Michel under the Benedictines, became the supreme pilgrimage site for those seeking the archangel's patronage of their imperial ambitions. Childebert III, Charles Martel, Charlemagne, Louis the Pious are but a few of the rulers

---

66 Kantorowicz, *Laudes Regiae*, 14 (emphasis mine).

67 For a detailed discussion of the sequence of saints, apostles, martyrs, and acclamations in the *laudes*, see Kantorowicz (31–53).

68 Kantorowicz notes a parallel inversion of the order of saints and apostles in the liturgy of the Coptic Jacobites. He suggests that "such 'Egyptian' symptoms are not rare in Gaul" and "may be accounted a survival, a Gallican remnant of earlier days, or, more likely, a later importation carried on the wave of Eastern influence in the sixth and seventh centuries" (52–53). Kantorowicz's suggestions are supported by the conclusions of Johannes Quasten, "Oriental Influence in the Gallican Liturgy" (*Traditio* 1 [1943]: 55–78), whose study appeared too late to be included in the first edition of Kantorowicz's book. Both views, however, support the hypothesis that sixth-century Gaul was the meeting-ground for Eastern and Western traditions.

69 *Culte*, 35 (my translation): "une image religieuse, – surhumane, mais liée aux intérêts terrestres, – éternelle, immatérielle, mais incorporée en un mythe dramatique, où la lutte et le triomphe le passé et le future se rejoignent."

who made at least one pilgrimage to the site of St. Michael's church on Mont Tombe seeking the archangel's patronage.

Thus, the continental migration of the archangel's cult would follow the established pattern of imperial appropriation from Gaul across the Rhine into the eastern territories of Lotharingia.[70] This eastward migration began first as part of the Anglo-Saxon mission to the Germanic territories under Boniface and continued later as part of the Carolingian imperial heritage. The Ottonian emperors dedicated a number of churches to St. Michael, and in the established pattern of the Lombard and Carolingian rulers appropriated the archangel's patronage for themselves and their political ambition. Perhaps the most striking example of this appropriation is the eleventh-century legend of the emperor Henry II's vision on Monte Gargano (*BHL* 5950). According to the legend, St. Michael, Gabriel, and all the angels would celebrate mass once a week at midnight in the grotto-chapel. Wishing to witness this angelic mass while on a visit to Monte Gargano, the emperor Henry II hid in a corner of the sanctuary. Discovered during the course of the office, Henry was invited by St. Michael to kiss the Gospel book used to celebrate the angelic mass. The emperor did not escape unscathed, however; as punishment for his audacity, Henry was struck lame for the remainder of his life. The legend is clearly part of an elaborate imperial myth meant to identify the emperor with the archangel and his celestial authority.

Summary

From this survey of the three principal cultic centers of Michaeline devotion, it is clear that the cult of the St. Michael spread from its origins in the ancient Near East to the West sometime in the fourth and fifth centuries, following in the legendary footsteps of Greek heroes to southern Italy. In Italy, the cult landed on the site of an ancient healing center associated with Calchas and Podaleirius. When the Garganic promontory was threatened by an incursion of Byzantine troops from Naples, the Lombard duke of Benevento mustered his forces to protect the sanctuary of the archangel. Thus, the cult of St. Michael was appropriated by the Lombards and transformed from a cult characterized by miraculous healings into an enterprise of nationalist expansion. Sometime in the sixth century, the cult spread to Merovingian Gaul, where it eventually flourished under the Carolingian dynasty, who adopted St. Michael as the patron saint of their imperial ambitions.

Although the imperial appropriation of the legends and cult became the established paradigm for the continental migration of the cult, this pattern does not adequately account for the establishment and development of the cult in Ireland and Anglo-Saxon England. Irish missionaries first came in contact with the cult of St. Michael on their continental peregrinations and particularly in Gaul, which served as the meeting ground of Eastern and Western religious traditions, and brought back to Ireland with them a tradition of devotion to the archangel. St. Columbanus first established Luxeuil in Gaul, and then near the end of his life traveled to Italy where he founded Bobbio in

---

[70] For an introduction to the cult in the Germanic territories, see Christian Wilsdorf, "La Diffusion du culte de Saint Michel en Allemagne," *MSM*, 3, 389–92.

613.[71] Certainly the many Irish missionaries who studied at Bobbio were likely to have returned to their homeland familiar with continental traditions of devotion to St. Michael. St. Patrick's tenure at Lérins some time in the early fifth century suggests a similar scenario. St. Michael became one of the most popular saints in Ireland, a fact which is attested by the large number of Irish liturgical and paraliturgical texts which mention the archangel.[72] Many of these Irish texts testify to St. Michael's currency in the elaborate eschatology of the Irish church.

From Ireland, a tradition of devotion to the archangel had spread to Northumbria and Mercia by the seventh century. Much of the evidence for the eighth and ninth centuries is found in liturgical and paraliturgical texts.[73] The calendars and prayers of this period reflect Irish influence. This influence becomes increasingly diffuse in the ninth and tenth centuries as a more general devotion to the archangel becomes the norm.[74] Indeed, the evidence of liturgical books suggest that the practice of devotion to St. Michael had taken on a more normative character by the late ninth and early tenth centuries.

The body of material surveyed in these first two chapters charts the development, diffusion, and consolidation of the archangel's principal roles from their literary origins in the Old and New Testament eras to their political appropriation by the Lombards and Carolingians. These roles constitute the thematic coordinates for the further elaboration of the archangel's character in the medieval English legends. In these legends, the archangel is most often characterized as an eschatological hero responsible for protecting the souls of the faithful in life, conveying their souls to heaven in death, for slaying Antichrist, and for summoning the dead to the Judgment on the Day of Doom. The chapters in the next section will first examine the English vernacular translations of the archangel's hagiographic foundation-myth and then focus on the representations of the archangel in the body of medieval English legends.

---

[71] For a general introduction to the subject of Insular contacts with Gaul in the fifth century, see Nora Chadwick, "Intellectual Contacts between Britain and Gaul in the Fifth Century," in *Studies in Early British History*, ed. H. M. Chadwick *et al.* (Cambridge, 1959): 189–263.

[72] For a full discussion of Irish devotion to St. Michael, see Chapter Two of my dissertation, "The Cult of Saint Michael the Archangel in Anglo-Saxon England," 103–32.

[73] I discuss this body of evidence and its Irish affiliations in "Feasts of Saint Michael the Archangel in the Liturgy of the Early English Church: Evidence from the Eighth and Ninth Centuries," *Leeds Studies in English* n.s. 31 (2000): 55–79.

[74] I am currently working on the evidence of a liturgical cult from this late period in an essay entitled in draft, "Evidence of a Liturgical *Cultus* of Saint Michael the Archangel in the Anglo-Saxon Church of the Tenth and Eleventh Centuries."

Part II

The Archangel in Medieval English Legend

3

Vernacular Versions of the Hagiographic Foundation-Myth

Ic eom michahel se heahengel godes ælmihtiges and ic symle on his gesihðe wunie.[1]

Ælfric's homily for September 29

Although never formally canonized by the church, St. Michael enjoyed considerable popularity from the earliest days of his cult in the ancient Near East.[2] As we have seen, at his cultic centers across Asia Minor, the archangel was invoked in accordance with his stature as a healer long before formal liturgical festivals became the normative means of expressing devotion to him. After the Eastern church began to formalize devotions to St. Michael, possibly in the late fourth or early fifth centuries (i.e., in the aftermath of the first Council of Laodicea), the archangel came to enjoy a number of different feast days in the East.[3]

Traditionally in the West, however, St. Michael has been celebrated on two principal feast days, May 8 and September 29, both of which originated with the cult of the archangel in Italy. Though no longer celebrated in the Roman calendar, the date May 8 holds special significance for the cult of St. Michael since it allegedly marks the day of both the archangel's legendary apparition to consecrate his own church and his intercession on behalf of the Sipontans in their victory over the pagan Neapolitans. The special feast instituted to commemorate this victory spread over the entire Latin

---

[1] Ælfric's homily for September 29 is published in Peter Clemoes, *Ælfric's Catholic Homilies: The First Series*, EETS SS 17 (Oxford, 1997) at 466: "I am St. Michael the archangel of God Almighty and I abide forever in his sight."

[2] The issue of the canonization of an angel, of course, would be a problematic one. Although there could not possibly be any bodily relics since the archangel is an incorporeal being, Mont-Saint-Michel claimed to possess the archangel's sword and shield (on which, see Jean LaPorte, "L'Épée et le Bouclier Dits 'De Saint Michel,'" *MSM*, 2, 397–410). St. Michael has been provided with a *vita*-of-sorts in the hagiographical foundation myth of Monte Gargano (*BHL* 5948) reviewed in the previous chapter.

[3] For example, September 6 marks the miracle at Chonae in the Greek, Russian, and Ethiopic churches (*AASS, Septembris* VIII, 7). June 8 in the Menology of Sirletus commemorates the dedication of Constantine's church to St. Michael at Sosthenion (*AASS, Septembris* VIII, 7). In the Ethiopic church, St. Michael is celebrated on June 6 and the twelfth day of every month (E. A. W. Budge, *The Book of Saints of the Ethiopian Church*, 6 vols. [Cambridge, 1928]: vol. 4, 986–92 [June 6]; and each volume for the twelfth day of the month).

Church but was later abandoned in favor of the feast of September 29.[4] The September date became the main feast of St. Michael, associated with the dedication of a church to the archangel on the Salarian Way, six miles north of Rome.

By the late ninth and early tenth centuries, however, the evidence of liturgical books suggests that the practice of devotion to the archangel in early medieval England had been largely stabilized in favor of the September 29 feast day. The ecclesiastical reforms of the tenth century further standardized these practices. From the tenth century, liturgical devotions to the archangel took on a more normative character and were highly regularized up until the Reformation. But what picture does the vast assortment of literature in Old English, Anglo-Norman, and Middle English paint? As might be expected, the representation of the archangel in this body of literature finds its fullest expression in the vernacular versions of the hagiographic foundation-myth (*BHL* 5948) of Monte Gargano. In its survey of these vernacular translations this chapter uncovers a pattern of expansion and elaboration of the archangel's traditional roles.

Translations of *BHL* 5948 in Old English

Although the Old English renderings of this myth occur primarily in homiletic texts associated with the archangel's principal feast day of September 29, the earliest references occur in a pair of notices for both of the May and September feast days in the ninth-century *Old English Martyrology*, a collection of commemorative entries arranged according to the liturgical calendar.[5] The entry for May 8 is brief, consisting of only 42 words, and shows no sign of the sort of elaboration of detail found in other entries.[6]

> On ðone eahteþan dæg þæs monðes bið þæt S<an>c<t>e Michaheles cirice ærest funden wæs on ðæm munte Gargano, þær se mon wæs ofscoten mid his agenre stræle, mid þy þe he wolde ðone fearr sceotan se stod on þæs scræfes dura.[7]

The entry abstracts the barest essentials of the Monte Gargano legend from the popular Latin account (*BHL* 5948). The use of the verb *findan* (to find, discover) in this entry, however, suggests a familiarity with certain continental descriptions of the May feast.

---

[4] For a full discussion of the establishment of St. Michael's feast days in the West, see my "Feasts of St. Michael the Archangel," especially 56–59. M. E. Ruggerini proposes only a slightly different scenario in "St. Michael in the *Old English Martyrology*," *Studi e materiali di Storia del'le Religioni* 65 (1999): 181–97.

[5] The standard edition is Günter Kotzor, *Das altenglische Martyrologium*, 2 vols., Abhandlungen der Bayerischen Akademie der Wissenschaften, phil.-hist. Kl., n.s. 88.1–2 (Munich, 1981). An earlier edition and translation can be found in G. Herzfeld, *The Old English Martyrology*, EETS OS 116 (London, 1900).

[6] As several scholars have shown, the text of the *Old English Martyrology* is likely to have been composed in two steps (C. Rauer, "The Sources of the *Old English Martyrology*," *ASE* 32 (2002): 89–109 at 90, n. 4). The first step consisted of compiling a register of saints' feast days with only the essential details of each entry. This step would be followed by the addition of supplemental details. Such a scenario would suggest that the May 8 entry in the *Old English Martyrology* represents the first stage of composition.

[7] Kotzor, *Das altenglische Martyrologium*, II, 96: On the eighth day of this month was St. Michael's church first found on mount Gargano, where the man was shot with his own arrow, with which he would shoot that bull that stood in the door of the cave.

In a Corbie martyrology of the early ninth century, May 8 is marked as "inventio sancti Michaelis archangeli in monte Gargano."[8] Similarly, a manuscript of the *Liber Pontificalis* describes the discovery of the church of St. Michael using the term *inventio*: "Huius temporibus inventa est aecclesia sancti angeli in monte Gargano."[9] According to the Toronto *Dictionary of Old English*, the verb *findan* can gloss the Latin term *invenire*, the verbal form of *inventio*.[10] Given the essential "Latinity" of the Old English Martyrologist, to borrow a phrase from J. E. Cross,[11] it is likely that the author was familiar with such continental sources as the Corbie martyrology. As recent scholarship has shown, the Old English Martyrologist was certainly familiar with the *Liber Pontificalis*.[12]

The notice for September 29 in the *Old English Martyrology*, however, is infinitely more illuminating. Not only does this entry shed some light on the martyrologist's method of composition,[13] but it also provides an interesting point of comparison with an anonymous homily, entitled "In Praise of St. Michael" by its editor, in CCCC MS 41.[14]

On ðone .xxviiii. dæg þæs monðes bið S<an>c<t>e Michaelis cirican gehalgung in Tracla þære ceastre in Eraclę ðære mægðe. Feonda menigo com to þære ceastre ond hy ymbsæton. Þa ceasterware þurh þreora daga fæsten ánmodlice bædon [God] fultumes, ond bædon þæt he him þone ætywde þurh S<an>c<t>e Michahel. Þa ðy þriddan dæge stod S<an>c<tus> Michahel ofer ðære ceastre gete ond hæfde fyren sweord in his honda. Þa wæron ða fynd abregede mid þy egesan ond hy gewiton ónweg, ond þa ceasterwara wunedon gesunde. Ond þær wæs getimbred S<an>c<t>e Michaheles cirice, ond seo wæs gehalgod on ðone dæg þe we mærsiað S<an>c<t>e Michaheles gemynd.[15]

J. E. Cross has shown that the account printed under September 29 differs in significant details from the Latin account of the legend. Cross has pointed out that while the *Old English Martyrology* notice for September 29 and the St. Michael homily in Corpus 41 (§

8 *AASS, Septembris* VIII, 6B.
9 L. Duchesne, *Le liber pontificalis*, 255, n. 2.
10 *Dictionary of Old English*, ed. Angus Cameron, Ashley C. Amos, Antonette diPaolo Healey, Sharon Butler, Joan Holland, David McDougall, and Ian McDougall (Toronto, 2003) s.v. *findan*.
11 J. E. Cross, "The Latinity of the Ninth-Century Old English Martyrologist," in P. Szarmach, ed., *Studies in Earlier Old English Prose* (Binghamton, NY, 1982): 275–99.
12 J. E. Cross, "On the Library of the Old English Martyrologist," in M. Lapidge and H. Gneuss, eds., *Learning and Literature in Anglo-Saxon England* (Cambridge, 1985): 227–49 at 243; Rauer, "The Sources of the *Old English Martyrology*"; and the vast body of work on the sources of the *Old English Martyrology* (and other Old English texts) compiled by the contributors to the *Fontes Anglo-Saxonici* Project, available on the World Wide Web at <http://fontes.english.ox.ac.uk>.
13 See J. E. Cross, "An Unrecorded Tradition of St. Michael in Old English Texts," *N&Q* n.s. 28, no. 1 (February 1981): 11–13; and "The Latinity of the Ninth-Century Old English Martyrologist."
14 Raymond J. S. Grant, *Three Homilies from Cambridge, Corpus Christi College 41* (Ottawa, 1982).
15 Kotzor, *Das altenglische Martyrologium*, II, 223–24: On the twenty-ninth day of this month was St. Michael's church consecrated in the town of Tracla in the province of Eraclae. A host of enemies came to the town and surrounded it. The citizens through a three-days' fast steadfastly prayed to [God] for help and prayed that he make a revelation to them through St. Michael. Then on the third day St. Michael stood over the gate of the town and had a fiery sword in his hand. The enemies were gripped with terror, and they withdrew, and the citizens remained unhurt. And there was built St. Michael's church, and it was consecrated on the day when we honor the memory of St. Michael.

23)[16] relate the same story, they each present new information not found in the other. Cross therefore concludes that they are each independently derived from an "unrecorded story about St. Michael (very probably in Latin) which was circulating in England by the ninth-century date of the Martyrology."[17]

The text reveals of this notice is comprised of three distinct layers of narrative. The first layer (M[1] and M[2]) is typical of other entries in this martyrology and serves as introduction and conclusion for the entry.[18] The second layer (S[1] and S[2]) comprises the details of the legendary account of the battle of the Sepontans against the pagan Neapolitans found in *BHL* 5948.[19] The two S-layers envelope the third layer (G) which consists of an image from the legend of St. Michael's appearance on the summit of the Moles Hadriani before the procession led by Gregory the Great.[20] Thus, the entry can be visualized in the following envelope pattern: M[1]–S[1]–G–S[2]–M[2].

M[1], which opens the notice, contains two anomalies: the names of the town, Tracla, and of the province, Eraclæ. In his note to this entry, the editor G. Herzfeld suggests that this might be a confusion resulting from a misreading of a source martyrological entry.[21] Herzfeld cites the Hieronymian martyrology and that of Usuard as two possible sources of the anomaly.[22] Perhaps the most likely source of the confusion, however, would be an entry similar to that found in the roughly contemporary martyrology of Hrabanus Maurus. The relevant portion of the entry for September 29 reads, "Dedicatio ecclesiae sancti Angeli Michaelis in monte Gargano in Thracia civitate Eraclea natale Eutici [Eutichii] Plautii."[23] The order of the two elements of the

---

16 Grant, *Three Homilies*, 63: Þis is se halga heahengel Sanctus Michael se ðe com on fultum þam crystenan, swa hit sægð in Actum Apostolorum, þæt on sumere ceastere ðære nama wæs Træleg and æghwelce geare hæðen here ayddon ða ceasterware. Ða gecwædon ða ceasterware him betweonum ðreora daga fæsten, and þa þæt fæsten geendod wæs, ða com him to Sanctus Michael, and he wæs to gefeohte gearu. Ða stod he ofer ðæs ceasteres burugate, and hæfde him ligen sweord on handa, and he aflimde ða elðeodligan sona þæt hi flugon on oðer ðeodland and hi næfre ma ðær oðeowdon. (This is the holy archangel St. Michael who came to the assistance of the Christians, as it says in the Acts of the Apostles, in a certain town whose name was Træleg and whose townspeople a heathen army oppressed every year. Then the inhabitants of the town agreed among themselves on a fast of three days, and, when the fast was ended, St. Michael came to htem, ready for battle. Then he stood over the town's main gate, holding a flaming sword in his hand, and he straightway put the strangers to flight so that they fled to another country and nevermore appeared there.)

17 Cross, "An Unrecorded Tradition," 13.

18 M begins "On ðone .xxviiii. dæg" and ends "in Eraclę ðære mægðe." M begins "Ond þær wæs getimbrod" and ends "we mærsiað S<an>c<t>e Michahelesgemynd."

19 S begins "Feonda menigo" and ends "þurh S<an>c<t>e Michahel." S begins "Þa wæron ða fynd" and ends "ceasterwara wunedon gesunde."

20 G comprises the sentence: "Þa ðy þriddan dæge stod S<an>c<tus> Michahel ofer ðære ceastre gete ond hæfde fyren sweord in his honda."

21 Herzfeld, *Old English Martyrology*, 236.

22 *Ibid.* The eleventh-century Ricemarch psalter and martyrology, which is one of the variant manuscripts of the Hieronymian martyrology consulted by the Bollandists, could represent an entry similar to the Old English Martyrologist's source (H. J. Lawlor, *The Psalter and Martyrology of Ricemarch*, HBS 47 [London, 1914]). The entry for September 29 reads, "In Tracia civitate Eraclae natale Eutici et Plauti et dedicatio basilicae beati archangeli Michaelis" (*AASS, Novembris* II, 532). Less likely is Herzfeld's suggestion of the martyrology of Usuard, which reads, "In monte Gargano, venerabilis memoria beati archangeli Michaelis, ubi ipsius consecrata nomine habetur ecclesia, vili facta scemate, sed cæesti prædita virtute. In Thracia, natalis sanctorum Eutici, Plauti, et Eraclæ" (*PL* 124: 517–18).

23 *PL* 110: 1171.

entry (i.e., the mention of the dedication of Michel's church before the mention of the martyrdom of Eutichus and Plautus) suggests the possibility of the misunderstanding. Thus, despite Cross's objection to Herzfeld's conclusion, it is possible that even a skilled reader of Latin might conflate the two elements of this entry.

As Cross suggested, the sources of *BHL* 5948 clearly inform this entry. The S[1] and S[2] portions of the entry are abstracted from those sources, summarizing details found in the "Liber de Apparitione."[24] Another legendary apparition, however, seems to have influenced the central image of the entry. St. Michael and his fiery sword in the G section are almost certainly related to the legend of St. Michael's appearance above the Moles Hadriani in which St. Michael is seen sheathing a bloody sword atop the mausoleum. M[2], the conclusion of the entry, is typical of other endings in the Martyrology, in reminding the reader of the significance of the feast day.

In his exemplary work on the sources of the *Old English Martyrology*, J. E. Cross has shown that the Martyrologist was at the very least a competent Latinist and an excellent abstracter of details, "who often echoed snatches of speech verbatim, and who reflected images from [his] sources."[25] Although the entry for September 29 does not contain any "snatches of speech verbatim," the composite nature of the notice is certainly in keeping with the Martyrologist's method of composition and suggests the use of three separate sources.

Aside from the notices in the *Old English Martyrology*, which are essentially abstracts of the legend, the two earliest vernacular[26] accounts of the hagiographic foundation-myth of the archangel's grotto-sanctuary on the summit of Monte Gargano in Anglo-Saxon England occur in the anonymous Blickling homily 16, "To Sanctæ Michaheles mæssan"[27] and Ælfric's homily for September 29, "Dedicatio Ecclesie Sancti Michahelis Archangeli."[28]

Blickling homily 16 for St. Michaelmas has received much close inspection because it contains a passage that is reminiscent both of the *Visio Pauli* and of the description of Grendel's mere in *Beowulf* (lines 2719–33), a connection first pointed out by Richard

[24] See Appendix A, section 2 of the "De apparitione" text.

[25] J. E. Cross, "On the Library of the Old English Martyrologist," 229.

[26] The hagiographic foundation-myth is first mentioned in a Latin homily once attributed to Bede but now acknowledged to be spurious (*Homeliae subdititiae*, Homily CI, *PL* 94: 502–503, on which see E. Dekkers, *Clavis Patrum Latinorum* [Turnhout, 1995]: 451 [1368] and J. Machielsen, *Clavis Patristica Pseudepigraphorum Medii Aevi. Opera Homiletica*, vol. 1 [Turnhout, 1990]: 616 [4073]). In this homily, the apparition of St. Michael on Monte Gargano is commemorated. The homily repeats the essential elements of the legend with little elaboration, aside from a first-person address by the archangel to the bishop of Sepontus instructing him to bring the people to the cave for worship.

[27] Richard Morris, *The Blickling Homilies*, EETS OS 58, 63, 73 (London, 1974–80; repr. as one volume 1967, 1990): 196–210. The homily is numbered 17 in Morris's edition. Morris's numbering, however, must be modified since he numbered 16 a fragment which is now recognized to belong to homily 4 (R. Willard, *The Blickling Homilies*, 38–40, especially note 82). The Blickling homily for St. Michael's feast will be referred to here as homily 16. The Blickling manuscript has been reproduced in photographic facsimile as volume 10 of the EEMF series, ed. R. Willard (Copenhagen, 1960). Homily 16 appears at fols. 120r–127r12.

[28] The earliest edition of this homily is by Benjamin Thorpe, *The Homilies of the Anglo-Saxon Church. The First Part, containing the Sermones Catholici or Homilies of Ælfric*, 2 vols. (London, 1844): I, 502–19. The standard edition now is Peter Clemoes, *Ælfric's Catholic Homilies: The First Series*, EETS SS 17 (Oxford, 1997): 465–75.

Morris.[29] The passage records a vision attributed to St. Paul in which "swearte saula" (black souls; i.e., sinners) dangle from trees on a cliff overlooking an ocean filled with "nicras" (water-monsters).

> Swa sanctus paulus wæs geseonde on norðanweardne þisne middangeard þær ealle wætero niðergewitad and he þær geseah ofer ðæm wætere sumne harne stan and wæron norð of ðæm stane awexene swiðe hrimige bearwas and ðær wæron þystrogenipo and under þæm stane wæs niccra eardung and wearga and he geseah þæt on ðæm clife hangodan on ðæm isgean bearwum manige swearte saula be heora handum gebundne and þa fund þara on nicra onlicnesse heora gripende wæron swa swa grædig wulf and þæt wæter wæs sweart under þæm clife neoðan and betuh þæm clife on ðæm wætre wæron swylce twelf mila and ðonne ða twigo forburston þonne gewitan þa saula niðer þa þe on ðæm twigum hangodan and him onfengon ða nicras.[30]

Although the scene is clearly indebted to a version of the *Visio Pauli*, its occurrence in the homily is not altogether surprising; in fact, it is carefully anticipated (whether this is a deliberate narrative strategy on the part of the author or not is another question). Several of the distinctive features of the episode are mentioned in the legendary account of St. Michael's apparitions. These features include a cliff, a rimy wood, dark mists, the distance of twelve miles, and even St. Paul himself. In the description of St. Michael's church (Morris, 207/10–28), the stones of the church are said to protrude steeply from it as if from a cliff ("ða stana swa of oðrum clife stæðhlyplice ut sceoredon"). In this same passage, the summit of the mountain is said to be covered with a rimy woods ("mid hsomige [hrimige?] wuda oferwexen"). Earlier, during the battle against the Neapolitans (Morris, 203/8–9), the summit is shrouded in dark mists ("mid þystro-genipum þæs muntes cnoll eal oferswogen wæs"). At the beginning of the homily (Morris, 197/20–22), the distance from the city walls of Siponto to the summit of the mount is said to be twelve miles ("Þonne syndon from þære burge weallum twelf mila ametene up to þæm hean cnolle"). The episode itself is prefaced, perhaps even prompted, by a paraphrase of St. Paul's Letter to the Hebrews 1:14:

> Qui ad ministrum summis. Englas beoð to ðegnunge gæstum fram Gode hider on world sended, to ðæm ðe þone ecean eðel mid mode and mid mægene to Gode

---

[29] Morris, *Blickling Homilies*, vi–vii. Charles Wright provides a comprehensive review of the scholarship on this scene (*The Irish Tradition*, 116–36).

[30] The passage appears in Morris's edition from page 209 at line 29 to page 211 at line 5 (henceforth indicated as follows: page number/line number). The scene as it appears here was first transcribed directly from the manuscript by Rowland Collins ("Blickling Homily XVI," 62) and quoted and translated by Wright (*The Irish Tradition*, 117): "So St. Paul was looking at this northern [part of the] world, where all waters go down, and there he saw over the water a grey rock, and to the north, grown exceedingly out of the rock, were frosty groves, and in that place were mists and darkness, and under the rock was the abode of water-monsters and wolves. And he saw that on the cliff many black souls were hanging on the icy groves, bound by their hands; and the (hellish) enemies of those (black souls), in the likeness of water-monsters, were taking hold of them even as a greedy wolf (would do); and the water was black under the cliff from beneath. And between the cliff and the water were such (black souls) for twelve miles, and when the boughs broke, then the souls that were hanging on the boughs went down and the water-monsters took them." In the EEMF facsimile edition, the scene occurs at folios 126v–127r.

geearniað, þæt him syn on fultume ða þe wið þæm awergdum gastum syngallice feohtan sceolan.[31]

The description of the "awergdum gastum" (accursed spirits) prompts the homilist to exhort his audience to entreat St. Michael and all angels for protection against all hell-fiends ("þæt hie us syn on fultume wiðhelsceaðum"). It seems then that the reference to St. Paul, which occurs in the Latin source of BHL 5948, may have provided the logical segue to the episode while the individual details (cliff, rimy woods, etc.) may have prompted the homilist to compose the scene.

Charles Wright has argued that the so-called Visio Pauli episode in Blickling 16 must "derive from two separate scenes . . . that must have been conflated in the homilist's source."[32] Wright points to a ninth-century redaction of the Visio Pauli (Redaction 11),[33] which combines several features of the scene (the hanging trees and the body of water filled with monsters), as an example of the type of source the Blickling homilist must have had before him.[34] The Insular, and probably Irish, origins of Redaction 11 suggest that the source of this scene in Blickling 16 may have originated in the Celtic sphere.[35]

The homily features St. Michael in several of his traditional roles. Noteworthy in this regard is the reference to the healing capabilities of a "swiðe wynsum ond hluttor wæta" (very pleasant and clear stream).[36] In keeping with the tradition of St. Michael's role as healer of the sick and wounded, the stream is said to cure "manige men of feforadle and on mislicum oðrum untrumnessum" (many men with fever-sickness and with various other infirmities).[37] The homily closes with an appeal to St. Michael "þæt he ure saula gelæde on gefean" (that he bring our souls into bliss), reference to the representation of St. Michael as psychopomp.[38]

Although Ælfric was an advocate of the reforms of the tenth-century Benedictine revival, a movement which sought in part to counter the uncritical acceptance of heterodox material in the anonymous homiletic tradition represented by the Blickling and Vercelli homilies, his homily on the dedication of St. Michael's church is characterized by both such heterodox material as the legend of the archangel's appearance on Monte Gargano and such traditional material as the Roman teaching on guardian angels. Since Ælfric generally avoided the use of apocryphal literature in his homilies, it is not surprising that St. Michael appears only once in his writings.[39] His homily for

---

[31] Morris, 209/22–27: Qui ad ministrum summis. Angels are as ministering spirits, sent hither into the world by God, to those who with might and main merit from God the eternal kingdom; so that they (the angels) should be a help to those who shall constantly contend against accursed spirits.

[32] The Irish Tradition, 121.

[33] This redaction was first published by M. E. Dwyer, "An Unstudied Redaction of the Visio Pauli," Manuscripta 32 (1988): 121–38.

[34] Wright, The Irish Tradition, 131–32. Certain details preclude this text from being the ultimate source of the episode (e.g., the trees in Redaction 11 are "fiery" whereas in the Blickling homily they are "icy").

[35] Charles Wright, "Some Evidence for an Irish Origin of Redaction XI of the Visio Pauli," Manuscripta 34 (1990): 34–44.

[36] Morris, Blickling Homilies, 209.

[37] Ibid., 209.

[38] Ibid., 211.

[39] In a text thought to have been partially written by Ælfric, "Visions of Departing Souls," St. Michael appears in his role as psychopomp ushering souls before the Lord that they may be judged. Given

September 29 marks the traditional feast day of St. Michael, and is found in twelve manuscripts, which reflects how widely this text was known.[40] The homily begins as a Monte Gargano homily, repeating the essential information of BHL 5948 in a fairly close translation of the Latin source. Max Förster first identified Ælfric's source of the Monte Gargano legend as a homily in a version of Paul the Deacon's homiliary "augmented" with additional homilies.[41]

The inclusion of the Monte Gargano legendary material in this homily is at odds with Ælfric's professed distrust of apocryphal material.[42] Yet, as if to mitigate the effect such legends might have on his audience, Ælfric uses the Euangelium portion of the homily to frame the various tales of St. Michael's apparitions on Monte Gargano in the context of an exegetical commentary on Matthew 18:1–10, the traditional reading for the third nocturn of Michaelmas. For his instructional commentary, Ælfric relies heavily on Haymo of Auxerre's exegetical commentary on this passage.[43] As several critics have pointed out, Haymo's homilies are often little more than "a cancatenation of patristic texts, embellished with occasional quotations from Scripture and illustrated with incidents from Church history."[44] Such a compilation suited Ælfric's didactic aims, given his position as an occasionally polemical reformer of the anonymous homiletic tradition, and may have quelled his anxiety over using the Gargano legendary material.

The second clause of Matthew 18:10, "Ic secge eow þæt heora englas symle geseoð

---

the nature of St. Michael's roles in this homily, however, it is not surprising that the passage in which St. Michael is mentioned is not one of those thought to have been composed by Ælfric. The homily has been edited by John C. Pope, Homilies of Ælfric: A Supplementary Collection, vol. 2, EETS OS 260 (London, 1968): 771–81.

[40] For a list of these manuscripts, see N. Ker, Catalogue of Manuscripts containing Anglo-Saxon (Oxford, 1957), Appendix C, 512–13; and A Plan for the Dictionary of Old English, eds. R. Frank and A. Cameron (Toronto, 1973): 57.

[41] Originally compiled at the request of Charlemagne as part of his ecclesiastical reforms and comprised largely of patristic sermons adapted for reading, Paul the Deacon's homiliary had added to it many new homilies in succeeding centuries. These subsequent versions are known as "augmented" homiliaries. The text of BHL 5948 is such an additional text since the original version of Paul the Deacon's homiliary did not contain a text for the archangel's September 29 feast (J. Leclercq, "Tables pour l'inventaire des homiliares manuscrits," Scriptorium 2 [1948]: 195–214 at 205–14). Förster first pointed out Ælfric's source in his doctoral dissertation at the University of Berlin. The dissertation was subsequently published in two parts, Über die Quellen von Aelfrics Homiliae Catholicae, I Legenden (Berlin, 1892), and "Über die Quellen von Aelfrics exegetischen Homiliae Catholicae," Anglia 16 (1894): 1–61. The homily itself is in the augmented version of Paul the Deacon's Homiliary printed by Migne in PL 95: 1522–25 (Pars Aestiva 56). For a convenient summary of Förster's work and the identification of additional sources, see Cyril Smetana, "Aelfric and the Early Medieval Homiliary," Traditio 15 (1959): 163–204. Smetana briefly discusses the homily on St. Michael at page 194.

[42] For a cogent review of the evidence of Ælfric's distrust of the vernacular homiletic tradition's use of apocryphal and therefore unreliable materials, see Joyce Hill, "Reform and Resistance: Preaching Styles in Late Anglo-Saxon England," in De l'homélie au sermon: histoire de la prédication médiévale, ed. Jacqueline Hamesse and Xavier Hermand, Publications de l'Institut d'Études Médiévales: Textes, Études, Congrès 14 (Louvain-la-Neuve, 1993): 15–46.

[43] Förster was also the first to identify a homily by Haymo as the source of Ælfric's commentary (Legenden, 24). Haymo's homily is printed in PL 95: 1525–30 (Pars Aestiva 58).

[44] Cyril Smetana, "Aelfric and the Homiliary of Haymo of Halberstadt," Traditio 17 (1961): 457–69 at 457.

mines Fæder ansyne seðe on heofonum is" (I say unto you, that their angels ever look upon the countenance of my Father who is in heaven), prompts Ælfric to comment on the doctrine of guardian angels. Quoting various passages from the Old and New Testaments, culminating in Daniel 10:13, Ælfric traces the development of the doctrine. Ælfric brings the homily to a close by praising St. Michael as the "singallice cristenra mann gefylsta on eorðan, and þingere on heofonum to þam Ælmihtigan Gode" (constant supporter of Christian men on earth and intercessor in heaven with Almighty God).[45] Thus, Ælfric's use of the Monte Gargano legendary material and his reliance on Haymo's exegetical commentary reflect a syncretic union of two seemingly antithetical points of view and suggest several conclusions. First, it seems likely that Ælfric made use of a source which contained both types of material. And second, the legendary character of the Monte Gargano material is in keeping with the heterodox tradition of the anonymous homilies of the Blickling and Vercelli collections, suggesting the possibility that Ælfric may have used a source text very like Blickling 16 (or its source text).

Over a hundred years ago, Förster briefly noted the similarities between Blickling homily 16 and Ælfric's homily for September 29.[46] Although a cursory analysis of the texts indicates that they do not correspond exactly to one another, the structural similarity and verbal agreement of the texts suggest that the relations of the two texts deserve to be more closely studied.[47] The broad strokes of the narrative of BHL 5948 in the two homilies exactly parallel each other. Both texts follow the three-fold arrangement of the "De apparitione" narrative: the story of Garganus and his bull; the description of the Neapolitan campaign; and the establishment of the archangel's church.[48]

The amount of verbal agreement (words and phrases shared by the two texts) suggests that these texts are closely related. Paleographically, the manuscript of the Blickling Homilies (Princeton University Library, W. H. Scheide Collection MS 71) is dated to the latter half of the tenth century (homily 11 contains an internal reference to the year 971). While most critics agree that the composition of the homilies must have taken place even earlier, possibly as early as the reign of King Alfred (871–899), the consensus opinion is that the homilies are "at least a generation earlier than Ælfric's earliest publication of his work around 990."[49] Given the range of dates for the composition of the homilies in the Blickling collection, then, it is worth exploring the possiblity that Ælfric could have used Blickling 16 (or something very much like it) as the exemplar for the account of the archangel's legendary apparitions on Monte

---

[45] Smetana, "Aelfric and the Homiliary of Haymo of Halberstadt," 518.

[46] Förster, Legenden, 195.

[47] The call for such a study has most recently been made by E. Gordon Whatley in his entry for "Michael archangelus" (under the generic heading "Acta Sanctorum") in SASLC, 343–46 at 345.

[48] For a discussion of the "De apparitione" text and its layers of narrative accretion, see Chapter Two, 37–41.

[49] Milton McC. Gatch, Preaching and Theology in Anglo-Saxon England: Ælfric and Wulfstan (Toronto, 1977): 8. In The Apocryphal Gospels of Mary in Anglo-Saxon England (Cambridge, 1998), however, Mary Clayton rightly points out that there is no conclusive evidence to argue that the habit of using apocrypha (as in the anonymous homilies of the Blickling and Vercelli collections) was exclusively a pre-Reform activity. She notes, for example, that "Ælfric's predecessors and contemporaries in the reform period were clearly interested in and well acquainted with apocryphal gospels of Mary's death and assumption and on her nativity": 149.

Gargano in his homily for Michaelmas.[50] Corroborating evidence for such a conclusion can perhaps be found in the verbal agreement of the two texts.

Many of the verbal parallels differ only by the use of one or two words, as in the following examples:[51]

Blickling 16:   "*þonne is seo circe on Campania þæs landes gemæro*" (The church is on the border of the lands of Campania);

Ælfric: "Seo dun stent *on Campania landes gemæron*" (The mountain stands on the borders of the land of Campania);

Blickling 16:   "*Wite þu eac þæt se mon se þær mid his agenum* stræle *ofsceoten wæs þa þæt wæs mid minum willan gedon*" (Know also that the man who was shot with his own arrow, that that was by my will done);

Ælfric: "*Wite ðu gewislice, þæt se mann ðe mid his agenre flan ofscoten wæs, þæt hit is mid minum willan gedon*" (Know for certain that the man who was shot with his own arrow, that it was done with my will);

Blickling 16:   "*ic on his* gesihþe *simle* stonde" (in his sight I stand forever);

Ælfric: "*ic symle on his* gesihðe wunige" (in his sight I abide forever);

Blickling 16:   "*On þa ilcan tide Naepolite . . .*" (At the same time the Neapolitans . . .);

Ælfric: "*þa on ðære ylcan tide Naepolite . . .*" (Then at the same time the Neapolitans . . .);

Blickling 16:   "*mid þystro-genipum þæs muntes cnoll eal oferswogen wæs*" (with dark mists the summit of the mountain was all covered);[52]

Ælfric: "*þæs muntes cnoll mid* þeosterlicum *genipum eal oferhangen wæs*" (the summit of the mountain with dark clouds/mists was all overhung).

At other places the homilies differ in wording only by the alteration of word order and phrasing:[53]

Blickling 16:   "*Ic þonne gelyfe se heahengel* ures Drihtenes *micele swiðor sohte and lufode þære heortan clænesse þonne þara stana frætwednesse*" (I therefore believe that the archangel of our Lord much more sought and loved cleanness of heart than the adornment of stones);

Ælfric: "*Ic gelyfe þæt se heah-engel* mid þam geswutelode þæt he *micele swiðor sohte and lufode þære heortan clænysse þonne ðæra stana frætwunge*" (I believe that the archangel would thereby manifest that he much more sought and loved cleanness of heart than the adornment of stones);

Blickling 16:   "*Se biscop þa ðær* gesette gode *sangeras* and mæssepreostas and manigfealdlice ciricean þegnas þa þær seoððan *dæghwamlice mid gelimplicere endebyrdnesses* weorðode" (The bishop then assigned there good singers and masspriests and manifold church ministers who afterwards worshipped there daily in fitting manner);

[50] Although it is possible, it seems unlikely. I propose a more plausible source-type below.

[51] This and subsequent lists are by no means exhaustive. Other examples occur at Morris, 201/4–5 and Clemoes, 466/28–29; Morris, 203/5–6 and Clemoes, 467/52–53; Morris, 205/13 and Clemoes, 467/73; and Morris, 207/13–14 and Clemoes, 468/97–98.

[52] On the word "þystro-genipum," see Rowland L. Collins, "Six Words in the Blickling Homilies," in *Philological Essays: Studies in Old and Middle English Language and Literature in Honor of Herbert Dean Merritt*, ed. James L. Rosier (The Hague, 1970): 137–41 at 141. Collins argues that "the noun *þystrogenip* should enter the lexicon as 'dark mist.'"

[53] Other examples occur at Morris, 207/21–23 and Clemoes, 468/101–3; Morris, 207/36, 209/1–3 and Clemoes, 469/114–17; Morris, 209/4–5 and Clemoes, 469/117–18; and Morris, 209/6–9 and Clemoes, 469/118–20.

Ælfric: "*Se biscop ða ðær Godes ðeowas gelogode, sangeras,* and ræderas, and sacerdas, þæt hi *dæghwamlice ðær Godes þenunge mid þæslicere endebyrdnysse gefyldon*" (The bishop then placed God's servants there, singers, and readers, and priests, that they perform daily there God's service in suitable manner).

The striking verbal echoes of many of these examples seem to substantiate the suggestion that Ælfric may have used an exemplar similar to Blickling 16. As these examples also indicate, however, Ælfric's syntax is frequently different than that of Blickling 16, suggesting the more likely possibility that Ælfric and the Blickling Homily represent indepedent translations of the same Latin text.

Despite the structural and verbal agreement of the two texts, Ælfric's text is in general more compressed than that of Blickling 16. Structurally, Ælfric's homily has no introduction while the Blickling homily opens with a call to honor the archangel, which describes in metaphorical terms the archangel's church: the church stands glorified in "sundorweorþunge þurh godcundra mægen" (in special privileges through divine power) and is "mid ece mægene geweorþod" (honored with everlasting virtue). These descriptions serve to remind the listeners of the special virtue of honoring the archangel. Ælfric's homily contains no such exhortations.

Other examples of compression in Ælfric's homily can be found in the following three passages.[54] The first passage describes the release of the fateful arrow by the enraged Garganus:

Blickling 16:   "Þa genam he his bogan and hine gebende and ða mid geættredum stræle ongan sceotan wiþ þæs þe he geseah þæt hryþer stondan" (Then he took his bow and bent it and then with poisoned arrow began to shoot towards where he saw the bull stand);

Ælfric: "and gebende his bogan and mid geættrode flam hine ofsceotan wolde" (and bent his bow and with a poisoned arrow would shoot him).

The second passage is St. Michael's first direct speech address to the bishop of Siponto:

Blickling 16:   "and min nama is Michael; ic eom heahengel Heofoncyninges and ic on his gesihþe simle stonde" (and my name is Michael; I am the archangel of Heaven's King and in his sight I stand forever);

Ælfric: "Ic eom Michael se heah-engel Godes Ælmihtiges and ic symle on his gesihðe wunige" (I am Michael the archangel of God Almighty and I abide forever in his sight).

The third passage is St. Michael's reply to the bishop of Siponto concerning the consecration of the church:

Blickling 16:   "min is þonne þæt ic mid arwyrðnesse tacne æteowe and gecyþe hine purh hine [me?] sylfne hie gehalgode and gebletsode" (I, on my part, will appear by a solemn token, and manifest it, that I myself have hallowed and consecrated it);

---

54 Other examples include the Pope's reply to the bishop of Siponto concerning the consecration of the church (Morris, 205/23–32 and Clemoes, 467–8/77–81) and the description of the discovery of the archangel's footprints by the north door of the grotto-chapel (Morris, 203/34–36, 205/1–4 and Clemoes, 467/65–68).

Ælfric: "ic þonne geswutelige hu ic ða stowe ðurh me sylfne gehalgode" (I will then show how I through myself hallowed the place).

In each passage, Ælfric's homily compresses the longer Blickling episode into a passage which includes all the essential details but none of the convoluted syntax.

In other passages, especially those the author would have found theologically troubling, Ælfric's homily omits or emends the offending elements. In one such scene in the Blickling homily, for example, the bishop of Siponto instructs the citizens "to Sancte Michaele þæt hie wilnodan þæt God gecyþde þæt mannum bemiþen wæs and bedigled" (to St. Michael that they entreat that God make known that which was concealed and hidden from men). It is likely that Ælfric would have found troubling the notion of entreating the archangel to discover God's purpose, especially since the archangel has no connection with the cave yet at this point in the narrative. In his homily, Ælfric omits St. Michael from the passage and has the bishop instruct the citizens to entreat God directly: "Se biscop ða funde him to ræde þæt hi mid þreora daga fæstene swutelunge þæs wundres æt Gode bædon" (The bishop then found it advisable that they should ask from God an explanation of the miracle with a fast of three days).

Similarly, in the first vision scene in the Blickling homily, St. Michael tells the bishop that by his signs he is the creator and guardian of the grotto where the bull was found: "and eac gecyþe on eallum ðæm tacnum þe þær gelimpeð þæt ic eom ðære stowe on sundran scyppend and hyrde" (and also show by all those signs that occur there that I am of that place especially the creator and guardian). Reluctant to accept uncritically the Blickling homilist's representation of St. Michael as the active agent of the "signs" and creator of the grotto, Ælfric maintains the archangel's authority as guardian of the place, but has transformed him into a passive witness of God's power of miracles: "ic wolde mid þære gebicnunge geswutelian þæt ic eom ðære stowe hyrde; and ealra ðæra tacna ðe ðær gelimpað ic eom sceawere and gymend" (I would by that sign manifest that I am the guardian of the place; and of all the miracles which happen there, I am the watchman and keeper). It is interesting to note that in each of these two passages Ælfric's text agrees in large part with the Latin texts of BHL 5948, a fact which will be explored further below. Although these examples of compression and omission do not entirely rule out the possibility that Ælfric used a source text similar to the Blickling homily or its source, they suggest that at the very least he redacted his source text heavily.

In addition to the verbal agreement and the examples of compression, there are also several differences between the two texts. The two most obvious differences are that Blickling 16 includes the interpolated scene from the *Visio Pauli* which Ælfric's homily does not, and the Ælfric homily contains a gospel lesson (on Matthew 18:1–10) not included in the Blickling homily. There are two other, more significant, differences, however, which suggest that the two texts were copied from two separate source texts. The first example occurs in the section covering the Neapolitan campaign. In the Blickling homily, St. Michael tells the bishop that the Sipontans should be prepared to fight the enemy at "þriddan tide on morgene" (at the third hour in the morning). In Ælfric's homily, however, the battle is set for "ane tid ofer undern." Although Thorpe translates Ælfric's passage as "one hour after morning," the term "undern" generally means "the third hour of the day" in Old English.[55] Thus, Ælfric most likely meant that

---

[55] Bosworth-Toller lists several other examples in Ælfric of the use of the term "undern" to mean

the battle would take place at the fourth hour of the day, a detail which corresponds to the Latin accounts of *BHL* 5948.

The second example occurs in the section on the establishment of St. Michael's church. After the grotto-chapel has been discovered and the two altars installed, the bishop of Siponto seeks the Pope's advice on the consecration of the church. In the Blickling homily, the Pope replies that the citizens of both Siponto and Rome should make a four-day fast, praying to the Trinity for guidance on the issue (Morris, 205/23–32). In Ælfric, the bishop enjoins only the citizens of Siponto to make a three-day fast and pray to the Trinity for guidance (Clemoes, 468/81–4). Interestingly, in this instance the Blickling homily is closer to the Latin accounts than Ælfric's homily. Although these differences are minor and could conceivably be attributed to scribal error, they suggest the use of two different exemplars (i.e., two different redactions of *BHL* 5948) in the composition of the vernacular accounts.

The exemplars for both these texts are most likely to have been in Latin. In addition to the two vernacular accounts, there are at least four Anglo-Latin recensions of *BHL* 5948.[56] Two are found in the manuscripts of the so-called "Cotton-Corpus" Legendary (London, BL, Cotton MS Nero E.i, pt. 2, fols. 147r–148v [xi^{med}, xi^{2}] and Salisbury, Cathedral Library, MS 222, fols. 179v–180v; *olim* Oxford, Bodleian Library, MS Fell 1 [xi^{ex}]).[57] In an article based on the research of his doctoral dissertation, Patrick Zettel has suggested that this mid-eleventh century English Legendary represents a collection of hagiographic texts very similar to the one which Ælfric may have used as the source for some of the saints' lives in his *Catholic Homilies* and *Lives of the Saints*.[58] Zettel believes the Cotton-Corpus Legendary was written on the continent in the late ninth century and introduced sometime in the tenth century to Anglo-Saxon England, where it circulated widely.

In his doctoral thesis, Zettel briefly examines the similarities between the Ælfric Michaelmas homily and the Cotton-Corpus text of *BHL* 5948.[59] He notes that although Ælfric's recension does not correspond exactly to that of Cotton-Corpus, the Legendary

---

"third hour of the day" (*An Anglo-Saxon Dictionary*, s.v. *undern*). Bosworth-Toller also notes several instances of the word in the Blickling homilies.

[56] There remain many Anglo-Latin homiliaries which have not yet been examined. The work begun by the late J. E. Cross and continued by Thomas N. Hall in this field may yet uncover additional copies of *BHL* 5948.

[57] Although both Wilhelm Levison ("Conspectus codicum hagiographicorum," *MGH SRM7* [1920]: 529–706 at 545–46) and Neil Ker ("Membra Disiecta, Second Series," *British Museum Quarterly* 14 [1939–40]: 82–83) first suggested the unity of the collection of manuscripts known as the "Cotton-Corpus Legendary," Patrick Zettel coined the title in his doctoral dissertation ("Ælfric's Hagiographic Sources and the Latin Legendary Preserved in BL MS Cotton Nero E.i + CCCC MS 9 and Other Manuscripts," [Oxford, 1979]) and the article, "Saints' Lives in Old English: Latin Manuscripts and Vernacular Accounts: Ælfric" (*Peritia* 1 [1982]: 17–37). More recently the Legendary has been discussed by Rosalind Love, who edits three saints' lives from the collection (*Three Eleventh Century Anglo-Latin Saints' Lives: Vita S. Birini, Vita et miracula S. Kenelmi, and Vita S. Rumwoldi* [Oxford, 1996]: xviii–xxiii). For a brief discussion of the manuscripts and a list of the contents of the Legendary, see Peter Jackson and Michael Lapidge, "The Contents of the Cotton-Corpus Legendary," in *Holy Men and Holy Women: Old English Prose Saints' Lives and their Contexts*, ed. Paul E. Szarmach (Albany, 1996): 131–46.

[58] "Saints' Lives in Old English," 22.

[59] "Ælfric's Hagiographic Sources," 182–84.

does contain readings closer to Ælfric than to the printed editions he consulted.[60] Of six instances of close correspondence between Ælfric and Cotton-Corpus which Zettel points out, one is particularly striking as it also occurs in Blickling 16.[61] The passage describes the miraculous water dripping from the roof-stone behind the altar:

Blickling 16:   "þæt þa biggengan þe *on ðære stowe* stille wunodan" ([used by] the inhabitants who still lived in that place);

Ælfric: "þæt gecigdon ða ðe *on þære stowe* wunodon, stillam, þæt is, dropa" (which those who dwelt in that place called "stilla," that is, drop);

Cotton-Corpus: "quam incolae *loci illius* stillam vocant" (which the inhabitants of that place call "stillam").

Although Zettel points out that the Cotton-Corpus text "provides a source reading which is marginally closer to Ælfric than any of the three printed editions" he consulted, which each have "quam incolae stillam vocant,"[62] it would seem that the Blickling homily is in fact closer to the Cotton-Corpus text. It is possible that Ælfric's wording is simply a translation of "incolae," and although the Blickling homilist seems to have been confused by his Latin source,[63] his wording shares the redundancy of the Latin phrase underlined above. Although it is possible that Ælfric's wording is borrowed from the Blickling homily, the fact that the confusion over the Latin "stillam" does not occur in Ælfric's text is yet another indication that Ælfric's wording cannot have derived from that of the Blickling homily.

The existence of two additional copies of *BHL* 5948, uncovered several years ago by the late J. E. Cross and Thomas N. Hall, has shed some doubt on Zettel's hypothesis that the Cotton-Corpus Legendary represented the source for Ælfric's hagiographical writings.[64] A full copy of the text is found in Salisbury, Cathedral Library, MS 179 (fols. 91v–92r; xi^ex), an augmented version of Paul the Deacon's homiliary.[65] The other copy unfortunately is just a fragment, comprising roughly one-third of the total text of *BHL* 5948, found in Canterbury, Cathedral Library, MS Addit. 127/1 (2v; xi^1).[66] It is followed by a second fragment comprising a portion of Haymo of Auxerre's homily, "In festo S. Michaelis archangeli."[67] Haymo's homily is an exposition of Matthew 18:1–10 and is Ælfric's explicit source for the *Evangelium* portion of his homily on the

---

[60] For his thesis, Zettel consulted the editions of *BHL* 5948 in B. Mombritius, *Sanctuarium seu vitæ sanctorum*, 2nd ed., 2 vols. (Paris, 1910): II, 219–20; *AASS, Septembris* VIII, 61–62; and G. Waitz, *MGH SRL*, 541–43. He did not consult the edition of Surius.

[61] I wish to thank Gordon Whatley for first directing my attention to these passages.

[62] "Ælfric's Hagiographic Sources," 184. On the printed editions Zettel consulted, see note 61 above.

[63] The Blickling homilist perhaps misread his source. He translates the word "stillam" (drop) from his Latin source as the English adverb "still" (i.e., at or up to the time indicated).

[64] For a discussion of these findings, see J. E. Cross and T. N. Hall, "The Fragments of Homiliaries in Canterbury Cathedral Library MS Addit. 127/1 and in Kent, County Archives Office, Maidstone, MS PRC 49/2," *Scriptorium* 47 (1993): 186–92.

[65] According to Cross and Hall, all homiliaries based on Paul the Deacon's "composed or known in Anglo-Saxon England, except one" (the exception is Saint-Omer, Bibliothèque Municipale 202) were "augmented" versions of Paul the Deacon's homiliary ("Fragments of Homiliaries," 186).

[66] The fragment begins "Memoriam beati archangeli Michaelis..." and ends "...D<e>i archangel<u>s ep<isc>opu<m> per" (*ibid.*, 189).

[67] This fragment begins "paruulos d<omi>n<u>s suos uolebat" and ends "in hoc seculo carnaliter uiuens se solum p<er>dat" (*ibid.*, 189). Haymo's homily is printed in *PL* 118: 770–76 (the Canterbury fragment is found at 772C–74A).

dedication of the archangel's church. Since the Cotton-Corpus Legendary text does not contain Haymo's exegetical homily, it seems more likely that the two Canterbury fragments taken together represent a full text which resembles closely the sort of text (most likely an augmented version of Paul the Deacon's homiliary) Ælfric must have used for his Michaelmas homily.[68]

Translations of *BHL* 5948 written in the Anglo-Norman Period

Of Norman devotion to the archangel warrior, there is a great deal of evidence. The Anglo-Saxon Chronicles relate that Duke William arrived in England on either "the eve of Michaelmas" (Worcester Chronicle) or on "St. Michael's Day" (Laud/ Peterborough Chronicle). Given St. Michael's popularity as commander of the angelic host, such strategic planning could hardly have been a coincidence. At the Battle of Hastings, Robert of Mortain, Duke William's half-brother, fought under the standard of St. Michael. Devotion to the archangel increased when the Normans conquered southern Italy and took possession of Monte Gargano, thereby uniting under the same authority the two most famous centers of the cult of St. Michael in Europe.

When William arrived in England, he was committed to reforming the English Church. The vigor of the tenth-century reform movement had waned by the middle of the eleventh century, and many irregularities in ecclesiastical practices were evident. In one of his first politico-ecclesiastical maneuvers, William sought the removal of the English Archbishop of Canterbury, Stigand, who had been uncanonically appointed. Stigand was deposed by a Papal Legate in 1070, and William brought Lanfranc, an Italian who had first been Prior of the monastery of Le Bec and then Abbot of William's own foundation of St. Stephen's, Caen, to England to replace him. Together William and Lanfranc sought to reform the English monasteries by tightening their observance of their rules and to rid them of the vestiges of English nationalism which had taken refuge there. Thus, William used the reform of the church as an agent of colonization, and by the end of his reign (1087) the English episcopate had been almost entirely Normanized. Despite William's militant aims of monastic reform and colonization, there was a degree of continuity between the late Anglo-Saxon and Anglo-Norman churches in the realm of the veneration of local and popular saints. The cults of St. Cuthbert at Durham, St. Edmund in his Suffolk borough, and St. Ætheldreda at Ely, to name only a few, were all eagerly taken up by the Normans.[69] The cult of St. Michael, already firmly established in Anglo-Saxon devotions, likewise prospered under the Normans.

The textual evidence of the Anglo-Norman period reflects the sociological reality of a "bilingual" culture. One of the immediate effects of the Conquest was to introduce an alien aristocracy and a military caste, both of which were French-speaking. During the course of his reign, William also introduced new, continental personnel into the higher

---

[68] I am presently working on a detailed analysis of the correspondences between Blickling, Ælfric, the Salisbury text, and the two Canterbury fragments in order to substantiate more fully this hypothesis.

[69] S. J. Ridyard, "*Condigna Veneratio*: Post-Conquest Attitudes to the Saints of the Anglo-Saxons," *Anglo-Norman Studies* 9 (1987): 179–206.

ranks of the existing ecclesiastical hierarchy. This cadre was also French-speaking, and for the first hundred years or so after the Conquest, the division of classes meant a division of languages. This linguistic division is of great significance for the texts of this period. On the one hand, those texts of the early Anglo-Norman period (1066–1150)[70] which seem to have been aimed at lay audiences (e.g., homilies) were produced in the English vernacular, or in other words a late variety of Old English. On the other hand, those texts of the later period (1150–1250), which are more artful, less plainly didactic, were written in Anglo-Norman. Nevertheless, in all these texts that St. Michael is assigned one or more of three principal roles. He is recognized as the guardian of Christians and their bodies after death. He is known for his victory over the dragon of Revelation 12:7. But perhaps most significantly for a study of his the development of his legendary persona, St. Michael is acknowledged as a powerful intercessor on behalf of mankind.

Although St. Michael appears in numerous liturgical calendars[71] between the Conquest and the mid-thirteenth century, the earliest textual evidence containing an explicit reference to the archangel is from a manuscript of the early twelfth century (British Library, Cotton Vespasian MS D. xiv).[72] The texts are all copied in Old English and the vast majority of them are taken from the manuscripts of Ælfric's homilies (principally Cambridge, University Library MS Gg. 3. 28.). The homily for the Festival of St. Michael is no exception. In its original form, the homily is a Monte Gargano homily (*BHL* 5948), repeating the essential information of the foundation-myth reviewed in Chapter Two. As preserved in this twelfth-century manuscript, however, the homily lacks the legendary material and only reproduces the *Euangelium* portion of Ælfric's homily. In this segment of the homily, Ælfric explicates Matthew 18: 1–10 (the reading for the third nocturn of Michaelmas), principally by quoting Haymo of Auxerre's commentary on the passage. Ælfric also summarizes traditional patristic teaching on guardian angels and archangels, describing St. Michael in particular as the "prince of the Hebrew folk,"[73] a paraphrase of Daniel 12:1. The homily ends by

---

[70] In *From Latin to Modern French* (Manchester, 1952), M. K. Pope divides the history of Anglo-Norman into two periods, the period of development and the period of degeneracy. This section focuses primarily on the literature of the period of development, which she argues spanned roughly the years 1066 to ca. 1250. This period she further subdivides into two stages. The early stage comprises the half century or so after the Conquest when the French spoken in England can hardly be distinguished from that spoken in the west of France. The later stage marked a period in which the language was beginning to be modified by its isolation from France. Although Pope is studying the evolution of the French language, her division of the history of the Anglo-Norman language into stages is useful for an analysis of the effects the state of the language had on the production of religious texts in Anglo-Norman. I have modified her dates slightly, extending the early period by forty years, as her divisions seem not to contain the linguistic differences found in the texts reviewed here.

[71] The September 29 (III kl. Oct.) feast is marked in virtually all of the calendars printed by F. Wormald in his volumes *English Kalendars before A.D. 1000* and *English Benedictine Kalendars after A.D. 1100*, vols. I and II, HBS 72, 77, 81 (London).

[72] For a description of the manuscript, see Neil Ker, *A Catalogue of Manuscripts containing Anglo-Saxon*, pp. 271ff. All of the homiletic pieces of this manuscript have been published in an edition by Rubie D.-N. Warner entitled *Early English Homilies from the Twelfth Century MS Vespasian D. xiv*, EETS OS 152 (London, 1917).

[73] Warner, *Early English Homilies*, 65: þæs Ebreiscen folcas ealdor.

praising St. Michael as the "constant supporter of Christian men on earth, and their intercessor in heaven with Almighty God,"[74] citing two of his principal roles.

The Impact of the *Legenda Aurea* of Jacobus de Voragine

For the later dissemination of the legends of St. Michael the archangel, the importance of the work known as the *Legenda Aurea*, or Golden Legend, cannot be overestimated. Dated about 1260, the authorship of the *Legenda Aurea* is commonly attributed to Jacobus de Voragine. Jacobus was an Italian Dominican friar, who late in life became Archbishop of Genoa.[75] Although he wrote several other volumes, the *Legenda Aurea* was by far his most important work.[76] A collection of texts about saints and the festivals of the church year, the Latin *Legenda Aurea* is extant in over 800 manuscripts, but it was also translated into numerous vernaculars, including Italian, French, German, Dutch, and English.[77]

As a member of Order of Friars Preachers, Jacobus would no doubt have been concerned with the practice of preaching, with the *ars praedicandi*.[78] It seems likely that one of the purposes of the *Legenda Aurea* was to serve as a resource for his fellow preachers, a spiritual quarry for suitable and exemplary material to include in sermons.[79] Thus, each chapter follows a systematic pattern of exposition that would facilitate the search for such materials. A patchwork of material from Scripture, the Church Fathers, Isidore of Seville, and some less authoritative sources, the chapter on St. Michael serves an example of Jacobus's usual method of presentation, at least for those chapters focusing on saints (as opposed to festivals of the church year). Jacobus opens the chapter on the archangel with a preface in which he offers an etymology and an interpretation of the significance of his name. Jacobus reproduces Isidore of Seville's etymology of the archangel's name: "Michael is interpreted, who is like God."[80] From this etymology, Jacobus declares that "when something requiring wondrous powers is

---

74 *Ibid.*: se mære heofonlice ængel beo singallice cristenra manna gefylsta on eorðan, and þingere on heofone to þan Ælmightigan Gode.

75 For more on Jacobus and his life, see E. C. Richardson, *Materials for a Life of Jacopo da Varagine* (New York, 1935).

76 The first Latin text of the *Legenda Aurea* was edited by T. Graesse, *Legenda aurea vulgo historia lombardica dicta* (Leipzig, 1850). The most readily available translation is William Granger Ryan, *The Golden Legend: Readings on the Saints*, 2 vols. (Princeton, 1993). The preeminent study of the *Legenda Aurea* and its history is Sherry L. Reames, *The Legenda Aurea: A Reexamination of its Paradoxical History* (Madison, WI, 1985). See also A. Boureau, *La légende dorée* (Paris, 1984).

77 The earliest English translation was published by William Caxton in 1483. It is available in a modern edition, *The Golden Legend or Lives of the Saints as Englished by William Caxton*, 7 vols. (London, 1931).

78 Works which discuss the medieval practice of *ars praedicandi* (the art of composing and delivering not only sermons but also arguments and speeches) include G. R. Owst, *Literature and Pulpit in Medieval England: A Neglected Chapter in the History of English Letters and of the English People* (Oxford, 1961) and *Preaching in Medieval England: An Introduction to Sermon Manuscripts of the Period c. 1350–1450* (New York, 1965); H. L. Spencer, *English Preaching in the Late Middle Ages* (Oxford, 1993); and J. J. Murphy, *Rhetoric in the Middle Ages: A History of Rhetorical Theory from Saint Augustine to the Renaissance* (Tempe, AZ, 2001).

79 A. Boureau discusses such a possibility at some length (*La légende dorée*, 21–25).

80 W. M. Lindsay, ed., *Isidori Hispalensis Episcopi, Etymologiarum sive Originum Libri XX*, 2 vols. (Oxford, 1911): I, 275: Michael interpretatur, Qui sicut Deus.

to be done, Michael is sent, so that from his name and by his action it is given to be understood that no one can do what God alone can do: for that reason many works of wondrous power are attributed to Michael."[81] Sanctioned by the authority of the etymology, Jacobus presents a fantastical list of the archangel's wondrous deeds, battles, and intercessions. Many of these examples find their way into later recensions of the archangel's legendary history.

After these prefatory remarks, Jacobus presents the principal categories of exposition for the rest of the chapter. In St. Michael's case, the chapter is organized around four categories: the archangel's apparitions, his victories, his dedications, and his commemorations. Each of these categories is divided into three or four subdivisions, which themselves are often subdivided further. This process of enumeration is typical of the rhetorical strategy of the works devoted to the practice of preaching. In the section on apparitions, the story of Garganus and his bull is retold, as is the story of Mont Tombe. The second element of the Garganic foundation-myth, the battle of the Sipontans against the Beneventans, falls under the second category, the archangel's victories. In this same place, St. Michael's role in casting Lucifer and his followers out of heaven is related. The third element of the foundation-myth, St. Michael's dedication of the Garganic church, is presented in the category devoted to the archangel's dedications. Thus, all the elements of the Garganic foundation-myth are found in Jacobus, but they are divided up, intermingled with other legendary material and presented in different sections of his chapter on St. Michael. Although the narrative of the Garganic myth is broken into discrete episodes, virtually all of its details have been faithfully preserved from the legendary sources of *BHL* 5948.

The impact of the *Legenda Aurea* on the development of St. Michael's legendary history, particularly in the later Middle Ages, is immeasurable. Virtually every aspect of the later St. Michael legends was influenced by this work. The *Legenda Aurea* was the source text for many of the details found in these later legends, and in many instances provided the structure and organization for their retelling.

Translations of *BHL* 5948 in Middle English

One of the most popular Middle English texts of the late thirteenth and fourteenth centuries in England was a collection of readings for the feasts of the church, homilies, and saints' lives known by the conventional title *South English Legendary*.[82] Among the

---

[81] Ryan, *The Golden Legend*, 201.

[82] The "definitive" edition has been edited by Charlotte D'Evelyn and Anna J. Mill, *The South English Legendary*, 3 vols. EETS 235, 236, and 244 (London, 1956–59). An earlier edition based on a single manuscript was edited by Carl Horstmann, *The Early South-English Legendary, or Lives of Saints*, EETS OS 87 (London, 1887). Manfred Görlach has produced the most extensive modern study of the South English Legendary and its manuscripts (*The Textual Tradition of the South English Legendary*, Leeds Texts and Monographs NS 6 (Leeds, 1974)). Most recently, Thomas R. Liszka has tackled the thorny issue of what sort of text or texts the *South English Legendary* represents ("The South English Legendaries," in *The North Sea World in the Middle Ages: Studies in the Cultural History of North-Western Europe*, ed. Thomas R. Liszka and Lorna E. M. Walker [Dublin, 2001]: 243–80). Liszka argues that modern editors have misrepresented the textual tradition of the South English Legendary by selectively choosing texts to include in their editions. In a series of Appendices, Liszka has published the

texts in this anonymous collection is a St. Michael text which falls into three sections, generally designated in modern editions as Michael I, II, and III. The subject matter of Michael I and II follow the general outlines of the hagiographic myths of Monte Gargano and Mont Tombe (*BHL* 5951) respectively.[83] The subject matter of Michael III is scientific in nature and encyclopedic in scope, covering such topics as the four elements, the weather, the heavens, and even the nature of man's soul and his death. Although the "Michael III" has generally been dismissed as having no relation or relevance to the first two parts, some critics have argued for the vertical or associative unity of all three sections of the *South English Legendary* "St. Michael."[84]

The content and structure of Michael I are well-unified and follow the chronology established by the Garganic foundation-myth. The story of Garganus and the bull is followed by a description of his apparition to the bishop of Siponto in which St. Michael reveals his custody of the mount. The narrative then turns to St. Michael's support of the Sipontans in their battle with the "Saracines" (i.e., the pagan Neopolitans). Michael I closes with a description of the church which the archangel constructs and dedicates in honor of the victory over the Neapolitans.

Two popular collections of vernacular texts of the fourteenth and fifteenth centuries were the *Festial* of Johannes Mirkus and the anonymous *Speculum Sacerdotale*. John Mirk was prior of the Augustinian abbey of Lilleshall in Shropshire and is the author of three extant works: the *Festial* (ca. 1382–70); a collection of practical advice known as the "Instructions for Parish Priests" (ca. 1400); and the *Manuale Sacerdotis* (ca. 1414).[85] Mirk's *Festial* is a collection of discrete vernacular homilies for the major festivals of the church year intended for use by parish priests and includes a homily for St. Michael's feast of September 29. Evidence of the popularity of the *Festial* can be deduced from the fact that 18 editions of the text were printed in the late fourteenth and early fifteenth centuries. Mirk relied heavily on hagiographic legends and popular romances as source material for his homilies and his homily for St. Michael's feast day reflects this reliance.

Entitled "De Festo Sancti Michaelis et eius Solempnitate" by editorial convention, Mirk's homily for September 29 is relatively short (only some 100 manuscript lines in length).[86] The homilist divides his text into three sections, dealing consecutively with

---

actual contents of the various manuscripts of the South English Legendary in an effort to disabuse readers of the myth of a "definitive" text of the *South English Legendary* ("The South English Legendaries," 261–80).

83 The order of the "Michael" texts in the *South English Legendary* is a matter of some debate. As Liszka has pointed out, in some manuscripts of the *South English Legendary*, Michael II does not fall under the September 29 date but under its proper calendrical position, commemorating the feast of the archangel on Mont Tombe.

84 D'Evelyn and Mill, the principal modern editors of the text, and Görlach dismiss Michael III as having no connection to the first two sections. Gregory Sadlek, however, has argued for the essential unity of the three sections ("The Archangel and the Cosmos: The Inner Logic of the *South English Legendary*'s 'Michael'," *Studies in Philology* 85 [1988]: 177–91). Although Sadlek relies heavily on the flawed analysis of Olga Dobiache-Rojdestvensky, his premise that St. Michael's traditional association with natural phenomena suggests a continuity between the three sections is valid. On St. Michael's association with natural phenomena, see Appendix C.

85 Little is known about John Mirk; his birth and death dates are not recorded. The *Festial* has been edited by Theodore Erbe, *Mirk's Festial: A Collection of Homilies*, EETS ES 96 (London, 1905; repr. 1987).

86 Erbe, *Mirk's Festial*, 257–60.

St. Michael's appearance on earth, the miracles he has worked, and his victories in battle.[87] In its organization, Mirk's text follows the pattern established by the *Legenda Aurea*. In the first section, Mirk attributes to Gregory the Great the medieval common-place about St. Michael which follows Jacobus's etymology of the archangel's name in the *Legenda Aurea*: "When God would perform a wonderful thing or deed, then he would send St. Michael as his agent."[88] As in the *Legenda Aurea*, all manner of miracles are next attributed to the agency of St. Michael: the archangel escorted Moses and Aaron into Egypt, he parted the Red Sea, and he protected the Israelites for forty years in the desert. In the second section, Mirk describes the misadventures of the rich man Garganus and his wayward bull. Acknowledging as it does an anonymous source text,[89] Mirk's text is a close rendering of the *Legenda Aurea* version of the Garganic myth. In an intriguing, and perhaps nationalistic twist, Mirk follows the Garganic myth with a rendering of an apparition of St. Michael to "another bishop at a place that is now called Michael's Mount in Cornwall."[90] Although there indeed is a tradition of an apparition by St. Michael in Cornwall,[91] the details of the account in Mirk's *Festial* are identical to those narrated in the *Legenda Aurea*, where they are associated with Mont Tombe. In the third section of Mirk's St. Michael homily, on his victories in fighting, the battle of the Sipontans and the Neapolitans is narrated.

Similar in purpose and scope to Mirk's *Festial* is an early fifteenth-century, anonymous collection of homilies known as the *Speculum Sacerdotale*.[92] In contrast to Mirk, however, the author of the *Speculum Sacerdotale* seems to have been mostly interested in producing a resource volume from which parish priests might cull material for their own homilies. Indeed, the editor of the *Speculum Sacerdotale*, Edward Weatherly has noted a fundamental difference in the kinds of stories the two works choose to relate: "Most of the stories in the *Festial* teach a moral; those in the *Speculum Sacerdotale* attempt to arouse devotion through wonder at the miraculous."[93] In the case of the St. Michael legends presented in these two texts, it would seem that both are interested in arousing "devotion through wonder at the miraculous."

The vast majority of the material in the *Speculum Sacerdotale* is based on the *Legenda Aurea*. Although much of the material in the chapter on "St. Michaell" derives from this source, the anonymous compiler of the *Speculum* reunites the various elements of the Garganic foundation-myth and presents them in their traditional order.[94] The three phases of the Garganic story (Garganus and the bull, the Sipontans victory over the Beneventans, and the dedication of the church) are followed by the prefatory material

---

[87] *Ibid.*, 257: he ys wondurfull yn aperyng, he ys mervelus yn miracles worchyng, and victorys yn his feghtyng.

[88] *Ibid.*: as Seynt Gregory sayth, when God wold do wondurfull þyng or dede, þen he sendyþe forþe Saynt Mychaell as hys banrer.

[89] In the second section, Mirk says "as we redyn," a reference presumably to the *Legenda Aurea*.

[90] Erbe, *Mirk's Festial*, 258: He aperet also to anoþer byschop at a place þat ys callet now Mychaell yn þe mownt yn Corneweyle.

[91] The apparition in Cornwall is designated "Miracula in Monte S. Michaelis in Cornubia" (*BHL* 5955b). On this apparition and St. Michael's Mount in Cornwall, see G. H. Doble, *Miracles at St. Michael's Mount in Cornwall in 1262* (St. Michael's Mount, 1945) and J. R. Fletcher, *Short History of St. Michael's Mount* (St. Michael's Mount, 1951).

[92] Edward Weatherly, *Speculum Sacerdotale*, EETS OS 200 (London, 1936; repr. 1988).

[93] *Ibid.*, xli.

[94] *Ibid.*, 210–15.

from the *Legenda Aurea*. The etymology and significance of St. Michael's name, and the list of legendary accomplishments are themselves followed by a catalog of the archangel's heavenly roles (prince of angels, custodian of Paradise, psychopomp, etc.).

Perhaps most intriguing, however, is the closing episode of the homily. Citing an unnamed source, the compiler launches into a fantastical tale of the archangel's defeat of a dragon who has been laying to waste a country "in the right part of Asia" with the "venomous blast" of his breath. So oppressed are the inhabitants of this region that many flee to other countries, leaving the land behind forsaken and like a desert. Those who remain in the region pray to God that he might save them from the dragon.[95] The Lord answers their prayers by sending St. Michael in the form of a bird to defeat the dragon. Needless to say, St. Michael is victorious and dismembers the dragon in twelve parts. A chorus of a thousand voices celebrates the victory, proclaiming "Salvation, honor, power, and authority to the almighty God forever." In order to avoid sickness from the rotting carcass, the inhabitants, who have now returned, drag the dead dragon with twelve oxen into the sea.[96] In the name of God and in honor of St. Michael, the inhabitants erect a church where they provide food for 150 men each day. On the site of the archangel's victory over the dragon a further miraculous occurrence is manifest: the marks of his claws can be seen in the hard stone as if they had been made in soft earth.[97]

This odd tale can be traced back to a Latin exemplar designated "Apparitio et victoria in Asia" (*BHL* 5956b). The late J. E. Cross first drew attention to the Latin exemplar of this episode in a collection of homiletic materials found in several Anglo-Saxon manuscripts, the earliest of which is Cambridge, Pembroke College MS 25 (Bury St. Edmunds, s. xi), a manuscript which preserves a copy of the so-called *Homiliary of Saint-Père*.[98] Most recently, Christine Rauer has productively examined this

---

[95] *Ibid.*, 214: And we rede that he wrou3t this meruelouse and grete vertu whiche schall nowe be tolde. In the ri3t parti of Asye there was a dragon hauynge his reste at a grete mowntayne come in the forsaid countre of Asye, and þe venomous blaste of this dragon slow3e alle peple that euer it towchid in so myche that the peple and inhabitours of the londe lafte and forsoke here heritages and possessions and flow3e in-to other coste3, and countrees. So as this peple þou3t a-monge hem-self howe that here londe was forsake and lafte as a deserte, as God 3aue hem grace they turnyd hem with alle here hertis vnto almighty God and askyd helpe of Ihesu Crist.

[96] *Ibid.*, 214–15: And then God sent the holy aungel Mi3hel to helpe hem in the likenes of a brydde hauynge a bry3te brennynge swerde for to kylle this dragon . . . And when he hadde þe victorie and hadde i-slayne and departed this dragon in-to xii. parties, there was herde a voice of a thowsande sayinge and cryinge: "Salus, honor, vertu, and power be euer to almy3tty God." And when the peple so thonkyne and glorifying here God were commen a3eyn to here countres and habitaciouns, they my3t vnneþe drawe þe lefte party of this dragon by xii. oxen vnto the see, for they dide carye hym theder that the peple ne here bestes schulde no3t be strangelyd with the stynke of his careyne.

[97] *Ibid.*, 215: And then in the same place the peple dide make after here promyssion and behotynge a grete chirche in the name of God and in honoure of Seynt Mi3hell, in the whiche chirche are foundyn and fedde vnto this day cl. men, and l. are sette there-in for [to] praye and make deuciouns vnto God, and l. for to rede and write, and l. for to ordeyne and puruey for here necessaries and to be a-bowte the occupaciones of the house. And also it is no3t to be for3ete to telle you howe þat in the same place where Seynt Mi3hel stode in the forme of a byrdde when he slow3e þe dragon, his clawes of his feete may be sey there in a harde stone as he hadde stoned on a softe mouable grounde or myrre, for grace, of whiche victorye done in the forsaide place God yche day scheweþ in it grete miracles and meruayls vncessyngly.

[98] J. E. Cross, "An Unpublished Story of Saint Michael the Archangel and its Connections," in *Magister Regis: Studies in Honor of Robert Earl Kaske*, ed. A. Groos (New York, 1986): 23–35, and *Cambridge, Pembroke College MS 25: A Carolingian Sermonary Used by Anglo-Saxon Preachers*, King's College London Medieval Studies 1 (London, 1987). Also on the *Homiliary of Saint-Père*, see H. Barré, *Les homéliaires carolingiens de l'école d'Auxerre*, Studi e Testi 225 (Vatican, 1962): 17–25; R.

episode in light of other secular and hagiographical accounts of dragon-fights.[99] Rauer observes that this episode (which she refers to as **Mi1**) was "demonstrably circulating in Anglo-Saxon England for an unknown period sometime between the early ninth century and the late tenth century" and suggests that it might have been a source for the extant vernacular homilies on St. Michael and, through them, the dragon-episode in *Beowulf*.[100] What is perhaps most striking is that aside from an Irish vernacular version (designated **Mi3** by Rauer), which removes the battle from "Asia" and locates it on Monte Gargano, the Middle English text in the *Speculum Sacerdotale* seems to be the only other vernacular account of this dragon fight.[101]

Summary

The Michaeline hagiographer, in fashioning the foundation-myth of the Garganic sanctuary, created a compelling narrative of angelic intervention and efficacy. The evidence of the texts examined in this chapter suggests that these elements of the myth resonated with the medieval English. Although the earliest renditions of the various elements of the myth follow the narrative of Garganic account quite closely, some of the texts (e.g., the *Old English Martyrology*) include additional legendary materials. The inclusion of additional material suggests a process by which the traditional range of legends attributed to the agency of the archangel might evolve. In other cases, such as Blickling Homily 16, the traditional association of the archangel with a figure of great religious stature (in the case of Blickling 16, St. Paul) may have inspired the homilist to compose additional material. In the latter period, many of the legends became regularized, partly through the enormous influence of the *Legenda Aurea*. Despite the normalizing effect of the *Legenda Aurea*, some St. Michael texts continued to exhibit their own inspired expansion of the roles attributed to St. Michael. The *South English Legendary* "St. Michael" is a case in point, particularly the cosmological section of the text.[102] Nevertheless, in all of the vernacular versions of the Garganic hagiographical foundation-myths examined in this chapter, St. Michael acts as guardian and defender of the faithful, as slayer of evil, and as benevolent judge of all that is good. And it is to a closer examination of these roles that the next two chapters are devoted.

McKitterick, *The Frankish Church and the Carolingian Reforms 789–895* (London, 1977): 107–108; and F. Dolbeau, "Du nouveau sur un sermonnaire de Cambridge," *Scriptorium* 42 (1988): 255–57.

[99] C. Rauer, *Beowulf and the Dragon: Parallels and Analogues* (Cambridge, 2000): see especially chapter 4, 116–24.

[100] *Ibid.*, 123–24. Rauer includes the text and translation of this (**Mi1** occurs at 158–61) and many other dragon-fight episodes. Although I am inclined to agree with Rauer in her contention that **Mi1** may have influenced vernacular representations of St. Michael, the fact that no other vernacular versions of the episode exist leaves the matter open for further discussion.

[101] Rauer indicates that two slightly different Latin accounts of this dragon fight exist (118). The Irish vernacular version is edited and translated by R. Atkinson, *The Passions and the Homilies from Leabhar Breac: Text, Translation, and Glossary*, 2 vols., Royal Irish Academy: Todd Lecture Series 2 (Dublin, 1887): II, 213–19. I discuss this homily and Irish representations of St. Michael in general in my dissertation (127–32).

[102] Unfortunately, a detailed study of the *South English Legendary*'s "Michael III" is beyond the scope of this work. This text merits far greater attention than it has received.

4

The Archangel as Guardian and Psychopomp

Þis is se halga heahengel Sanctus Michael goda hirde ðæs
dryhtenlican eowdes, se ðe ne læteð wulf ne ðeof nanewuht
gewirdan on his hlafordes heorde.[1]

Anonymous, "In Praise of Michael" homily, CCCC MS 41

The notion that a guardian spirit watches over each human enjoys a long history in
Judeo-Christian tradition.[2] As the epigraph from the anonymous Old English homily
"In Praise of St. Michael" suggests, the concept was firmly established in Anglo-Saxon
England. Indeed, for the Anglo-Saxons, St. Michael was the preeminent guardian of the
bodies and souls of the faithful. Ælfric, in the *Euangelium* portion of his homily for St.
Michael's feast day, September 29, reflects on the doctrine of guardian angels.[3]
Commenting on the second clause of Matthew 18:10,[4] Ælfric declares, "By these words
is manifested that over every believing man an angel is set as a guardian who shields
him against the devil's machinations and supports him in holy virtues."[5] From a patch-
work of quotes on the roles and charges of angels through salvation history, Ælfric
reaches the conclusion that "It is now credible that the archangel Michael has care of
Christian men, he who was prince of the Hebrew folk when they believed in God."[6]
The inclusion of this material in Ælfric's homily indicates the degree to which St.
Michael's role as a guardian spirit was firmly established by the tenth century in
England.

According to Christian tradition, St. Michael was also charged with the conveyance
of the souls of the faithful to heaven at death. Several additional verse-paragraphs of

---

[1] This verse-paragraph appears on page 408 of the manuscript. This and two other homilies from the
manuscript are edited and translated by Raymond J. S. Grant, *Three Homilies from Cambridge, Corpus
Christi College 41* (Ottawa, 1982) at 60–61: "This is the holy archangel St. Michael the good shepherd
of his lord's flock, who permits neither wolf nor thief to do any injury to his lord's herd."
[2] On this doctrine, see Chapter One, 14–15, and especially n. 22.
[3] On Ælfric's homily, see Chapter Three, 55–63.
[4] Peter Clemoes, *Ælfric's Catholic Homilies: The First Series*, EETS SS 17 (Oxford, 1997). The second
clause in Old English reads, "Ic secge eow þæt heora englas symle geseoð mines fæder ansyne seðe
on heofonum is" (I say unto you that their angels ever look upon the countenance of my Father who
is in heaven) at 473.
[5] *Ibid.*: Mid þysum wordum is geswutelod þæt ælcum geleaffullum menn is engel to hyrde geset þe
hine wið deofles syrewungum gescylt and on halgum mægnum gefultumað.
[6] *Ibid.*: Is nu geleaflic þæt se heahengel michahel hæbbe gymene cristenra manna se þe wæs þæs
ebreiscan folces ealdor þa hwile hi on god belyfdon. In the course of his exposition, Ælfric quotes
Psalm 91:11–12; Acts 12:15; Tobit 12:12; Deuteronomy 32:8; and Daniel 10:13.

the Corpus 41 homily suggest that one of the archangel's most common roles in early medieval England was as psychopomp, or conveyor of the souls of the faithful to heaven at death. Verse-paragraph 14 suggests that it is St. Michael "who leads the soul of each and every true man through the gates of eternal life into the kingdom of heaven."[7] The two last verse-paragraphs (27 and 28) of this homily also refer to St. Michael in this role. In verse 27, St. Michael is said to conduct "the holy souls into the kingdom of heaven" after the Final Judgment. The homily closes with a plea that St. Michael receive the souls of the faithful and lead them into "the heavenly kingdom of the Lord."[8]

Scattered references to St. Michael in the role of psychopomp occur frequently in Anglo-Saxon liturgy, particularly in prayers.[9] St. Michael's role as psychopomp is also acknowledged in early English versions of the Gospel of Nicodemus, in which he escorts the soul of Adam to Paradise. References also abound to the archangel in this role at various points in the "Michael" section of the Middle English *South English Legendary*. So prevalent was the notion of St. Michael as psychopomp that in *Piers Plowman* Truth promises safe conduct to heaven for any man who lives his life in the service of good works:

> And y shal sende ʒow mysulue seynt Mihel myn Angel
> That no deuel shal ʒow dere ne despeyre in ʒoure deynge
> And sende ʒoure sowles þer y mysulue dwelle
> And abyde þer in my blisse body and soule for euere.[10]

In this tradition, the archangel's most important charge as psychopomp was the body and soul of the Virgin Mary. There exists a large store of early English legendary material with regard to the Virgin's assumption and St. Michael's role in it. It is clear from this brief catalogue of references to St. Michael's role as psychopomp in early English literature that the tradition is rich and vast. As this chapter demonstrates, the archangel's popularity is due in large measure to his stewardship of human souls, both as a guardian in life and as psychopomp at death.

Early References to St. Michael as Psychopomp

Although the Roman missionaries Augustine, Birinus, and Theodore were probably familiar with Italian devotions to St. Michael and possibly introduced such devotions to the archangel in their services, the earliest evidence of St. Michael's influence in early medieval England is found in the writings of the Venerable Bede.[11] In *HE*, Bede

---

[7] Grant, *Three Homilies*, 60–61: Þis is se halga heahengel Sancte Michael se ðe anra gehwilces soðfæstes mannes saule gelædeð þurh þa gatu þæs ecan lifes to hefena rice.

[8] *Ibid.*, 64–65. Verse 27 reads, "þonne ða halgan saula to heofona rice he gelædeð." Verse 28 reads, "biddan we þonne halgan heahengel Sanctus Michael þæt ura saula sie anfenge and hi gelæde on heofoncund rice to þam dryhtene."

[9] See Chapter Two, notes 73 and 74.

[10] George Russell and George Kane, eds. *Piers Plowman: The C Version* (Berkeley, CA, 1997): 371, Passus IX, lines 36–40.

[11] St. Michael is mentioned in Bede's *Martyrology* (ed. Dom Jacques Dubois and Genevieve Renaud, *Edition pratique des martyrologes de Bède, de l'anonyme Lyonnais et de Florus* [Paris, 1976]) where his feast

recounts that St. John of Beverley, bishop of Hexham in Northumbria (687–705), was in the habit of retiring to a "remote dwelling" on the other side of the River Tyne from Hexham where there was an "oratory" dedicated to St. Michael to read and pray.[12] J. M Wallace-Hadrill remarks that "This oratory . . . was clearly a remote spot suitable for contemplation. Hence the dedication to St. Michael, who is often to be found presiding over hermits' fastnesses where his protection against evil spirits was especially welcome."[13] Bede also narrates the story of a healing which the bishop performed at the site: he enabled a dumb youth (*adulescens mutus*) "to reveal the secrets of his thoughts and wishes to others which he could never do before."[14] Although St. Michael is not invoked and does not appear in the story of the healing, the fact that it took place at a site dedicated to the archangel is typical of his traditional role as guardian of the faithful and is reminiscent of the long tradition of healing associated with the archangel.

The earliest Anglo-Saxon reference in which the archangel acts expressly as a psychopomp is found in the *Life of Wilfrid*, bishop of York, by Stephen of Ripon (formerly Eddius Stephanus),[15] and corroborated by Bede.[16] According to Stephen of Ripon, while returning to England from a visit to Rome in 705, Wilfrid fell gravely ill and was taken "ad Meldum civitatem" [to the town of Meaux]. St. Michael appeared to him on the fifth day of his illness to inform him that the Virgin Mary had interceded on his behalf and that he would recover from his illness. The archangel urged Wilfrid to found a church in Mary's honor and then disappeared with the promise to return in four years.[17] Wilfrid recovered from his illness and upon his return built two churches,

day, September 29, commemorates the dedication of a church in his honor. There is some confusion as to which church was dedicated on this day. Although Bede does not declare which church dedication was commemorated, traditionally this date was associated with the dedication of the church on the Salarian Way.

12 Colgrave and Mynors, *Bede's Ecclesiastical History*, 457–59 at 456: "Est mansio quaedam secretior, nemore raro et uallo circumdata, non longe ab Hagustaldensi ecclesia, id est unius ferme miliarii et dimidii spatio interfluente Tino amne separata, habens clymiterium sancti Michahelis archangeli, in qua uir Dei saepius, ubi opportunitas adridebat temporis, et maxime in Quadragesima manere cum paucis atque orationibus ac lectioni quietus operam dare consuerat." Bede uses the Latin word *clymiterium* which is found only in *HE*. It is translated in the Old English version of the *HE* as *gebædhus and ciricean* or "prayer-house and church" (Thomas Miller, *The Old English Version of Bede's Ecclesiastical History of the English People*, EETS OS 95 and 96 [London, 1890–91; repr. Kraus Reprints, 1978]: vol. 96, 388). Colgrave follows Miller in rendering the Old English translation of the Latin *clymiterium* as "oratory."

13 J. M. Wallace-Hadrill, *Bede's Ecclesiastical History of the English People: A Historical Commentary* (Oxford, 1988): 175.

14 *HE*, 458.

15 B. Colgrave, *The Life of Bishop Wilfrid by Eddius Stephanus* (Cambridge, 1927): 120ff.

16 The story of Wilfrid's life and death is told in Book V, chapters 19–20 of *HE*, 517–33.

17 Colgrave, *Life of Wilfrid*, 120, 122: Quinta demum die, mane illucescente, ecce angelus Domini in veste candido sancto pontifici nostro apparuit, dicens: 'Ego sum Michael summi Dei nuntius, qui misit me ad te indicare, quod tibi adduntur anni vitae pro intercessione sanctae Mariae genetricis Dei semperque virginis et pro subditorum tuorum lacrimis, ad aures Domini pervenientibus; et hoc tibi erit signum, quod ab hac die in dies melioratus sanaberis et ad patriam tuam pervenies, tibique substantiarum tuarum carissima quaeque redduntur, et in pace vitam consummabis. Paratus quoque esto, quia post IIII annorum spatium iterum visitabo te. Iam enim memento quod in honore sancti Petri et Andreae apostolorum domos aedificasti, sanctae vero Mariae semper virgini intercedenti pro te nullam fecisti. Habes hoc emendare et in honorem eius domum dedicare.' Et post haec verba angelus Domini assumptus ab oculis eius discessit.

one dedicated to St. Michael and the other to the Blessed Virgin. Wilfrid died exactly four years later in 709, and Stephen of Ripon declares that St. Michael returned with a band of angels to escort the good bishop to heaven.[18] In this episode, St. Michael identifies himself as "Dei nuntius" (God's messenger) and performs his traditional role of psychopomp in conducting Wilfrid's soul to heaven. In his account of Wilfrid's death, Bede omits the reference to St. Michael's role in conveying the bishop's soul to heaven.

Although he does little more than point out an intriguing parallel between Wilfrid's four-year reprieve and an angelic vision St. Columba experienced near the end of his life, the historian Henry Mayr-Harting has suggested an Irish connection for the passage: "When the holy angels who had been sent to conduct his soul from the flesh were already in sight, Columba had a sudden vision that four years had been added to his life."[19] Since St. Michael is not mentioned in the Irish text, it is possible that Stephen of Ripon simply elaborated on an established type-scene by adding the archangel. The addition of four years to both Wilfrid and Columba's lives, for example, may be patterned to some extent on the story in 2 Kings 20:6 (Vulgate 4 Kings 20:6) in which King Hezekiah receives a similar reprieve on his deathbed and fifteen years are added to his life. The exact repetition of the four-year reprieve accompanied by the vision of the angels, however, may have suggested to Mayr-Harting a degree of influence, or at the very least, a common source for the scene.

The episode of Wilfrid's illness and the archangel's visit is also related in Alcuin's "Versus de patribus regibus et sanctis Euboricensis ecclesiae," and three other accounts of Wilfrid's life: the metrical "Breviloquium vitæ beati Wilfridi" by Frithegod; the "Vita Wilfridi episcopi" by Eadmer; and the "Breviloquium vitæ sancti Wilfridi" also attributed to Eadmer.[20] Although these four accounts differ from each other in interesting ways, they are all essentially based on Stephen of Ripon's account of the episode. In the two metrical accounts of Alcuin and Frithegod, the episode is necessarily compressed to accommodate the constraints of the poetic form. Nonetheless, Alcuin's description of the scene embellishes several details in Stephen of Ripon's account. Where Stephen says St. Michael appeared to the bishop "in veste candida" (in shining

---

18 Colgrave, *Life of Wilfrid*, 142: Sapientes autem qui illic aderant dixerunt, certe se scire, angelorum choros cum Michaele venisse et animam sancti pontificis in paradisum deducere.

19 Henry Mayr-Harting, *The Coming of Christianity to Anglo-Saxon England*, 3rd ed. (University Park, PA, 1991): 144. The passage in Adomnán's *Life of St. Columba* which narrates this vision reads as follows: "For I saw holy angels sent from the high throne to meet and conduct my soul from the flesh. But see now, they have suddenly been held back, and are standing on a rock beyond the strait of our island; they wish to approach, in order to summon me from the body, but they are not allowed to come nearer, and will presently return to the highest heavens. Because what the Lord granted me when I asked it with my whole strength, that I should pass to him from the world on this day, he has changed, more quickly than speech, answering in preference the prayers of many churches for me. And it has so been granted by the Lord to the prayers of those churches that, although against my will, four more years from this day shall be added to my sojourn in the flesh. This day, grievous to me, was justly the cause of my sorrow today. After the end of the four coming years in the life, by God's favour I shall, with a sudden departure and no preceding bodily distress, joyfully depart to the Lord, with the holy angels who will come to meet me at that time." (A. O. and M. O. Anderson, *Adomnán's Life of Columba* [Oxford, 1991]: 217.)

20 Alcuin's text has been edited and translated by Peter Godman, *The Bishops, Kings, and Saints of York* (Oxford, 1982). The other three texts have been edited by James Raine, *The Historians of the Church of York and its Archbishops* (London, 1879): 105–59 at 152 (Frithegod); 161–226 at 216 (Eadmer's "Vita Wilfridi episcopi"); and 227–37 at 234 (Eadmer's "Breviloquium vitæ beati Wilfridi").

raiment), Alcuin describes the archangel as "niveo nimium praeclarus amictu/ et . . . flammigero" (resplendent in snow-white garb/ with fiery countenance).[21]

In addition to the two notices for the archangel's traditional feast days reviewed in Chapter Three, St. Michael appears as a psychopomp in three other notices recorded in the ninth-century *Old English Martyrology*: April 24, St. Wilfrid; June 2, St. Erasmus; and July 19, St. Christina. The entry for St. Wilfrid is straightforward since it is abstracted from Stephen of Ripon's *Life of Wilfrid* and matches the account of Bede mentioned above. The notices for Sts. Erasmus and Christina, however, are more intriguing. St. Erasmus was bishop of Formiae and was martyred there ca. 300 CE[22] His feast occurs in the Hieronymian Martyrology[23] and the early Irish *Martyrology of Œngus*, where he is listed as bishop of Antioch,[24] a detail also found in the *Old English Martyrology*. According to the legendary tales of St. Erasmus, the Emperor Maximianus heard of the hermit saint's fame and attempted to force him to worship a golden idol. Presumably angered at the sight of the holy man, however, a dragon came out of the idol and devoured a third of the assembled crowd. For inciting the idol to anger, Erasmus was thrown in jail, where at midnight St. Michael appeared to him and led him out of the town to an awaiting ship which took him to Formiae. As J. E. Cross has shown, the account in the *Old English Martyrology* agrees in its broad details with Latin sources.[25]

The case of St. Christina is slightly more complicated.[26] The *Old English Martyrology* lists her feast day as July 19, while most other early martyrologies list her feast as July 24.[27] The entry falls neatly into two sequences of events, each detailing St. Christina's relationship with her father, Urbanus. St. Michael appears in the second sequence. Furious at his daughter's public profession of faith in Christ, Urbanus has a stone fastened around Christina's neck and has her thrown in the sea. God's angels save her

---

[21] The passage in Stephen occurs at page 122 of Colgrave's edition. The passage in Alcuin occurs at page 52 in Godman's edition. The translations in parentheses come from the editions of each work.

[22] A convenient summary is provided in David Hugh Farmer, *The Oxford Dictionary of Saints*, 3rd ed. (Oxford, 1992): 159–60.

[23] *AASS, Novembris* II.

[24] Whitley Stokes, *The Martyrology of Œngus*, HBS 29 (London, 1905).

[25] J. E. Cross, "Source, Lexis, and Edition," in *Medieval Studies Conference Aachen 1983, Language and Literature*, eds. Wolf-Dietrich Bald and Horst Weinstock, Bamberger Beiträge zur englischen Sprachwissenschraft 15 (Frankfurt am Main, 1984): 25–36. The *Fontes Anglo-Saxonici* database indicates that the "probable direct source" for the St. Erasmus notice is the anonymous "Passio S. Erasmi" (C. Rauer, "The Sources of St. Erasmus (Cameron B.19.097)," 2000, *Fontes Anglo-Saxonici: World Wide Web Register*, accessed June 2004).

[26] The *Fontes* database indicates that the entry for St. Christina is derived from multiple sources, principally Aldhelm's "De virginitate" (prose) and the anonymous "Passio S. Christinae" (C. Rauer, "The Sources of St. Christina (Cameron B.19.130)," 2000, *Fontes Anglo-Saxonici: World Wide Web Register*, accessed June 2004).

[27] J. E. Cross discusses this discrepancy in his article, "An Unrecorded Variant of the 'Passio S. Christinae' and the 'Old English Martyrology'," *Traditio* 36 (1980): 163, n. 17. Cross argues that this discrepancy could easily arise from a scribal corruption of the text; in other words, a scribe wrote "xiiii k. Aug." (July 19) for "viiii k. Aug." (July 24). In private correspondence with me, Prof. Cross elaborated on the likely source of the error: "By extending the two downward strokes of his 'v,' a scribe could easily write 'xiiii' for 'viiii' " (dated August 30, 1994). Furthermore, in his article, Cross points out that the corruption of the date of St. Christina's feast day also shows up in another ninth-century English text, the calendar in Oxford, Bodleian Library, Digby MS 63 (printed in F. Wormald, *English Kalendars before A.D. 1100*, HBS 72 [London,1934]: 8). It must be noted, however, that it is quite conceivable that the discrepancy arose from scribal miscopying.

from drowning, and she walks with them over the sea. At midnight, Christ appears to her and baptizes her thrice-fold in the sea. Christ then gives her to St. Michael, who leads her safely back to land. The next morning, Urbanus sees Christina walking across the sea to the city. The entry ends by noting Christina's martyrdom. In the entries for SS. Erasmus and Christina, St. Michael plays a traditional role as their guardian angel, protecting the two saints by leading them away from danger.

St. Michael in the Narratives of the Assumption of the Virgin Mary

Although the doctrine of the Assumption of the Virgin Mary has no warrant in scripture, a group of apocryphal works concerning the final fate of Mary, perhaps originating in Egypt, began to circulate around the fourth century in several different languages (principally Syriac, Coptic, Greek, and Latin).[28] While the Syriac form of the legends influenced the Irish tradition of Assumption apocrypha, the Latin versions of this apocryphon are the most important for the legends of the Assumption which made their way to early medieval England.[29] The principal Latin versions of the Assumption thought to have been known in Anglo-Saxon England are Transitus Mariae B[1], Transitus Mariae B[2], Transitus Mariae C, and Transitus Mariae E.[30] The two principal Anglo-Saxon texts which refer to St. Michael's roles in the Assumption of the Virgin are Blickling homily 13 and the Assumption homily in CCCC MS 41.[31]

The first critic to attempt to unravel the convoluted account of the Assumption in Blickling homily 13 was Rudolph Willard, who in two articles argued that the homily derives from two Latin apocrypha.[32] The first Latin source he identified is a variant of

[28] For a summary of the complicated textual history of the Assumption apocrypha, see Mary Clayton, *The Cult of the Virgin Mary in Anglo-Saxon England*, CSASE (Cambridge, 1990): 8–10, and especially *The Apocryphal Gospels of Mary in Anglo-Saxon England*, CSASE 26 (Cambridge, 1998); and Simon Claude Mimouni, *Dormition et Assomption de Marie: Histoire des Traditions Anciennes* (Paris, 1996).

[29] For a succinct discussion of the Latin versions relevant to the study of Anglo-Saxon knowledge of Assumption apocrypha, see Mary Clayton, "De Transitu Mariae," *SASLC: Trial*, 41–43.

[30] Transitus Mariae B has been edited by Constantin Tischendorf, *Apocalypses Apocryphae Mosis, Esdrae, Pauli, Iohannis item Mariae Dormitio* (Leipzig, 1866): 124–36. Following Tischendorf, I will refer to alternate readings as "MB" variants. Transitus Mariae has been edited by Monika Haibach-Reinisch, *Ein neuer 'Transitus Mariae' des Pseudo-Melito* (Rome, 1962): 63–87. Mary Clayton reprints Haibach-Reinisch's edition of Transitus B, but without the variants, in her *The Apocryphal Gospels of Mary in Anglo-Saxon England*, 334–43. Transitus Mariae C has been edited by Dom André Wilmart, *Analecta Reginensia* (Rome, 1933): 325–57. Transitus E is a variant of Transitus B and is found in Milan, Biblioteca Ambrosiana, MS Lat. 58. Tischendorf has printed excerpts from it in the prolegomena to his *Apocalypses Apocryphae* (xliii–xlvi). Rudolph Willard first designated this text Transitus Mariae E ("On Blickling Homily XIII: 'The Assumption of the Virgin,'" *Review of English Studies* 12 [1936]: 4).

[31] Blickling homily 13 appears in Morris, *Blickling Homilies*, 82–96. The Blickling manuscript has been reproduced in photographic facsimile as volume 10 of the EEMF series, ed. R. Willard (Copenhagen, 1960). Homily 13 on the Assumption appears at folios 84v7–98v9. The Corpus 41 homily on the Assumption has been published by Grant, *Three Homilies*, 18–33. Most recently, Mary Clayton has edited and translated both homilies (the Assumption homily in Corpus 198 for Blickling 13 and the Corpus 41 Assumption homily) in *Apocryphal Gospels of Mary*, 239–314 and 213–36, respectively. Quotations from the Corpus Assumption homily are taken from Clayton's edition.

[32] The two articles are "On Blickling Homily XIII: 'The Assumption of the Virgin,'" *Review of English Studies* 12 (1936): 1–17, and "The Two Accounts of the Assumption in Blickling Homily XIII," *Review of English Studies* 14 (1938): 1–19.

Transitus C, which comprises a summary account of the Assumption. Willard showed that the Blickling Assumption homily begins by following closely the narrative of the Transitus C variant, in which Mary's body is conducted to heaven by St. Michael separately from her soul. This narrative is then abandoned in favor of an account which describes the corporal assumption in greater detail. Willard concluded that the motivation for combining these two texts was to achieve "a story of equal richness throughout, from the annunciation of death to Mary's reception in Paradise."[33] He was unable to identify positively the source of this secondary material, but suggested that it must have been "a text which was related to [Transitus B and Transitus E], though neither of them as we know them."[34] Mary Clayton identifies the second source of homily 13 as a slightly different version of the Transitus B narrative, designated "Transitus Mariae B²" by its editor.[35] Clayton argues that the motivation for the joining of the two texts "seems to have been the desire to reaffirm the assumption of the resurrected body and soul, rather than the desire for greater narrative fullness, as Willard suggested."[36] At several key junctures, an examination of St. Michael's various roles in the homily sheds light on the complicated textual history of homily 13.

St. Michael first appears in a passage the translator mistranslated from his Latin source. As Clayton has shown, in the apostle John's description of how he was transported to the Virgin Mary's side, the translator mistook the Latin words *me* and *me hic* for abbreviations of *Maria* and *Michahel*.[37] As a result, the Old English is confused, seeming to indicate either that St. Michael transported the apostle to Mary's side or that the Assumption itself had begun even before the Virgin's death with St. Michael's arrival to convey her soul to heaven.

As in most of the Assumption legends, St. Michael is in fact entrusted with the Virgin's soul at her death. When Christ arrives just before Mary's death, St. Michael, the prince of all angels, is singing hymns with all the angels, keeping vigil over the Virgin as she rests.[38] At her death, Christ passes the Virgin's soul to St. Michael, who receives it "mid ealra his leoma eaჳmodnesse" (with the humility of all his limbs).[39] Clayton has shown that a similar phrase originates in the Latin source text [Transitus C: *exceptis omnibus membris*] as a reference to Mary's physical state after death.[40] She argues that the phrase is meant to indicate that "Mary's soul had a human form but without sexual differentiation" and concludes that the translator mistakenly transferred the description to St. Michael.[41]

After Mary's death, Christ tells the apostles to carry the Virgin's body to a new tomb they will find on the other side of the city. As the procession makes its way through the city the next day, a crowd of angry Jews attempts to steal the body. After the account of this confrontation, the apostles arrive at the tomb where they bury Mary's body.

[33] Willard, "The Two Accounts," 5.
[34] *Ibid.*, 8.
[35] "Blickling Homily XIII Reconsidered," *Leeds Studies in English* 17 (1986): 25–40 at 26.
[36] *Ibid.*, 29.
[37] *Ibid.*, 31–32.
[38] Morris, *Blickling Homilies*, 147: Michahel se heahengle se wæs ealra engla ealderman, he wæs ymen singende mid eallum þæm englum, mid þy þe Hælend wæs ingongende. (Michael the archangel, who was the prince of all angels, was singing hymns with all the angels when the Lord entered.)
[39] *Ibid.*
[40] "Blickling XIII," 33.
[41] *Ibid.*

Christ's immediate arrival with a company of angels signals the insertion of a second assumption narrative in the homily. In this second account of the assumption of Mary's soul, St. Michael is once again entrusted with the Virgin's soul and conveys it to Paradise. Following the account of the second assumption, the translator changed source texts. From the second arrival of Christ and the heavenly host at Mary's tomb (this time at the third hour of the third day) to its conclusion, the homily is a fairly faithful translation of Transitus Mariae B², as Mary Clayton has convincingly demonstrated.[42]

In a scene prefiguring the role the apostles will play at Judgment, Christ asks the apostles what they would have Him do with Mary's body. The apostles reply that they would have Him raise her body from the dead.[43] The Lord then commands the archangel Gabriel to remove the stone from before Mary's tomb.[44] St. Michael immediately approaches at the command of the Lord and presents before Him the soul of the Virgin.[45] At Christ's command, Mary's body arises from the tomb. The Lord kisses her and passes her body into the keeping of St. Michael, who lifts her up into the clouds before the presence of the Lord.

The role of St. Michael in this homily is an ancient one in Assumption apocrypha. Despite the several anomalies discussed, the archangel is essentially a psychopomp, entrusted with the conveyance of both Mary's body and soul to heaven. It is the anomalies, however, which provide a tantalizing clue as to the source text of the homily. Although Clayton has demonstrated conclusively that the Transitus B² text is the source text for Blickling homily 13, the principal manuscript does not contain the stone episode. Therefore, the ultimate source text can be further narrowed to one of the set of B² manuscripts which does relate the episode: MSS T, F, O¹, O², and V. As indicated in Table 2, these manuscripts preserve the order of the anomalies in the Old English: the stone episode with Gabriel and the presentation of Mary's soul by St. Michael at the tomb.

In a note to the stone episode in homily 13, Willard astutely remarks on the appropriateness of the division of labor between the archangels in this episode.[46] On the one hand, according to Judaic and Christian traditions of angelology, St. Michael is the supreme angelic psychopomp. On the other hand, Gabriel, whose name means "the strength of God" according to Isidore of Seville (*Etymologiae* VII.v.10),[47] is the appropriate archangel to perform the task of removing the stone from the entrance of Mary's tomb. As is indicated in Table 2, however, the assignment of these tasks is confused in yet another Old English Assumption homily, namely that found in CCCC MS 41.

---

[42] *Ibid.*, 33ff.

[43] As Clayton points out, a mistranslation of the source text means that the apostles have only asked for the resurrection of Mary's body and not its assumption (*ibid.*, 34).

[44] Although the principal manuscript of Transitus B does not relate this episode, it does occur in several variant manuscripts of both Tischendorf's B text (the MB variants) and Haibach-Reinisch's B text. For a summary of the manuscript anomalies, see Table 1 above (29), and the textual notes to the opening lines of chapter 16 in the Haibach-Reinisch edition (85).

[45] Although it would seem more logical that St. Michael present Mary's body, the source text, Transitus B, agrees with the Old English translation: "Statimque iubente Domino accedens Michael archangelus, praesentavit animan sanctae Maria coram Domino" (Haibach-Reinisch, 85). It would seem that the reason for the presentation of Mary's soul at this point is so that the soul might witness the conveyance of its body to heaven.

[46] Willard, "The Two Accounts," 14, n. 6.

[47] W. M. Lindsay, ed., *Isidori Hispalensis Episcopi, Etymologiarum sive Originum Libri XX*, 2 vols. (Oxford, 1911): I, 275: "Gabriel Hebraice in linguam nostram vertitur *fortitudo Dei*."

Table 2. Summary of anomalous archangel roles in the Assumption narratives

Texts	Angel who rolls stone	Psychopomp
Blickling Homily XIII	Gabriel	Michael
Transitus B	Michael	Michael
MB Variants of B	Gabriel	Michael
Transitus B2 (mss T, F, O1, O2 and V)	Gabriel	Michael
Transitus E	No mention of stone	Michael
CCCC 41	Gabriel	Gabriel presents the soul of Mary before the Lord, but Michael conveys her body to heaven.

The vernacular Corpus 41 homily on the Assumption has been shown by several critics[48] to depend, albeit loosely, on Transitus B[1].[49] Recently, however, Mary Clayton has argued convincingly that the Old English homily corresponds much more closely with Transitus B[2].[50] Despite the close correspondence of many aspects of the Assumption homily in Corpus 41 and Transitus B[2], an examination of the role of St. Michael in the Old English homily reveals an anomaly between the two texts.[51]

As in Blickling 13, in the Corpus 41 homily on the Assumption of the Virgin, St. Michael is presented in the role of guardian and conveyor to heaven of the Virgin's soul, a role he performs in some of the Coptic and Syriac accounts of the Assumption, and in the two Transitus Mariæ texts.[52] In the third year after Christ's ascension,[53] an angel of the Lord appears to Mary. The angel informs her that her death is imminent and gives her a palm branch to be placed on her bier. Mary beseeches the angel that the apostles gather beside her. The angel declares that they will come to her "from the

---

[48] Principal among these is Rudolph Willard in *Two Apocrypha in Old English* (Leipzig, 1935): 3, and "The Two Accounts" (2); H. L. C. Tristram, *Vier altenglische Predigten aus der heterodoxen Tradition, mit Kommentar, Übersetzung und Glossar sowie drei weiteren Texten im Anhang* (Freiburg, 1970), who points out that the Old English of the Corpus 41 homily and the Latin of Tischendorf's Transitus B text do not always correspond; and R. Grant, *Three Homilies* (Ottawa, 1982): 13–16.

[49] C. Tischendorf, *Apocalypses Apocryphae*, 124–36.

[50] "The Assumption Homily in CCCC 41," *N&Q* n.s. 36 (1989): 292–94. In this article (293), Clayton also points out that Transitus B is the older of the two versions of the Pseudo-Melito and was known in England from at least the first half of the eighth century as Bede quotes from it in his *Retractatio in Acta Apostolorum* (ed. M. L. W. Laistner, CCSL 121 [Turnhout, 1983]: 134–35).

[51] Clayton discusses three anomalies: the year of Mary's death, the angel's assurance to Mary that the apostles will be brought from Paradise to her bedside, and St. Michael's roles ("The Assumption homily," 293–95).

[52] St. Michael performs this function in another Corpus 41 homily as well. In verse-paragraph 13 of the "In Praise of St. Michael" homily, it is the archangel "to whom the Lord entrusted St. Mary's soul after her death when he committed her to him" (þam dryhten befæste Sancta Marian saule æfter hire forðfore, and he hi him bebead) (Grant, *Three Homilies*, 60–61).

[53] Transitus B puts the Virgin's death in the second year after Christ's ascension. Clayton remarks that the Corpus homily is unique in assigning it to the third year and that the date "must stem from a misreading of .iii. for .ii." ("The Assumption Homily," 294).

glory of Paradise," and they are miraculously transported to her side.[54] Once the apostles have assembled and the vigil has begun, Christ and a great host of angels comes to Mary, who is fearful of an encounter with dark spirits after her death. Christ comforts her by telling her that although she will likely encounter the prince of darkness, she will have nothing to fear since she will be escorted to paradise by the heavenly host. Mary then gives thanks to God and sends forth her spirit. Her soul rises from her body shining, and Christ passes it into the protection of St. Michael who is acknowledged as "neorxnawonges hyrde, ealdormon, Ebrea ðeode" (guardian of paradise, the chief of the Hebrew people).[55] In keeping with his traditional roles as psychopomp and guardian of souls of the living and the dead, St. Michael is entrusted with the protection and conveyance of Mary's soul. In the Latin Transitus B[1], but not Transitus B[2], the archangel Gabriel accompanies St. Michael and the soul of the Virgin Mary to paradise.[56] The names and roles of these two archangels are significant because they are later confused in the Old English text.

After Mary's soul is entrusted to St. Michael, Christ assigns the body of the Virgin to St. Peter for burial with the injunction that the body be buried for three days, at which point He will return. Christ then departs amid the singing and rejoicing of the heavenly host. Mary's body is transported to a sepulcher "in þa swiðran healfe þære ceastre" (on the right-hand side of the city).[57] As in Blickling homily 13, Christ, accompanied by the angels, returns at the third hour of the third day and asks the apostles what they would have Him do with Mary's body. Peter and the apostles reply that it is just that Mary's body be raised into heaven.[58] It is at this point that the Old English text confuses the names and roles of the archangels.

In Tischendorf's principal text, Transitus B[1], St. Michael returns with Mary's soul and is commanded to move the stone from in front of the sepulcher (see Table 2).[59] Christ then raises the body of Mary. In this version, however, St. Michael does not receive the reunited soul and body of Mary for conveyance to heaven; the host of angels carries her into paradise. In most manuscripts of Transitus B[2], St. Michael returns with Mary's soul, but there is no mention of either the removal of the stone in front of the

---

54 The angel's assurance in the Corpus homily reads, "Nu todæge hi beoð genumene of neorhxnawonges gefean and her to ðe cumað" (This very day they will be taken from the joys of Paradise and will come here to you) (Clayton, *Apocryphal Gospels of Mary*, 216–19; also Grant, *Three Homilies*, 18). The *Transitus B* text reads, "Ecce hodie omnes apostoli per virtutem Domini assumpti huc venient" (Haibach-Reinisch, *Ein neuer "Transitus Mariae,"* 67). This anomaly is discussed by Clayton, who reviews Tristram's conjecture that the Corpus text may rely at this point on a parallel passage in the Greek "The Book of John concerning the Falling Asleep of Mary," in which Mary requests that all the apostles, "both those who have already gone to Thee and those in the world that is now" be brought to her side (A. Roberts and J. Donaldson, *Ante-Nicene Fathers*, vol. 8 [New York, 1903]: 587). Clayton concludes that Tristram's argument is ultimately unsatisfactory as it relies both on the "loss of part of a sentence and the knowledge of a detail which does not otherwise appear in any version of *Transitus B* or, indeed, in any known Latin apocryphon" ("The Assumption Homily," 294).

55 Clayton, *Apocryphal Gospels of Mary*, 222–23; also Grant, *Three Homilies*, 24.

56 The anomalies in the sequence of events are summarized in Table 1 above, 29.

57 Clayton, *Apocryphal Gospels of Mary*, 222–23; also Grant, *Three Homilies*, 24.

58 Mary Clayton argues that the justification for the corporal assumption of Mary lies in her "virginal maternity: that the body which had given birth without corruption should not suffer corruption in death" (*The Cult of the Virgin Mary*, 8).

59 Among Tischendorf's variants, MB depicts Gabriel as removing the stone from the sepulcher, an anomaly which the Old English follows.

sepulcher or the archangel Gabriel (see Table 2). In Transitus B², St. Michael is also restored to his role of psychopomp; the archangel conveys the reunited body and soul of Mary to paradise. Thus, despite several anomalies, St. Michael is the only angel to play a significant role in the principal texts of both Latin versions (B¹ and B²) of the Transitus B apocryphon.

In the Corpus homily, however, the various roles of the two angels are confused. In the Transitus B¹ text, its MB variants, and the B² text, St. Michael returns with Mary's soul so that it may be reunited with her body. Although St. Michael receives Mary's soul from Christ to be conveyed to heaven in the Corpus homily, he is not charged with bringing her soul back to be reunited with her body. As in the MB variants of Transitus B¹, the archangel Gabriel is first introduced to remove the stone from Mary's sepulchre. But it is also Gabriel who brings Mary's soul back for its reunion with her body. Furthermore, he makes the speech which in all the Latin sources is made by Christ and effects the corporeal reunification. This is in pointed contrast to Gabriel's role in Blickling homily 13. As Table 2 indicates, Gabriel is only introduced to remove the stone from before the Virgin's tomb. Once reunited, Mary's body and soul are entrusted by Christ to St. Michael, who immediately takes her up to heaven surrounded by the host of angels.

Thus, despite the anomalies of both the Blickling and Corpus texts, the principal role assigned St. Michael in the Anglo-Saxon Assumption texts is that of psychopomp. The relationship between the two Old English texts, however, deserves closer scrutiny. Based solely on an analysis of St. Michael's roles in the two texts, it seems clear that the two texts are closely affiliated and may derive from a common Latin source text.

Although most Assumption apocrypha of the later Middle Ages derive principally from the Latin Transitus Marie B tradition, the greatest purveyor of this tradition was the *Legenda Aurea* of Jacobus de Voragine. Two English texts of the Assumption which reflect influence of the *Legenda Aurea* are found in the *Festial* of John Mirk and in the anonymous *Speculum Sacerdotale*.

Mirk's Assumption homily follows the essential outline of the Latin Transitus Mariae B¹ tradition.[60] Christ sends an angel bearing a palm branch from Paradise to announce to Mary that on the third day she will be called to join her son in the "ioy and blysse without end" of heaven. At Mary's request, the apostles are transported to her side to await the third day. On the appointed day, Christ comes down with a "gret multitude of angyls" and ascends to heaven with the soul of his mother. After another three days, during which time Mary's earthly body is prepared and placed in its bier, Christ returns with St. Michael who bears Mary's soul in his arms. Christ commands the archangel to join Mary's body and soul together: "Myghell, do my modyr soule ageyne." Once Mary's body and soul are reunited, the host of heaven bears her to Paradise where she is crowned "qwene of Heuen, emperice of hell, and lady of þe worlde." The homily continues for some pages with material culled from the *Legenda Aurea*.

Similar in scope and purpose to Mirk's *Festial*, the *Speculum Sacerdotale* is a collection of sermons on the festivals of the liturgical year intended for use by parish priests.[61] The Assumption homily in this collection is a close rendering of the Transitus Mariae B² text (minus the Prologue), more faithful in many instances than that found in the

---

[60] The homily is number 53 in Erbe, *Mirk's Festial*, 221–27.
[61] Edward Weatherly, *Speculum Sacerdotale*, EETS OS 200 (London, 1936; repr. 1988).

Corpus 41 Assumption homily. Indeed, the *Speculum Sacerdotale* homily restores the Assumption chronology to the second year after Christ's Ascension (the Corpus 41 Assumption homily ascribes it to the third year). Unlike the Corpus homily, however, St. Michael only appears once in this homily. He is designated "proueste of paradise and prynce of the kynde of Hebrewes" and receives the soul of the Virgin Mary from Christ. Although the *Speculum Sacerdotale* homily on the Assumption does not depict St. Michael in the full range of his roles in the Transitus Mariae B² tradition (moving stones, uniting the Virgin's body and soul), it does suggest that his most important role is that of guardian and escort of the Virgin Mary's soul.

St. Michael in the Gospel of Nicodemus
(Descensus Christi ad inferos)

In addition to his stewardship over the body and soul of the Virgin Mary, St. Michael was also custodian of all human bodies and conveyor to heaven of all human souls. Perhaps the most influential New Testament apocryphon in the Middle Ages which portrayed St. Michael in these roles was the *Evangelium Nicodemi*, or Gospel of Nicodemus.[62] The Gospel of Nicodemus consists of two originally independent parts, the "Acta Pilati" and the "Descensus Christi ad inferos." The "Acta Pilati" narrates the dramatic events of Christ's trial before Pontius Pilate, while the "Descensus" depicts Christ's Harrowing of Hell. The earliest extant versions of the Gospel of Nicodemus in medieval England are a Latin text in an Anglo-Saxon manuscript (London, British Library, Royal MS 5.xiii) and three Old English translations. The earliest Old English translation is found in Cambridge, University Library, MS Ii.2.11, a manuscript which includes the West Saxon Gospels. The second Old English translation occurs in a twelfth-century collection of homilies now bound together with the *Beowulf* manuscript, London, British Library, Cotton MS Vitellius A.xv (pt. 1, fols. 60–86v). The third Old English translation is found in a twelfth-century collection of short homilies and theological tracts in Old English (London, British Library, Cotton MS Vespasian D.xiv). This manuscript contains an abridged recension of the "Descensus Christi ad inferos" entitled "De resurrectione Domini."[63]

St. Michael is featured in his roles as guardian of physical bodies and psychopomp

---

62 On the Gospel of Nicodemus, see Zbigniew Izydorczyk, *Manuscripts of the "Evangelium Nicodemi": A Census*, Subsidia Mediaevalia 21 (Toronto, 1993) and *The Medieval Gospel of Nicodemus: Texts, Intertexts, and Contexts in Western Europe*, ed. Z. Izydorczyk (Tempe, AZ, 1997).

63 Warner, *Early English Homilies*, pp. 77–88. Although it differs in some details, the version found in this manuscript is essentially the recension designated as "Latin A" by M. R. James in his *New Testament Apocrypha* (Oxford, 1924). For a discussion of this apocryphon in early medieval England, see J. E. Cross, ed., *Two Old English Apocrypha and their Manuscript Source: The Gospel of Nichodemus and the Avenging of the Saviour*, CSASE 19 (Cambridge, 1996), especially T. N. Hall, "The *Evangelium Nichodemi* and *Vindicta saluatoris* in Anglo-Saxon England" (36–81). See also W. H. Hulme, "The Old English Version of the Gospel of Nicodemus," *PMLA* (1898): 457–542; S. J. Crawford, *The Gospel of Nicodemus*, The Awyle Ryale Series (Edinburgh, 1927); K. A. S. Collett, "The Gospel of Nicodemus in Anglo-Saxon England" (unpublished Ph.D. dissertation, University of Pennsylvania, 1981); and J. J. Campbell, "To Hell and Back: Latin Tradition and the Literary Use of the 'Descensus ad Inferos' in Old English," *Viator* 13 (1982): 107–58.

in the "Descensus Christi ad inferos" portion of the Gospel of Nicodemus.[64] The subject of the "Descensus" portion is the continued interrogation by the Jewish council of Joseph of Arimathea, who, along with the purported author Nicodemus, was the most knowledgeable about the events surrounding the crucifixion and resurrection. Joseph explains the events of the Harrowing, describing in great detail how after the crucifixion Christ descended into the Hell and rescued the souls of the righteous, including two men, Karinus and Leucius, who were living in Arimathea. The Jewish council travels to Arimathea where they interrogate the two men and coerce each of them to write his account of the Harrowing. Miraculously, the two accounts agree word-for-word. According to the account, on the night of Christ's passion, a marvelous light appeared in hell, an event which provokes much comment from the patriarchs and prophets. Of most relevance to a discussion of St. Michael is Adam's request of Seth to tell the story of his journey to obtain the Oil of the Tree of Mercy. Christ arrives in Hell after Seth has told his story and binds Satan. Christ then takes Adam by the hand and conveys Adam and all the righteous to Paradise, where he turns them all over to St. Michael.[65] In Paradise, they meet Enoch and Elijah, who on the Last Day will return to earth to fight Antichrist. At the end of their narratives, Karinus and Leucius declare that they were commanded by St. Michael to return to earth and preach the good news of the Lord's resurrection. The two men hand their accounts over to the Jewish council and disappear.

Although the archangel appears at various points in the narrative of the "Descensus," St. Michael figures most prominently in the "Oil of Mercy" exemplum, in which Seth is sent by his father Adam to the Gates of Paradise to entreat God for the Oil of the Tree of Mercy to anoint Adam's body when he is sick and near death.[66] In the exemplum, St. Michael appears to Seth at the Gates of Paradise and tells him, "I am sent from the Lord to you, and I am set over the bodies of all men. Now I say to you, Seth, do not vex yourself by praying, spilling tears, that you need to obtain that oil of the tree of mercy that you can anoint your father Adam for his body's sores, for as yet five thousand and five hundred winters have not been completed, then you will be able to possess it, and he will become healed."[67] St. Michael's role as the guardian of human bodies is a familiar one for the archangel and can be traced back to the lost Jewish apocryphon known as the *Assumption of Moses* in which St. Michael fights with Satan over the body of Moses.[68] This apocryphon sanctioned the belief that St. Michael could

---

[64] The "Harrowing of Hell" was also the subject of several Old English poems, such as the Exeter Book "Descent into Hell," "Christ III," and "Christ and Satan."

[65] In a York Cycle miracle play, entitled "The Harrowing of Hell," St. Michael is represented binding Satan, who complains loudly, "Owt! ay! herrowe! helpe Mahounde!/ Nowe wex I woode oute of my witte!" (R. George Thomas, ed., *Ten Miracle Plays* [Evanston, 1966]: 130–44). In the play, Jesus also turns over the souls of the righteous to St. Michael (lines 385–92).

[66] For a discussion of the history and significance of this *exemplum*, see Esther Casier Quinn, *The Quest of Seth for the Oil of Life* (Chicago, 1962).

[67] The Cotton MS Vespasian D.xiv version printed in Warner, *Early English Homilies*, is quoted here: Ic eam asænd fram Drihtene to þe and ic eam asett ofer eal mænnisc lichame. Nu secge ic þe Seth, ne þeart þu swincan biddende, ne þine teares geotende, þ[æt] þu þurfe bidden þone ele of þan treowe þære mildheortnysse, þ[æt] þu Adam þinne fæder mide gesmerigen mote for his lichames sare, for get ne synden gefullede fif þusend wintre and þa fif hundred, þe sculen beon agane, ær þone he gehæled wurðe (83).

[68] On this apocryphon, see Johannes Tromp, *The Assumption of Moses: A Critical Edition with Commentary*, SVTP 10 (Leiden, 1993).

defend men at the terrible moment of death from attack by Satan, and from the second century on, St. Michael is assigned the task of conducting the souls of the faithful on the passage to heaven. Indeed, when Adam dies in this exemplum, God delivers him to St. Michael for conveyance to paradise: "Ælmightig God betæhte þa Adam Michaele, þan hehængle, and he heo gebrohte to neorxenewanga mid wulderfulre blisse."[69]

The story of Seth's journey to obtain the Oil of Mercy for his father clearly captured the popular imagination, for it is often repeated in Middle English writings. The exemplum most often appears in the Middle English versified versions of the Gospel of Nicodemus. Three manuscripts of the fourteenth and fifteenth centuries containing an assortment of metrical homilies, lives of saints, and other theological texts include versified versions of the Gospel of Nicodemus: London, British Library, Cotton MS Galba E.ix; London, British Library, Harley MS 4196; and London, British Library, Additional MS 32,578.[70] The story of St. Michael's roles in Seth's quest for the Oil of Mercy and at Adam's death in each of these manuscripts is virtually identical. The broad strokes of the narratives agree with the Latin A recension and the Old English translations of the "Descensus Christi ad inferos."

The story is altered slightly, however, in the "Canticum de Creatione" (Oxford, Trinity College MS 57) where Eve joins Seth in his journey to the gates of Paradise to obtain the Oil of Mercy.[71] Although both Eve and Seth pray at the gates of paradise, St. Michael addresses Seth only, telling him that he will have to wait 5500 years before he receives the Oil of Mercy for his father Adam. At Adam's death, St. Michael is charged with Adam's soul until the Last Days when "his sorrows will all turn into bliss."[72] Six days after Adam dies, Eve asks Seth to compose two accounts of her life. She asks that one be made on an earth tablet so that it might survive the destruction of the world by fire at Doomsday and one on a stone tablet so that it might survive destruction by

---

[69] Warner, Early English Homilies, 87: Almighty God delivered Adam to Michael the archangel and he brought him into Paradise with glorious bliss.

[70] These versions are edited and discussed by W. H. Hulme, The Middle English Harrowing of Hell and Gospel of Nicodemus, EETS ES 100 (London, 1907; repr. 1978). For other Middle English versions of the Gospel of Nicodemus, see A. W. Holden, "The Gospel of Nicodemus in Middle English Prose from British Museum MS Egerton 2658, John Rylands English MS 895, Bodleian Library MS Bodley 207, Stoneyhurst MS XLIII" (unpublished MA thesis, University of London, 1951); H. C. Kim, "The Gospel of Nicodemus Translated by John Trevisa" (unpublished Ph.D. dissertation, University of Washington, 1963); B. Lindström, ed., A Late Middle English Version of the Gospel of Nicodemus edited from British Museum MS Harley 149, Acta Universitatis Upsaliensis, Studia Anglistica Upsaliensis 18 (Uppsala, 1974); J. F. Drennan, "A Short Middle English Prose Translation of the Gospel of Nicodemus" (unpublished Ph.D. dissertation, University of Michigan, 1980); Z. Izydorczyk, "The Legend of the Harrowing of Hell in Middle English Literature" (unpublished Ph.D. dissertation, University of Toronto, 1985); C. W. Marx and J. F. Drennan, eds., The Middle English Prose Complaint of our Lady and Gospel of Nicodemus, Middle English Texts 19 (Heidelberg, 1987); D. C. Fowler, "The Middle English Gospel of Nicodemus in Winchester MS 33," Leeds Studies in English n.s. 19 (1988): 67–83; and Z. Izydorczyk, "The Unfamiliar Evangelium Nicodemi," Manuscripta 33 (1989): 169–91.

[71] Carl Horstmann, ed., "Canticum de Creatione," Anglia: Zeitschrift für englische Philologie 1 (1878): 287–331. The "Canticum" is a version of the pseudepigraphal "Vita Adae et Evae" in Middle English verse. The "Vita Adae et Evae" is translated in OTP, 2, 270–77. The "Canticum" contains the story of the fall of the angels with a full account of St. Michael's role in that battle (lines 236–312; 308–10). It also describes how St. Michael provides Adam with seeds and teaches him how to work the earth (lines 451–56; 313).

[72] Ibid., lines 887–88, 324: his sorwes alle/ Turnen in to blys.

water. At Eve's death, St. Michael appears to Seth and bids him not mourn longer than six days in order that he begin composing the account of his parent's lives.[73]

The Oil of Mercy exemplum is also told in the fourteenth-century Northumbrian poem, Cursor Mundi, a history of the world from Creation to Doomsday written in some 24,000 lines of Middle English verse.[74] In Cursor Mundi, Adam resides in Hell and has just heard from John the Baptist that Jesus was baptized in the river Jordan. The story of Jesus' baptism reminds him of St. Michael's response to his son, and he urges Seth to tell the story of his quest for the Oil of Mercy: "Son, tell us now all the truthfulness and nothing else that you heard from St. Michael the angel when I sent you to the gates of Paradise."[75] Once again, the details of the narrative correspond to the Latin A recension of the "Descensus," except for one minor difference. St. Michael tells Seth that he must wait 5100 years (as opposed to 5500): "When five thousand and five score years pass then shall God fulfill his promise."[76] At the Harrowing, Christ takes Adam by the hand and turns him over to St. Michael who leads all the righteous to Paradise: "Our Lord took Adam by the hand and gave him to St. Michael, who led him to that fellowship in Paradise."[77]

The exemplum is occasionally recounted as a prelude to the elaborate legend of the growth of the three trees, which become the single tree of the Holy Rood, from three seeds placed in Adam's mouth at death.[78] In these instances, the details of the exemplum agree largely with the version already discussed, except for yet another slightly different accounting scheme. This time, St. Michael tells Seth that he will not receive the oil until 5228 years have elapsed: "When five thousand years are gone, and two hundred and twenty, and also eight, all according to God's will."[79] At Adam's death, Eve and all their children lay across the corpse trying to revive him. St. Michael appears to the family and instructs them in how to bury Adam properly: "Weep no more, but be still, for thus it is my Lord's will that I shall teach you here you shall do with this corpse."[80] Following St. Michael's instructions, the family takes Adam's body to the Valley of Hebron where they are astounded at the sight of his grave. St. Michael assures them that all the dead must be buried in earth or stone.[81] Before they entomb the body of Adam, Seth remembers the three kernels the archangel had given him

---

[73] The account he composes is meant ostensibly to be the original text of the "Vita Adae et Evae."

[74] Richard Morris, ed., Cursor Mundi: A Northumbrian Poem of the XIVth Century, 6 vols. (London, 1874–93).

[75] Ibid., III, lines 17928–32: sone tell vs now al/ þe soþfastenes and no þing nele/ þat þou hardest of seynt mycchele/ þe aungel when I gan þe wyse/ to þo ʒatis of Paradis.

[76] Ibid., III, lines 17955–6: Whenne fyve þousonde ʒeer fyve skore biskille,/ þenne shal god his grante fulfille.

[77] Ibid., III, lines 18379–81: Vr lauerd adam bi þe hand light,/ And to sant Michael him bi-taght,/ In paradis þat felauscip he ledd.

[78] Richard Morris, Legends of the Holy Rood EETS OS 46 (London, 1881; repr. 1990): 67–72. In this same volume, Morris prints a legend of "The Invention of the Holy Cross" from the third edition of Caxton's Gilte Legende (1493) which relates the role of "saint mychell thaungell" in Seth's journey to Paradise for the Oil of Mercy (154).

[79] Ibid., lines 188–90, 67: When five thousand ʒere er went,/ Twa hundret and twenty þar-till,/ And also aght als es goddess will.

[80] Ibid., lines 353–56, 72: Wepes namore, bot bese still,/ For þus it es my lordes will,/ Pat I sal teche here ʒow vnto/ How ʒe with þis cors sall do.

[81] Ibid., lines 368–72, 72: Of þis thing haues no ferly,/ For als we now do him vnto/ So sal ʒe with ʒowre ded men do;/ Gers beri þam in erth or stane.

earlier, and he places them in his father's mouth. After a time, these seeds grow into three small saplings, which, according to the legends of the Tree Cross, grew together into the single tree from which the Cross was constructed.[82]

Summary

   Much of St. Michael's popularity in England during the medieval period was clearly due to his stewardship of human souls. The archangel's persona as a superhuman guardian spirit is long-lived and well-attested. In Old English texts, St. Michael is often invoked or represented as a protector of the faithful. In numerous prayers and in Bede, the archangel oversees the safe conduct through this world of the souls of the faithful. Ælfric, in his homily for St. Michael's feast day, traces the literary history of guardian spirits and confers on the archangel the status of supreme guardian. St. Michael's stewardship of the human soul extends beyond this life as well. St. Michael receives the souls of the faithful after death and conducts them to heaven. His most important charge in this capacity is clearly the soul of the Virgin Mary. In homilies on the Assumption of the Virgin, Christ himself entrusts the soul of His mother to St. Michael, an act which most certainly sanctioned belief in the archangel as the psychopomp *par excellence*. St. Michael's role in the conveyance of the souls of the righteous from hell in the legends of the "Harrowing" must also have further promoted the archangel's stature. Clearly, the numerous references to St. Michael in these roles underscore the widespread belief in his efficacy as guardian of the faithful and conveyor of their souls to heaven. Yet another aspect of St. Michael's involvement in the post-mortem fate of the soul is the subject of the final chapter.

---

[82] On the legends of the Holy Cross, see Mary Catherine Bodden, *The Old English Finding of the True Cross* (Cambridge, 1987); Stephan Borgehammer, *How the Holy Cross was Found: From Event to Medieval Legend* (Stockholm, 1991); Jan Willem Drijvers, *Helena Augusta: The Mother of Constantine the Great and the Legend of her Finding of the True Cross* (Leiden, 1992); Arthur S. Napier, *History of the Holy Rood Tree: A 12th Century Version of the Cross-Legend* (London, 1899); Allan Robb, "The History of the Holy Rood-Tree: Four Anglo-Saxon Homilies" (unpublished Ph.D. dissertation, University of Illinois, 1975); and Thomas Tipton, "Inventing the Cross: A Study of the Medieval English *Inventio Crucis* Legends" (unpublished Ph.D. dissertation, Northwestern University, 1997).

5

The Archangel and Judgment

Then schull ye all knel adowne, and pray to Seynt Michaell þat he apere to you, when ye schull passé out of þys world, and defende you from your enmyse, and bring you to þe ioye of paradise. Amen[1]

"De Festo Sancti Michaelis," *Mirk's Festial*

As the epigraph from Mirk's *Festial* suggests, all of St. Michael's roles (intercessor, psychopomp, defender of the faithful) are drawn into sharp focus at two moments of human vulnerability, at death and at the Final Judgment. As Chapter One indicated, St. Michael's efficacy in the present is eclipsed by that of the risen Christ, except at the moment of each human's death.[2] At that time, the archangel battles against devils for the custody of the soul of each person and supervises the individual post-mortem judgment of the soul.[3] St. Michael's efficacy, however, will be restored to its full glory at the end of Time, at the Final Judgment, as suggested by Revelation 12:7–9. After he defeats Satan in the final battle, St. Michael, along with Gabriel in some texts, will sound his trumpet to summon the dead to Judgment.[4]

A compelling feature of St. Michael's role at both the post-mortem and Final Judgments is his supervision of the weighing of the souls, or *psychostasis*. St. Michael's decisive role in the psychostasis is surprising as there is no scriptural warrant for his exercise of such an office. Already in the Book of Revelation and the apocryphal Revelation of St. John the Theologian, the archangel has acquired great eschatological status as leader of the celestial host that defeats Satan and his minions. The Epistle of Jude indicates that Christians were familiar with a legend, recorded in the Jewish apocryphal Assumption of Moses, in which the archangel contends with Satan for the body of Moses. As we have seen, this apocryphon sanctioned the belief that St. Michael could defend men at the moment of death from the attack of the devil. In the fourth-century CE Coptic text, the History of Joseph the Carpenter, the archangel receives the soul of Joseph for the post-mortem passage to heaven. St. Michael is entrusted with the soul of the Virgin Mary in the Assumption texts. The archangel's credentials as psychopomp and defender of the souls of the faithful are unquestionable. The association with the weighing of souls is more obscure and may lead back to Egypt where the weighing of

---

1 Erbe, *Mirk's Festial*, 260.
2 See especially 24–30.
3 This notion is sanctioned by Scripture; see Jude 9 and Zechariah 3:1–2.
4 See Appendix C.

the heart of the deceased is found in graphic detail in the *Book of the Dead*.[5] In the apocryphal Testament of Abraham, which is a text thought to have been composed in Egypt by a Jewish Christian during the second century CE, St. Michael conducts the patriarch on a guided tour of the next world in order to alleviate his fears about dying.[6] On the tour, Abraham sees an angel resplendent in light holding scales and weighing souls. St. Michael explains that what he is witnessing is the post-mortem judgment and retribution before the Lord. Although St. Michael is not the angel who actually weighs the soul in this text, it is clear from the context that the archangel is the official supervisor of the event. In later popular renditions of this post-mortem scene, St. Michael becomes associated with the angel who carries out the psychostasis. It would seem logical that the cause of this transference would be the archangel's long-standing reputation as the champion of mankind against the Devil. Ultimately, the post-mortem judgment of the soul came to have a double significance: it was both an unequivocal assessment of the morality of an individual's life and a contest between St. Michael and the Devil for the possession of the soul.

Although St. Michael is invoked in innumerable Old English prayers as a powerful intercessor on behalf of mankind, the prayers never appeal to the archangel specifically as weigher of souls. A dramatic expression of the motif of the archangel weighing souls, however, is found in a verse-paragraph of the anonymous Old English homily "In Praise of St. Michael" in Cambridge, Corpus Christi College MS 41. Verse-paragraph 26 reads,

> This is the holy archangel Michael who on the latter day at the end of the world and at the fearful judgment will then awaken the dead at the Lord's command; in an exceeding glorious voice he will call and will thus speak, "Surgite! Surgite! Arise! Arise!" And then will arise all the dead whom the earth swallowed up, or the sea drowned, or fire consumed, or wild animals devoured, or birds carried off on land, or worms gnawed in the earth.[7]

Another verse-paragraph of this homily also alludes to the archangel's role at the Final Judgment: "he is destined on the Day of Judgment to grant every man the recompense he has merited."[8] Clearly, St. Michael's roles in scenes of judgment and intercession are compelling and depictions of these scenes found there way into early English homiletic literature. In these scenes, the archangel acts in either or both of two capacities: as presenter of souls before the Lord for judgment and/or intercessor of behalf of the souls at judgment. This chapter examines the archangel's roles as an intercessor in scenes of judgment and as the slayer of Antichrist. These vivid depictions present St. Michael as a martial hero whose efficacy may even exceed that of Christ.

---

[5] For a discussion of the iconographic representations of St. Michael as weigher of souls, see Appendix D.

[6] On this apocryphon, see Chapter One, 17–18.

[7] Grant, *Three Homilies*, 65: Þis is se halga heahengel Sanctus Michael se ðe on þam neahstan dæge worulde ende and æt þam egesfullan dome he ðonne ða deadan aweceð mid dryhtenese hæse: beoruhtere stefene he clipað and þus cwið, "Surgite! Surgite! Arisað! Arisað!" and þonne arisað ealle ða deadan ðe eorðe forswealg, oððe sæ bescente, oððe fir forbærnde, oððe wildeor abiton, oððe fuglas on lande tobæren, oððe wirmas on eorðan fræten.

[8] *Ibid.*, 63: he sceal on domesdæge anra gehwelcum men his dæda edlean forgildan.

St. Michael in Scenes of Judgment and Intercession

A homily on the Last Judgment in CCCC MS 41 is concerned generally with the fate of the soul and contains a vivid description of Doom which is based largely on the apocryphal *Apocalypse of Thomas*.[9] More important for the study of St. Michael, however, is the inclusion in this homily of the apocryphon of the Seven Heavens, which describes the journey and trials of purgation of souls after death, can be found in many Jewish and early Christian sources.[10] From the Middle Ages, the apocryphon of the Seven Heavens is preserved in several versions: a Latin epitome, three Irish versions, and in the Corpus 41 homily on the Last Judgment.[11]

In the Corpus 41 homily, St. Michael performs plays a dual role. The archangel guards the door of the first heaven and presents the souls before the throne of the Lord in the seventh heaven. The first heaven is the "lyftlic" (air-like or aery) heaven, which

---

[9]   This homily is found on pages 287–95 of the manuscript. The text has been printed in part by M. Förster, "A New Version of the *Apocalypse of Thomas* in Old English," *Anglia* 73 (1955): 17–27, who prints the equivalent of manuscript pages 287–92 of the homily, and by R. Willard, *Two Apocrypha in Old English*, Beiträge zur englischen Philologie (Leipzig, 1935): 3–6, who picks up where Förster leaves off and prints all but a final portion of the homily. This final section of the homily remains unedited and contains a full account of the pains of hell and a brief comparison of these pains with the joys of heaven. On the Apocalypse of Thomas, see Milton McC. Gatch, "Eschatology in the Anonymous Old English Homilies," *Traditio* 21 (1965): 117–65; Mary Swan, "The *Apocalypse of Thomas* in Old English," *Leeds Studies in English* n.s. 29 (1998): 333–46; and most recently Charles D. Wright, "The *Apocalypse of Thomas*: Some New Latin Texts and Their Significance for the Old English Versions," in Kathryn Powell and Donald Scragg, eds., *Apocryphal Texts and Traditions in Anglo-Saxon England* (Cambridge, 2003): 27–64.

[10] The doctrine is discussed in terms of its relation to Greek, Oriental, Jewish, and Christian literature in the Preface (xxx–xlvii) to R. H. Charles and W. R. Morfill's edition of *The Book of the Secrets of Enoch* (Oxford, 1896).

[11] The Latin epitome of the apocryphon is among the *Apocrypha Priscillianistica* from a florilegium in Karlsruhe, Badische Landesbibliothek Aug. CCLIV, published by Dom De Bruyne, "Fragments retrouvés d'apocryphes priscillianistes," *RB* 24 (1907): 318–35. The three Irish versions of the apocryphon are found in sections 15–20 of the *Fís Adamnán*, Recension III of the *Tengua Bithnua*, and in the Liber Flavus Fergusiorum. For a fuller account of the Irish versions and their relation to the Corpus homily, see my essay, "Archangel in the Margins: St. Michael in the Homilies of Cambridge Corpus Christi College 41," *Traditio* 53 (1998): 63–91. In his study of the Seven Heavens apocryphon, Rudolph Willard (*Two Apocrypha*, 23, n. 113) notes that there is an allusion to the doctrine of the seven heavens in an unpublished Easter homily in CCCC MS 162 (384). Willard prints the relevant passage in his note. Willard also points out that the Seven Heaven apocryphon must have influenced another Old English homily, "Be heofonwarum 7 be helwarum," which describes hell in terms closely resembling the Latin and Old English versions of the apocryphon. Willard prints the passage (24) and analyzes its significance in relation to the other versions of the Seven Heavens apocryphon (25–28). Although the anonymous homily, "Be heofonwarum 7 be helwarum," is clearly related to the Corpus version of the apocryphon, it differs in significant details, particularly in its virtual neglect of St. Michael. The entire homily is printed in T. C. Callison, "An Edition of Previously Unpublished Anglo-Saxon Homilies in MSS CCCC 302 and Cotton Faustina A. ix" (unpublished Ph.D. dissertation, University of Wisconsin, 1973). There occur several references to the seventh heaven in two homilies of Pseudo-Wulfstan: Homily 43 and Homily 44 (A. Napier, *Wulfstan*, 207, line 2; 213, line 13; and 217, line 16). Yet another reference to the doctrine of the Seven Heavens occurs in a Rogationtide homily edited by J. Bazire and J. E. Cross, *Eleven Old English Rogationtide Homilies*, King's College London Medieval Studies 4 (London, 1990): 64, line 90.

is entered through the door "Abyssus."[12] Another door is mentioned in connection with this heaven: it is called "Sabaoth, þæt is, weoroda duru, for þon englas ðider ingað and manna sawla" (Sabaoth, that is, the Door of the Host, because angels and the souls of men enter thither).[13] St. Michael guards these doors, accompanied by two attendants, Equitas and Estimatio, who bear in their hands burning rods. Evidently the souls are to be disciplined at the hands of these personified Cardinal Virtues before proceeding to the next heaven.[14] In each succeeding heaven, souls are punished according to the severity of their sins until they reach the seventh heaven, the heaven of the Holy Trinity. In the seventh heaven, "Sanctus Michael agifeð þa sawla þæra soðfæstra and þæra sinfulra" (St. Michael delivers the souls of the truth-fast and the sinful) before the throne of the Lord so that they may be judged.[15]

Although the conception of Seven Heavens seems to have been commonplace in apocryphal and pseudepigraphal literature, many of the details in the Corpus homily are unique. Furthermore, in the Jewish and early Christian sources a system of doors and guardian angels for each heaven is lacking. The doors must have been added at a later date and were probably associated with guardian angels after that doctrine was affirmed in the writings of the Fathers of the Church.[16]

In particularly graphic terms, the Old English Pseudo-Wulfstan homily 29,[17] "Her is halwendlic lar and ðearflic læwedum mannum, þe þæt læden ne cunnon" (Here is a wholesome and useful lesson [for] unlearned men, who do not know Latin), describes the post-mortem judgment of an unworthy soul. The homily, which includes an address by a soul to its body at the hour of death, relates the tale of a holy man who is led on an otherworldly journey by some companions (presumably angels) and witnesses the evacuation of a soul from its body. The body is surrounded by devils who taunt the reluctant soul.

> But he dared not go out, because then he saw the fiendish spirits standing before him. Then one of those devils said to him: "What is your hesitation? Why aren't you willing to come out? The expectation is that St. Michael the archangel will come with the angelic throng and seize you from us."[18]

---

[12] The Seven Heavens portion of this homily is printed by R. Willard, *Two Apocrypha*, 4–6.

[13] *Ibid.*, 4/7–9. Willard compares eleven versions of this apocryphon and notes a close correspondence between the Latin, Irish, and Old English texts in the names of the seven heavens, the doors of the heavens, and the guardian angels, except in the instance of this second door in the first heaven. Here the Old English is unique in mentioning a second door.

[14] In each of the first two heavens, there are two attendants assisting the guardian angel. In the Corpus homily, these attendants are named as four Cardinal Virtues: Equitas and Estimatio are found in the first heaven, Continentia and Contentia in the second. The homily refers to these attendants as "youths" or "virgins."

[15] Willard, 5/50–51.

[16] For an overview of the subject of guardian angels in the Old Testament, see William G. Heidt, *Angelology of the Old Testament* (Catholic University Press, 1949): 40–50; and in the writings of the Fathers of the Church, see Jean Daniélou, *Les Anges et leur Mission*, trans. David Heimann as *The Angels and their Mission* (Westminster, MD, 1957): 68–82.

[17] Arthur Napier, *Wulfstan, Sammlung der ihm zugeschriebenen Homilien nebst Untersuchungen über ihre Echtheit* (Berlin, 1883): 134–43.

[18] *Ibid.*, 140/11–15: Ac heo ne dorst ut gan, forðam þe heo geseah þa awyrgedan gastas beforan hyre standan. Þa cwæð an þæra deofla to hyre: "Hwæt is þin þriding? Hwi nelt ðu ut gan? Wen ys, þæt Michael se heahengle cume mid engla þreatum and wyle þe geniman of us."

This devil continues to taunt the wretched soul, declaring that it does not deserve to be saved because it willingly participated in the debauchery of its body. The soul tries to assert that it was forced into such vile acts by its body. St. Michael, however, does not arrive to rescue the soul, and it suffers a horrible fate along with other wretched souls.

> Then devils led them and plunged them into the mouth of a fiery dragon, and he [the dragon] consumed them instantly and spewed them into the hottest fires of hell-torment.[19]

This gruesome depiction of the fate of a wretched soul is reminiscent of many similar scenes in Old English homilies.

St. Michael also figures in several homilies which feature intercession scenes. Generally, these scenes take place at judgment (either the post-mortem judgment or the Final Judgment) and involve the intercessions of three saints, most often the Virgin Mary and Saints Michael and Peter. Versions of the intercession motif are found in the homily for Easter in CCCC MS 41; Vercelli homily 15; two versions of the "Sunday Letter" (Pseudo-Wulfstan 45 and a homily in CCCC MS 140); and a Last Judgment homily in Oxford, Bodleian Library, Hatton MS 114.[20]

The fullest account of the intercession motif is found in the homily for Easter in Corpus 41.[21] As has been noted by several scholars, Ælfric dismissed as heretical the view that the Virgin Mary and some other saints could successfully intercede to rescue any of the sinners condemned to hell at the Last Judgment.[22] The Corpus homily is unique and problematic, however, in representing just this view. After relating Christ's Judgment of the sinful,[23] the homilist warns that the condemned souls are to be led off to hell. Beginning the intercession scene, the Virgin Mary rises, approaches the Lord, and asks Him that He grant her a third portion of the sinful souls. He does so, and Mary transfers her saved souls to Christ's right side. SS. Michael and Peter next

19 Ibid., 141/23–25: Þa deoflu hi ða læddon and bescutton hi anum fyrenan dracan innan þone muð, and he hi þærrihte forswalh and eft aspaw on þ a hatostan brynas hellewittes.
20 The CCCC MS 41 homily for Easter is found on pages 295–301 and has been printed by W. H. Hulme, "The Old English Gospel of Nicodemus," Modern Philology 1 (1904): 32–36 (610–14). Virtually the same text for Easter appears in CCCC MS 303 (fols. 72–75), where the Intercession scene is lacking. Vercelli 15 has been printed by Donald Scragg, The Vercelli Homilies, EETS OS 300 (Oxford, 1992): 253–65. Vercelli 15 is also printed in Vercelli Homilies IX–XXIII, ed. P. Szarmach (Toronto, 1981) and has been translated by Jean Anne Strebinger in The Vercelli Book Homilies: Translations from the Anglo-Saxon, ed. Lewis Nicholson (Lanham, MD, 1991): 97–103. Pseudo-Wulfstan 45 appears in A. Napier, Wulfstan, 226–32. The "Sunday Letter" homily in CCCC MS 140 is printed in R. Priebsch, "The Chief Sources of Some Anglo-Saxon Homilies," Otia Merseiana 1 (1899): 135–38. The Last Judgment homily in Oxford, Bodleian Library, Hatton MS 114 is printed in A. M. L. Fadda, Nuove omelie anglosassoni della rinascenza benedettina (Florence, 1977): 42–53.
21 Mary Clayton has treated this scene in an exhaustive article, "Delivering the Damned: A Motif in Old English Homiletic Prose," MÆ 55 (1986): 92–102.
22 Mary Clayton, "Delivering the Damned," 92, and Thomas D. Hill, "Delivering the Damned in Old English Anonymous Homilies and Jón Arason's Ljómur," MÆ 61 (1992): 75–82 at 75. Ælfric's condemnation is found in his homily "In Natale Sanctum Virginum" in Ælfric's Catholic Homilies: The Second Series, ed. M. Godden, EETS SS 5 (London: 1979): 333.
23 William H. Hulme, "The Old English Gospel of Nicodemus," Modern Philology 1 (1904): 35: Ic cweðe nu to eow, gewitað ge awirgede fram me in þæt ecce fyr; and ic eow betyne to dæg heofona rices duru to geanes, swa ge betyndon eowra dura togenes þearfum ð[e] an mine naman to eow cigdon. Nelle ic gehiran to dæg eowre stefne þe maðe ge woldon gehiran þæs earman stefne.

intercede each for another third of the souls, transferring in turn their company to Christ's right side. Devils carry off the remainder to hell,[24] as St. Peter locks the doors of hell behind them and throws the keys on the ground, "þa næfre siððan gode angeminde ne cumað" (so that never thereafter might the good-minded come there).[25] The homily ends with Christ's address to the good souls (a paraphrase of Matthew 25:35–40), and the Ascension of Christ and the good souls into heaven.

The intercession scene in the Corpus 41 homily has recently received attention from three critics. Mary Clayton has argued that the scene ultimately derives from a similar motif which occurs as an appendix to some versions of the *Apocalypse of Mary*.[26] This Apocalypse exists in two forms, one of which derives from Greek, with versions in Armenian, Ethiopic, Slavonian, Syriac, Latin, and Old Irish, while the other is found only in an Ethiopic witness.[27] In the *Apocalypse of Mary*, the Virgin Mary, St. Michael, and the apostles view the torments of hell immediately after Mary's bodily Assumption. The tortured souls of hell plead with each of the saints, who in turn intercedes on their behalf with Christ. After accusing the dreadful souls of forgetfulness, Christ grants them a respite of three hours because of the intercession of Mary, St. Michael, and the apostles.[28] Although it is clear that the *Apocalypse of Mary* is dependent on the *Apocalypse of Paul*, Mary Clayton argues that "The dependence of the Old English motif on the *Apocalypse of Mary* rather than on the better-known *Apocalypse of Paul* is clear from the non-appearance of Paul and the prominence of Mary in the Anglo-Saxon."[29]

Thomas D. Hill has noted that the motif of delivering the damned was current in

---

[24] The mathematics of this passage has troubled many critics as it seems illogical that there should remain any souls after the three intercessions of one third each. Given the identical rhetorical structure of each intercessory appeal, however, it is possible that the third portion that each saint acquires is not a third of the total number of sinners at the beginning of the scene, but rather a third of the sinners left after each successful intercession. This accounting scheme has the advantage of ensuring that some souls would remain to be damned.

[25] Hulme, "The Old English Gospel of Nicodemus," 35.

[26] "Delivering the Damned," 97. By this title, Mary Clayton refers to a group of texts in Syriac, Latin, and Greek. The Syriac text is the "Obsequies of the Holy Virgin," published by W. Wright, *Contributions*, 42–51.

[27] For the purposes of this study the most important versions of the Greek form are the Greek, Syriac, and Old Irish. The Greek Apocalypse is printed in M. R. James, *Apocrypha Anecdota*, vol. 1 (Cambridge, 1893): 109–26, and has been translated as "The Apocalypse of the Virgin, or the Apocalypse of the Holy Mother of God concerning the Chastisements," by A. Rutherford in *Ante-Nicene Fathers*, vol. 9, ed. A. Menzies (New York, 1903): 169–74. The Syriac version is printed in W. Wright, *Contributions to the Apocryphal Literature of the New Testament* (London, 1865): 42–51. The Old Irish version is printed in Charles Donahue, *The Testament of Mary: The Gaelic Version of the Dormitio Mariae together with an Irish Latin Version* (New York, 1942). The sole Ethiopic witness has been edited by M. Chaîne, "Apocalypsis seu Visio Mariae Virginis," in *Apocrypha de Beata Maria Virgine: Scriptores Aethiopici*, Series 1, vol. 7 (Rome, 1909): 43–68. For a succinct discussion of both forms of the Apocalypse with full bibliography, see R. Bauckham, "Virgin, Apocalypses of the," in *Anchor Bible Dictionary*, vol. 6 (New York, 1992): 854–56.

[28] The efficacy of the intercession of Mary and St. Michael is also a popular motif in Coptic homiletic literature where they are often associated with natural phenomena. For a description of St. Michael's association with the regular occurence of natural phenomena, see Appendix C. For a discussion of several Coptic homilies in which the Virgin Mary and St. Michael are depicted as intercessors whose advocacy before the Lord guarantees the rising and setting of the sun and other such natural phenomena as keep the world functioning properly, see my "Archangel in the Margins," 88–90.

[29] "Delivering the Damned," 96.

the early Christian world as St. Augustine condemns the view that the damned can be delivered in *De civitate dei* (Book xxi, Chapter 18), but concedes that "there are no patristic or apocryphal texts which could have served as a model to the Old English homilists who fashioned the narrative in the form in which it is preserved in Anglo-Saxon England."[30] Hill draws attention instead to a late medieval Icelandic poem which contains "an exact parallel to the Old English apocryphal motif as condemned by Ælfric."[31] Although St. Michael is not mentioned in Jón Arason's poem, *Ljómur*, Mary and the apostle John are portrayed interceding successfully on behalf of sinners at Judgment. Unlike its Old English counterpart, in which a portion of sinners is left unsaved after the intercession, however, the intercession in the Icelandic poem saves all of humankind, the evil and the good. Noting the common convention of citing Old Norse-Icelandic parallels to Old English texts, Hill discounts the view that a lost Latin text may have been the source of the intercession scene in both the Old English homilies and Arason's poem in favor of "the possibility that this motif was disseminated in the vernacular form from Anglo-Saxon England to Iceland, where it was preserved in mediaeval Icelandic religious tradition."[32]

In the most recent article on the currency of this motif, Sarah Cutforth explores the relationship between the two manuscript texts of the Easter homily in CCCC MSS 41 and 303 (fols. 72–75).[33] Cutforth points out that the Easter homily in CCCC MS 303, which is virtually identical in wording to the Corpus 41 homily, lacks entirely the intercession scene of Mary, St. Michael, and Peter. The passage omitted occurs in Corpus 41 between two sentences which repeat the same idea, namely, that the devil will seize the souls left and lead them to hell. Cutforth concludes that although the omission could have been the result of an eyeskip, it is more likely that "the omission reflects conscious scribal intervention designed to improve a passage which was theologically problematic."[34] Following Clayton, Cutforth underscores the theological significance of the successful intercession *after* the assembled sinners have been judged (i.e., after the *Discedite* passage): "the intercession of the saints occurs after Christ has condemned them to hell's eternity, providing the truly wicked with a further chance of redemption: theologically this is seen to undermine Christ's powers as Judge."[35]

Despite the apocalyptic nature of this homily, the homilist does not mention St. Michael's usual role as slayer of Antichrist at the end of time. Instead he stresses the efficacy of the archangel's intercession on behalf of sinners at Judgment. St. Michael's importance as intercessor is well attested in apocryphal and pseudepigraphal sources of both the Old and New Testaments.[36] So too in Anglo-Saxon sources is St. Michael acknowledged as a powerful advocate of humankind. In his homily for St. Michael's

---

30 "Delivering the Damned in Old English Anonymous Homilies and Jón Arason's *Ljómur*," *Medium Ævum* 61 (1992): 75–82 at 83.

31 *Ibid.*, 79.

32 *Ibid.*

33 "Delivering the Damned in Old English Homilies: An Additional Note," *N&Q* n.s. 40, no. 4 (December 1993): 435–37. Ker dates the marginalia of Corpus 41 to the same date as the Bede text or a little bit later. He dates CCCC MS 303 about a century later than the Bede, i.e., the first half of the twelfth century (*Catalogue of Manuscripts Containing Anglo-Saxon* [Oxford, 1957]: 45 and 105).

34 "Delivering the Damned," 436.

35 *Ibid.*, 437, and Clayton, "Delivering the Damned," 95–96.

36 See Appendix C. As has been shown in Chapter Four, St. Michael is also regarded as a powerful intercessor in many versions of the Assumption narrative.

feast day, Ælfric describes angels in general as "þeninggastum" (ministering spirits), and St. Michael in particular as "þingere on heofonum to ðam Ælmihtigan Gode" (intercessor in heaven with Almighty God).[37] In the homily for St. Michael's feast found in the anonymous Blickling collection, St. Michael is portrayed in his role as an intercessor on behalf of the Sipontans in their battle with the pagan Neapolitans. The archangel is also invoked in numerous prayers in Latin and Old English alike as a powerful intercessor on behalf of humankind.[38] The unique aspect of this homily's representation of St. Michael as an intercessor, then, lies in its transference of the scene of intercession to the Last Judgment. As has been discussed, the effectiveness of any intercession *after* Christ's judgment is theologically troubling. It has even been suggested that Ælfric's condemnation may have been in reaction to a Corpus-like text.[39]

The intercession scene in Vercelli 15 is essentially a paraphrase of the apocryphal *Apocalypse of Thomas*.[40] The homily begins by recounting the signs of Doomsday's arrival, emphasizing in particular the rise of idolatry more than its source does. An account of the events of the six days before Doom follows. This account breaks off in the middle of the signs for Sunday (one folio is missing). The homily concludes by departing from its Latin source to depict a scene in which the Virgin Mary, St. Michael, and St. Peter each intercede with Christ on behalf of a third portion of the sinners at Judgment.[41] Despite the apocalyptic nature of the homily, the homilist's principal concern seems to have been the efficacy of St. Michael's intercession on behalf of sinners.

In the intercession scene, St. Michael and Peter each fall at Christ's feet to utter an appeal for clemency which is reported in direct speech. Mary bases her intercession on her humble maternity of Christ, St. Michael bases his on his mighty dominion over heaven, and Peter does so on his possession of the keys of heaven and hell. After the intercessions, Christ calls the blessed souls on his right side to receive the kingdom of the Lord (Matthew 25:34). He then turns to the sinful band on his left side and banishes them to the eternal punishments of hell (Matthew 25:41). As devils drive the last of the sinful souls into hell, St. Peter locks the door of hell and tosses the key over his back into hell. Although there exist differences between the intercession scenes in Vercelli 15 and Corpus 41, the most significant of which is in the sequence of events, the scenes are clearly related. Donald Scragg has argued that despite the differences, the source for the intercession motif in both homilies is "undoubtedly the same."[42] While Mary Clayton concedes that the homilies must indeed be related, she argues that the theologically problematic order of events in the Corpus homily rules out the possibility that the two homilies were translated independently from the same source.[43]

---

[37] Clemoes, *Ælfric's Catholic Homilies*, 469 and 475.

[38] For a discussion of many of these prayers, see Chapter Three.

[39] Mary Clayton remarks that Ælfric may have been referring to a Corpus-like text, "as he specifies that no one can rescue a soul 'þe crist þus to cweð: Discedite . . .'" ("Delivering the Damned," 96).

[40] James, *ANT*, 555–62; and Elliott, *ANT*, 645–51. See also n. 9 above.

[41] In her article, "Delivering the Damned," Clayton analyzes the significance of the different treatments of the theme in Vercelli XV and in the Easter homily in CCCC MS 41.

[42] *The Vercelli Homilies* (251). See also Scragg, "Vernacular Homilies and Prose Saints' Lives before Ælfric," *ASE* 8 (1979): 223–77 at 231.

[43] Clayton, "Delivering the Damned," 96.

A similar intercession scene occurs in two Old English homilies based on the so-called "Sunday Letter" tradition.[44] Robert Priebsch has shown that Pseudo-Wulfstan homily 45, "Sermo angelorum nomina," and a homily in CCCC MS 140 both belong to the family of the first Latin recension of the Letter, the oldest form of the Letter.[45] According to the first recension, St. Michael carries from heaven to Jerusalem a Letter written by Christ, which urges upon its audience a strict observance of the Lord's Day. The Letter then travels by various routes through Bethlehem, Cappadocia, Monte Gargano, arriving finally at Rome. Although Priebsch contends that the Old English version of the Letter is a "translation" of the first Latin recension, Clare Lees has argued that the Old English version is in fact a rather free-form rendition of the Latin source.[46] Nevertheless, in the Latin and Old English homilies, the Virgin Mary, St. Michael, and SS. Peter and Paul intercede to avert the imminent destruction of the world. Thus, while the motif of the intercession, and even most of the characters involved, are related to those found in Corpus 41 and Vercelli 15, the ultimate aim of the intercessions differs and therefore rules out any direct relationship between the scenes.

The final example of the intercession motif occurs in a Last Judgment homily under the rubric, "Dominica II ebdomadae Quadragesime," in Oxford, Bodleian Library, MS Hatton 114. As in the Corpus and Vercelli scenes, the Virgin Mary, St. Michael, and St. Peter are present at the Last Judgment. First, St. Michael ushers a good soul before the Lord, and the soul is blessed. Then the archangel brings a sinful soul before the Lord, who condemns the soul to hell. The Virgin Mary intercedes on behalf of the sinful soul, but the outcome of her intercession is never reported.

Clearly, the motif of an intercession by the Virgin Mary, St. Michael, and St. Peter (and occasionally some number of the other apostles) at scenes of judgment (either the Last Judgment or the particular judgment) captured the popular imagination and found its way into the Old English homiletic prose of the ninth century.[47]

---

44 For a summary of the Sunday Letter tradition in Anglo-Saxon England, see Clare Lees' entry under "Sunday Letter," *SASLC: Trial*, 38–40.

45 "Chief Sources of some Anglo-Saxon Homilies," *Otia Merseiana* 1 (1899): 129–47, where he prints the Latin source from Vienna, Österreichische Nationalbibliothek lat. MS 1355 (fourteenth century). Priebsch also discusses this homily in passing in his full-length study of the various Heavenly Letter traditions, *Letter from Heaven on the Observance of the Lord's Day* (Oxford, 1936).

46 "The 'Sunday Letter' and the 'Sunday Lists'," *ASE* 14 (1985): 129–51 at 132. Deviations include a passage stressing the necessity of tithe-giving (Napier, *Wulfstan*, 230/16–20); and the inclusion in the Old English of a lengthy "Sunday List," a list of scriptural events which occurred on the Lord's Day (*ibid.*, 230/11–31).

47 For a description of similar scenes in Anglo-Saxon iconographic representations of St. Michael, see Appendix D. The impact of these scenes of intercession can also be seen in a formulaic protection clause included in many late tenth-century Anglo-Saxon charters. The clause invariably invokes the Virgin Mary, St. Michael, and St. Peter (occasionally with other saints) to guarantee adherence to the terms of the charter. The clause generally reads as follows: "Sca Maria 7 scs Michahel cum sco Petro 7 eallum Godes halgum gemiltsien þis haldendum gif hwa buton gewrihton abrecan wille God hine to rihtere bote gecerre. Amen." (May St. Mary and St. Michael, with St. Peter and all the saints of God, be merciful towards those who observe this. If anyone, without due cause, attempts to break it, may God turn him to due amendment. Amen.). Variations occur in the punishment suffered by those who break the clause: "wille God adiligie his noman of life bocum" (God shall blot out his name from the book of life).

St. Michael in the Vision of St. Paul

The principal Old English version of the Vision of St. Paul is a translation found in Oxford, Bodleian Library, MS Junius 85/86, a manuscript of the mid-eleventh century.[48] St. Michael appears in the context of the judgment of a good soul.[49] With the angelic throng, St. Michael praises the Lord as the good soul is brought before the throne. The good soul's guardian angel introduces the soul before the Lord and together the pair await the Lord's judgment. The Lord praises the soul for not displeasing Him on earth and promises to show the soul mercy. The soul is then passed into the charge of St. Michael, who conveys it to paradise where it will reside with all the saints.

The Old English version of the Vision of St. Paul closest to the translation in Oxford, Bodleian Library MS Junius 85/86 occurs in Pseudo-Wulfstan homily 46, entitled simply Larspell ("Homily").[50] As Healey has shown, in contrast to the Old English translation, homily 46 reverses the order of the going-out of the good and evil souls, suggesting that it is a later development.[51] In this homily, St. Michael does not appear at all in the context of the judgment of either the evil or good soul. Instead he is mentioned as a powerful intercessor by a devil taunting an evil soul: "Why won't you, unhappy one, acknowledge the Lord and pray to the holy Michael, and all the holy ones, that he be to you a helper?"[52]

A fuller account of St. Michael's roles in the Vision of St. Paul occurs in a homily once attributed to the Venerable Bede, but now generally recognized to be spurious.[53] In the homily, St. Michael guides St. Paul on his tour of Hell, answering his questions about each of the gruesome punishments they witness. In a brief allusion to the journey of a good soul to heaven, Michael is described as fulfilling his role as psycho-pomp, placing the soul in paradise. When the miserable souls in Hell beg St. Michael and Paul to intercede on their behalf, the heavens tremble and Christ descends from the clouds. For the sake of St. Michael and Paul, the Lord grants the souls in Hell a weekly respite for the duration of the Sabbath. The homily closes with an injunction to keep the Sabbath faithfully and avoid the sins for which the souls in Hell suffered grievously.

Given Ælfric's explicit denunciation of the Latin version of the Vision of St. Paul known to him, one can assume that none of the various Old English versions of the Vision would have met with the holy man's approval either.[54] The heterodox nature of

---

[48] The Old English translation was first treated in an article by A. M. L. Fadda, "Una inedita traduzione anglosassone della 'Visio Pauli,' " Studi Medievali 15 (1974): 482–95. The translation was then edited by Antonette diPaolo Healey, The Old English Vision of St. Paul, Speculum Anniversary Monographs 2 (Cambridge, MA, 1978). For a description of the manuscript, see N. R. Ker, Catalogue, 409–11, art. 336.

[49] Healey, The Old English Vision, 67–69/93–115.

[50] Napier, Wulfstan, 232–42.

[51] Healey, The Old English Vision, 43.

[52] Napier, Wulfstan, 240/11–14: Hwi noldest ðu, unsæglige, andettan þinum drihtne and biddan þone halgan Michael, þæt he wære þe fultumigend, and ealle halgan?

[53] Homelia C of the "Homeliæ Subdititiae," PL 94: 501–502, on which see Chapter Three, n. 26.

[54] Ælfric repudiates the Vision in his homily, "In Letania Maiore," printed in Clemoes, Ælfric's Catholic

the Vision in its vernacular versions, however, suggests that its popular appeal lay in its description of the ultimate fate of the soul at the moment of death.

Although popular in Anglo-Saxon England as a description of the fate of the soul at the moment of death, the Vision of St. Paul was to enjoy its greatest popularity in the twelfth and thirteenth centuries. In the Anglo-Norman period, the vision exists in Old English in a twelfth-century manuscript,[55] which is a compilation from earlier eleventh-century documents, and in two Anglo-Norman versions. In the Old English version, the essential details of the vision are embedded in a homily entitled "In Diebus Dominicis." From the vision, the preacher remarks that every Christian ought to hallow Sunday by taking rest on that day and faithfully observing his religious duties because Sunday has three virtues. The first is that on earth Sunday marks a day of rest from all labor. The second virtue is in Heaven, where the angels rest themselves more than on any other day. The third virtue is in Hell where the wretched are given a day of rest from their torments, a respite which St. Michael and Paul achieve on behalf of these souls. As the principal lesson of the sermon, however, is to impress upon the laity the importance of Sunday observance, the homily is brief and omits nearly all the details of the Latin and later French and Middle English versions of the Vision of St. Paul.

There are seven medieval French rhymed versions of the Vision of St. Paul.[56] Their manuscripts range in date from the twelfth century to the fourteenth century. Of the seven versions, there are two which fall within the scope of our period. The first is an Anglo-Norman "translation" by Adam de Ross which dates from the last quarter of the twelfth century.[57] Although there persists some debate as to his identification, it is generally agreed that he came from Ross-on-Wye in Herefordshire.[58] A study of the order of the various episodes in Adam's poem indicates that his source text was most likely the common Latin Redaction IV,[59] although the poet omitted one of the torments and elaborated on another one. The second version of the Vision of St. Paul which falls within the Anglo-Norman period is that by the Lincolnshire Templar Henri

---

Homilies, 317–24. The passage is quoted in Healey, *The Old English Vision* (41), who indicates that Aldhelm also disparaged the Latin Vision.

55 Lambeth 487, printed in Morris, *Old English Homilies*, 41–47.

56 For a discussion of these, see D. D. R. Owen's "The *Vision of St. Paul*: The French and Provençal Versions and their Sources," *Romance Philology* 12 (1958): 33–51.

57 The text has been published several times, from a single MS by A. F. Ozanam in *Dante et la philosophie catholique du treizième siècle* (Paris, 1839): 343ff.; and edited from all known sources by L. E. Kastner in "The Vision of Saint Paul by the Anglo-Norman *trouvère* Adam de Ross," *Zeitschrift für Neufranzösische Sprache* 29 (1906), and edited from the oldest fragment by Ian Short in "The Bodleian Fragment of the Anglo-Norman *Vision of St Paul* by Adam de Ross," *Studies in Medieval French Language and Literature presented to Brian Woledge in honour of his 80th Birthday*, ed. Sally Burch North (Droz, 1987): 175–89.

58 J. C. Russell identifies the poet with an Irish monk who lived in 1279 (*Dictionary of Writers of 13th Century England* [London, 1936]: 9–10). Given the dating of the poem to the last quarter of the twelfth century, this date is untenable. Professor M. D. Legge also favors an Irish connection, although she readily admits that of this there is no proof (*Anglo-Norman in the Cloisters* [Edinburgh, 1950]: 53–54, 122, and *Anglo-Norman Literature and its Background* [Oxford, 1963]: 274–75, 304).

59 There are two principal works on the Greek and Latin versions of the legend: H. Brandes, *Visio S. Pauli. Ein Beitrag zur Visionsliteratur, mit einem deutschen und zwei lateinischen Texten* (Halle, 1885), and T. Silverstein, *Visio Sancti Pauli: The History of the Apocalypse in Latin together with Nine Texts*, Studies and Documents 4 (London, 1935).

d'Arcy, produced sometime between the end of the twelfth and middle of the thirteenth centuries.[60] Henri acknowledges that his version is translated from the Latin and the poem's editor points out that it is very close to the same Redaction IV as used by Adam. Like his predecessor, Henri elaborates the poem only slightly, making no important changes to the story. One of Henri's changes, however, merits attention here. On two occasions, Henri expands on his Latin source to insist on the merits of regular and sincere churchgoing. At lines 64–69, he poignantly remarks on the suffering of those in the infernal river as being a result of their negligence of observing Sunday. Furthermore, he closes his poem with some thirty lines in praise of Sunday, a twenty-nine line expansion of his Latin source.[61] Taken in conjunction with the Old English homily on the significance of Sunday, it seems that the Visio Pauli must have been generally perceived as an effective instructional guide to the painful lessons of one's negligence of God's laws, especially in the observance of Sunday's privileges. But perhaps the most important aspect of these versions of the Vision of St. Paul for the cult of St. Michael is, once again, his role as an intercessor, in this case on behalf of the wretched souls in Hell.

Related to the versions of the Vision of St. Paul are a series of texts which describe in gruesome detail the Eleven Pains of Hell. In fact, these tales are versions of the Vision in miniature. While they differ in length and in some detail, the general impetus of the tales is the same: whosoever will hallow Sunday and observe God's laws will have joy and bliss in Heaven. There are three principal texts of these Pains: a text in Oxford, Jesus College MS 29 of the mid-thirteenth century, the mid-fourteenth-century Douce MS 302, and the late-fourteenth-century Vernon MS. The text of the Jesus College MS opens with alternating verses of Anglo-Norman and early Middle English, which would suggest a French source for the tale. The other two texts are in Middle English and closely resemble one another and the Latin text of Redaction IV.

Although there are a great many similarities in the accounts of these three versions, there differences are enlightening. The Jesus College MS describes the various torments of hell in full and gruesome detail, and seems to linger on the descriptions with a morbid sense of satisfaction. The most significant difference for a study of the legends of St. Michael is that the Jesus College MS makes no mention of the archangel at all. St. Paul's guide to the geography of hell never appears and once the torments of hell are visited, the tale comes to an end. In contrast, the description of the torments of hell in the Douce and Vernon manuscripts is much shorter and somewhat sketchy. In fact, it seems as though the descriptions of the pains of hell are only of an introductory character. They are followed by the summoning of the righteous and wicked souls

---

[60] This version was edited by L. Kastner, "Les versions françaises inédites de la Descente de saint Paul en enfer," Romania (1905): 385–95, who suggests that the poem was composed in the early thirteenth century. Paul Meyer examined the sole surviving manuscript (Paris, BN, fr. 24,862) and concluded that it was written in England in the middle of the thirteenth century (Notices et extraits des manuscrits de la Bibliothèque Nationale 35:1 (1896): 131ff). D. M. Legge shows that there was an important member of the Order of Templars called Henri d'Arci between 1160 and 1180. She assumes him to be the poet of this version (Anglo-Norman in the Cloisters, 55).

[61] The Latin is printed in Paul Meyer's article "La Descente de Saint Paul en enfer: Poème français composé en Angleterre," Romania 24 (1895): 365–75. The brief Latin injunction concerning the observance of Sunday is as follows: "Ideo, qui custodierint ipsum diem sanctum havebunt partem cum angelis Dei" (375).

before the throne of God and the prayers of the evil souls for mercy. These scenes naturally culminate in the true object of the poem's interest, the intercession of Saints Paul and Michael on behalf of the wretched souls, which results in the brief weekly respite for the damned until Doomsday. The differences between the Jesus College version and the versions of both the Douce and Vernon manuscripts can be accounted for by the fundamental difference in their aims. The Jesus College version, on the one hand, with its full descriptions of the pains of hell, seems to be intent on emphasizing these torments as a means of encouraging the observance of God's laws. The versions in the Douce and Vernon manuscripts, on the other hand, emphasize the remission of these torments obtained by the intercession of St. Paul and St. Michael.

St. Michael's Struggle with Antichrist

The literature on the subject of an eschatological adversary at the End of Time is vast and complex.[62] Although the term "Antichrist" only occurs in the two letters of the Apostle St. John (I John 2:18, 22 and 4:3; and II John 7) where it is applied almost generically to all enemies of the church, the earliest manifestations of a supreme and final eschatological enemy are found in Jewish (and possibly Near Eastern) tradition.[63] Early Christian commentators relied on a complex store of texts from the Old and New Testaments for their development of the persona of Antichrist.[64] In several of the dream visions of the Book of Daniel (chapters 7–12), the prophet describes four hideous beasts who devour each other (chapter 7) and a beast whose horns sprout smaller horns which will defeat the armies of heaven (chapter 8). In the final vision (chapters 10–12), an angel gives Daniel a detailed prophecy of future history which will only end with the death of the final king. According to this final vision, the adversary will be deceitful and destructive (11:21–22); he will defile the Temple (11:30–31); he will challenge God as His rival and equal (11:36); he will reign with impunity for three and a half years (this if the figure medieval commentators agree on, but see Daniel 7:25, 8:14, 9:27, 12:7, 11, 12); and establish his royal seat between the sea and mountain (11:45). It is here at his royal establishment that St. Michael will defeat the adversary, ushering in the Final Judgment. It is significant that St. Michael appears in this final vision as a powerful hero of supreme military prowess who will bring about the vindication of the Jews. St. Michael's role in the final defeat of Antichrist in all later

---

[62] A sense of the immense store of material on the subject can be gleaned from the following list of works: Wilhelm Bousset, *Der Antichrist in der Überlieferung des Judentums, des NT und der alten Kirche* (Göttingen, 1895), trans. A. H. Keane as *The Antichrist Legend: A Chapter in Christian and Jewish Folklore* (London, 1896); Norman Cohn, *The Pursuit of the Millennium* (Fairlawn, NJ, 1957); Josef Ernst, *Die eschatologischen Gegenspieler in den Schriften des Neuen Testaments* (Regensburg, 1967); Richard K. Emmerson, *Antichrist in the Middle Ages: A Study of Medieval Apocalypticism, Art and Literature* (Manchester, 1981); and most recently, Bernard McGinn, *Antichrist: Two Thousand Years of Human Fascination with Evil* (San Francisco, 1994). For an overview of English apocalypticism, see *The Apocalypse in English Renaissance Thought and Literature*, eds. C. A. Patrides and Joseph Wittreich (Ithaca, NY, 1984).

[63] Bousset stressed the Near Eastern mythological background of a battle between a primordial dragon and a god of creation (*Antichrist Legend*, especially chapter 1).

[64] For a survey of Antichrist in patristic thought, Bernard McGinn, *Visions of the End* (New York, 1979): 16–17, 22–24.

legends finds its ultimate scriptural warrant in this final vision of the Book of Daniel. In the Gospels, Jesus warns the disciples of false announcements of the end of the world and describes the true End, with reference to the prophecies of Daniel (see Mark 13:3–37, Matthew 24:4–36, and Luke 21:8–36). Jesus speaks of false Christs and false prophets who would appear as deceivers prior to the final age. St. Paul, in II Thessalonians (2:1–12), writes of the "man of Lawlessness" who will proclaim himself to be God, deceive those who are to perish, and finally be destroyed at the second coming. Finally, in Revelation 11, it is revealed that two witnesses will expose God's adversary and by slain by him, only to be resuscitated and taken to heaven. St. Michael's role in slaying the dragon of Revelation 12:7–9 underscores his authority as a martial hero whose success in battle straddles human history.[65]

Interestingly, early Christian commentators on this body of material concerning the character and identity of Antichrist added very little to the essential outline of the legend as it is found in Daniel 10–12, Revelation 11–12, and II Thessalonians. The principal expansion of the legend is the universal identification of the unnamed adversaries of the Lord in these texts with the "Antichrist" of Johannine epistles. Later additions include the naming the location of Antichrist's royal seat as Mount Olivet, and the identification of the Two Witnesses of Revelation 11 as the prophets Enoch and Elijah. Perhaps one of the most problematic additions to the legend for later commentators involves the agency of St. Michael's slaying of Antichrist. In and of itself, the defeat of the dragon in Revelation 12:9 by the archangel posed no theological dilemma for these commentators. The identification of the dragon with Antichrist, however, suggested the possibility that the archangel's efficacy was greater than that of Christ.[66] After all, the eschatological parallels between St. Michael's struggle with Satan at the beginning of time and a battle against Antichrist at the end of time are compelling. To avoid such a troubling transgression, many commentators on and purveyors of the Antichrist legend indicate that while St. Michael will indeed slay Antichrist, he will do so only through the agency of Christ.

Indeed, in his "De ratione temporum," the Venerable Bede is reluctant to commit either way, suggesting Antichrist will die either through the Lord or St. Michael.[67] After Bede, perhaps the most influential commentator on the legend was Adso of Montier-en-Der (ob. 992), whose *Libellus de antichristo* was written in the form of a letter to Queen Gerberga of France.[68] This text was to have the greatest impact on later medieval versions of the Antichrist legend.

In Anglo-Saxon England, there were several references to the legend. The

---

[65] On the significance of St. Michael's trans-temporal role in slaying the dragon, see Chapter One, 20–22.

[66] Bousset considered the notion that St. Michael would slay Antichrist to be a survival of an early Jewish tradition (*The Antichrist Legend*, 227–31).

[67] Bede, PL 90, col. 574: "Percusso autem illo perditionis filio sive ab ipso Domino sive Michaele archangelo." See also Haymo of Auxerre's *Expositio II Thess.*, PL 117, cols. 779–81.

[68] Adso's text appears in several places. In Latin, PL 101: 1291–97, and Ernst Sackur, *Sibyllinische Texte und Forschungen* (Halle, 1898). It has been translated by Bernard McGinn, *Apocalyptic Spirituality* (Paulist Press, 1979). On Adso and his *Libellus*, see D. Verhelst, "La préhistoire des conceptions d'Adson concernant l'Antichrist," *Recherches de théologie ancienne et médiévale* 40 (1973): 52–103; and Rangheri, Maurizio, "La *Epistola ad Gerbergam reginam de ortu et tempore Antichristi* di Adsone di Montier-en-Der e le sue fonti," *Studi Medievali* 14 (1973): 677–732.

anonymous Blickling homily 7 for Easter Sunday briefly recounts the events surrounding the crucifixion, the harrowing of hell, and Christ's ascension into Heaven.[69] As Max Förster first pointed out, the descriptions of the harrowing of hell and the release of Adam and Eve are taken from Pseudo-Augustine, Sermo 160.[70] Förster also noted the affinity between the passage in the Blickling homily in which Adam beseeches the Lord to unloose the fetters binding his soul and a similar passage in an account of the harrowing of hell found in the *Book of Cerne*.[71] The Blickling homily closes with an account of the six days before Doom. As one might expect, it is here that St. Michael plays a central role. On the sixth day, St. Michael will slay Antichrist and all his accursed followers for their disobedience and wickedness.[72] Operating in a heterodox tradition, the Blickling homilist had no compunction in assigning the full agency of the deed to St. Michael. On the seventh day, the day of Doom, St. Michael will blow the four trumpets to rouse the dead for Judgment.[73]

Operating in an equally heterodox environment, the anonymous homilist of the Corpus 41 homily, "In Praise of St. Michael," depicts the archangel slaying Antichrist and identifies him with Lucifer, the "ancient enemy that is the great serpent who at the creation of the earth was created brightest of the angels."[74] In an anonymous translation of Adso's *Libellus de Antichristo* once ascribed to Wulfstan,[75] however, the attribu-

[69] Morris, *The Blickling Homilies*, 82–96. The manuscript appears in photographic facsimile as volume 10 of the EEMF series (fols. 50r–58v20). For a discussion of the eschatology of this homily and others in the Blickling collection, see Milton McC. Gatch, "Eschatology in the Anonymous Old English Homilies," *Traditio* 21 (1965): 117–65.

[70] Max Förster, "Altenglische Predigtquellen, I," *Archiv* 116 (1906): 301–307. The Pseudo-Augustine sermon, 160, is printed in *PL* 39: 2059–61.

[71] Förster, "Altenglische Predigtquellen." The Blickling passage begins on page 87 of Morris's edition. The passage in question occurs on pages 197 and 198 of Kuypers' edition of the *Book of Cerne*.

[72] Morris, *Blickling Homlies*, 95: Swa þonne þy dæge cymeþ Sanctus Michahel mid heofonlicum þreate haligra gasta and þa þonne ofsleaþ ealle þa awergdan and on helle grund bedrifaþ for heora unhyrsumnesse Godes beboda and for heora mandædum. (Then on that day Saint Michael will come with a heavenly troop of holy spirits and then they will slay all the accursed and drive them into the abyss of hell for their disobedience of God's commands and for their wickedness.)

[73] In Blickling homily 14, however, it is said that as St. John had been Christ's crier in the world (i.e., the trumpet announcing his arrival), so too would he be the trumpet announcing Judgment once Christ had risen as Judge (Morris, 163).

[74] Grant, *Three Homilies*, 64–65: Þis is se halga heahengel Sanctus Micheal se ðe ær ðisse worulde ende ofslihð þone ealdan feond þæt is se micla draca se ðe æt frymðe midan gardes gesceapen þæs to ðam beorhtestan engle; ac he self hit forworhte mid ði he cwæð, "Ic hebbe min heahsetl to norðæle, and ic beo gelic þam heahstan cyninge." And þa gefeol he, and gehreas mid his werode on niwulnesse grund, efene se illca Antacrist se ær ðisse worlde ende cymeð on ðisne middan geard to ðam þæt he sceal gesamnian ða ðe his sindon. Þanne cymeð Sanctus Michael and hin ofslihð, forðon ðe hit æfre geðohte þæt he scolde gelic beon ðan heahstan cyninge. (This is the holy archangel St. Michael who before the end of the world will slay the ancient enemy that is the great serpent who at the creation of the earth was created brightest of the angels; but he himself forfeited this when he said, "I will lift up my throne to the north, and I shall be like unto the highest king." And then he fell, and he landed with his troop in the depth of the abyss, the very same Antichrist who before the end of the world will come to the earth in order to assemble those who are his. Then St. Michael will come and slay him, because he has ever thought that he ought to be equal to the highest king.)

[75] Arthur Napier prints it as part of a homily entitled, "De temporibus antichristo" (*Wulfstan*, 201): "swa hweðer swa he bið ofslagen þurh miht ures drihtnes agenes bebodes oððe Michael godes heahengel hine ofslea, þurh ðæs lifigendan godes miht he bið ofslagen and nâ þurh nanes engles mihte." In her edition of the homilies of Wulfstan, however, Dorothy Bethurum prints a homily by

tion is blurred: "Whether he is slain through the might of or the archangel Michael kills him, through the might of the life-giving Lord he will be slain, not through the might of any angel."

In the Anglo-Norman period, texts describing St. Michael's roles at the end of time are confined to translations of the Book of Revelation. This group of texts falls into two categories: those translations in prose and those in verse. The prose versions mostly derive from the thirteenth century.[76] Two slightly later versions exist in the library of Trinity College, Cambridge and in the Bodleian Library, Oxford.[77] Of the second category, there are three rhymed versions of the Apocalypse known. Both derive independently from the same French prose redaction. One version is extant in seven manuscripts and was edited by Paul Meyer in 1896.[78] Meyer dates the composition of the Apocalypse to the second half of the thirteenth century. The second version survives in a single fourteenth century copy of an earlier thirteenth century manuscript.[79] The third version is also found in an early fourteenth-century manuscript and thought by its editor to have been composed in the early thirteenth century.[80]

In his *Festial*, John Mirk follows the *Legenda Aurea* in ascribing additional roles to St. Michael at Judgment. Not only will the archangel slay Antichrist on Mount Olivet and raise the dead for Judgment, but he will also collect and present the instruments of Christ's Passion (the Cross, the nails, the spear, the crown of thorns) at the seat of Judgment.[81] Through their righteousness, these instruments sanction the damning to eternal punishment those who deny Christ's Passion. In the St. Michael homily in the *Speculum Sacerdotale*, which is also based on the *Legenda Aurea*, the archangel performs the same functions as in Mirk's *Festial*. The *Speculum* author, however, adds the comment that St. Michael is the defender of his "chosen children" and "therefore we are more bound to worship him."[82] Similarly, in the Middle English metrical version of the *Revelations of Methodius*,[83] preserved in a single manuscript of the fifteenth

---

this name but the passage in question is not found there (*The Homilies of Wulfstan* [Oxford, 1957]). Bethurum suggests that the text is in fact a translation of Adso's *Libellus*, which may or may not have been commissioned by Wulfstan (42).

[76] These have been discussed by L. Delisle and P. Meyer, *L'Apocalypse en français au XIIIe siècle* (Paris, 1901).

[77] These have been published by M. R. James, *The Trinity College Apocalypse* (London, 1909) and A. G. and W. O. Hassall, *The Douce Apocalypse* (London, 1961), respectively.

[78] *Romania* 25 (1896): 174–257.

[79] This text has been edited by Olwyn Rhys and Sir John Fox, *An Anglo-Norman Rhymed Apocalypse with Commentary* (Oxford, 1946).

[80] H. A. Todd, "The Old French Versified Apocalypse of the Kerr Manuscript," *PMLA* 18 (1903): 535–77.

[81] Erbe, *Mirk's Festial*, 258: He schal sle þe Antecryst yn þe mownt of Olyuete. He schal byd all þe ded ryse yn þe day of dome. He schall bring to þe dome þe crosse of Cryst, þe nayles, þe spere, þe crowne of þornes, and all oþer ynstrumentys of his passyon, forto schow how ryghtwysly þay schull be dampnet þat day þo þat settyth noght by Crystys passyon.

[82] Weatherly, *Speculum Sacerdotale*, 213: And he schall att the commanundement of God sle Antecrist beynge in the Mounte of Olyuete. And at the voyce of this Archangel Miȝhel dede men schall vprise. And he shall schewe and present in the day of dome the crosse, nayles, spere, and crowne of þorne. And for the chosyn children of god he schal stoned as here defensour. And þerfore we beþ the more bounden for to worschipe hym.

[83] The *Revelations* are attributed to the third-century martyr bishop Methodius, but they were actually written in Syriac by a pro-Byzantine monk sometime in the late seventh century. On the history of

century (London, British Library, Stowe MS 953), Antichrist is slain through the archangel's agency alone.[84]

In perhaps the fullest poetic rendition of the legend, the *Cursor Mundi* first depicts the return of Enoch and Elijah and their slaying at the hands of Antichrist. After a grim description of the last days, the poet proclaims that if St. Michael is to slay Antichrist then it will only be through the bidding of Christ and not through his own "vertu".[85] The text quickly moves into a detailed list of the "XV signis before þe dome." The most forceful representation of this legend, however, is the fifteenth-century Chester Cycle play entitled *Coming of Antichrist*,[86] itself based on a twelfth-century Latin original from the Kloster Tegernsee in Bavaria.[87] Although St. Michael is not mentioned in the Latin original, nor for that matter in any of the other English dramatic cycles which feature plays on the coming of Antichrist, the archangel commands a powerful presence in the Chester Cycle play. In the play, Antichrist appears and misrepresents himself as the Savior. Enoch and Elijah return to earth to confront the false savior, who in a long and occasionally tedious monologue pleads earnestly with the Two Witnesses. Antichrist finally becomes frustrated with the prophets, who continue to deny him, and slays them. The archangel appears at the same moment and proclaims an end to the reign of Antichrist: "Antichrist, now has come the day that you shall no longer rule."[88] At the end of his speech, a stage direction indicates the St. Michael kills Antichrist: "Tunc mychaell occidet antechristum et in occidendo dicat antechristus Help Help."[89] In vain, Antichrist calls on his former associates, innumerable devils, Satan, and Lucifer. After he dies, two forlorn devils come to mourn his death and eventually drag his soul to hell. As Antichrist is removed from the scene, Enoch and Elijah arise from the dead, and St. Michael invites them to join him in heaven's bliss. The archangel escorts the prophets to heaven and the play comes to a close.[90]

this text, see P. J. Alexander, "Byzantium and the Migration of Literary Works and Motifs: The Legend of the Last Roman Emperor," *Mediaevalia et Humanistica* n.s. 2 (1971): 47–68.

[84] Charlotte D'Evelyn, "The Middle English Metrical Version of the *Revelations of Methodius*," *PMLA* 33 (1918) 181: And as seynt Gregory dothe expres./ þe prynce of aungeelys seynt mychaell./ is antecryst to dethe xall dresse./ and sle þat felon false and fell./ and xall hym put in sory presse./ in-to þe deppest pyt in hell./ in endless peyn depe depresse./ þer with damnyd euer to dwell.

[85] Morris, *Cursor Mundi*, lines 22399–408: sant michel sal him quell/ In papilon, that mikel fell/ In þat stede in his aun stal;/ þat þis be soth ful wel mai fall/ For if sant michel cum to place,/ To dome before vr lauerd grace,/ Him sla it sal noght his vertu/ bot elles wit bidding o iesu.

[86] W. W. Greg, ed., *The Play of Antichrist from the Chester Cycle* (Oxford, 1935) and *The Chester Plays*, EETS ES 115 (Oxford, 1959): 412–20.

[87] The Latin text is found in Karl Young, *The Drama of the Medieval Church* (Oxford, 1961): 371–87. An excellent introduction and translation have been produced by John Wright, *The Play of Antichrist* (Toronto, 1967).

[88] Greg, *The Play of Antichrist*, 58: Antechrist nowe ys comyn they day/ reigne no longer thowe ne maye.

[89] *Ibid.*

[90] *Ibid.*: Ennoke and helye com ye anon/ my lorde wyll that ye with me gon/ to heuens blysse botthe blude and bon/ euer mo there to be/ Ye haue ben long for ye ben wyse/ dwelling in erthlye paradyce/ but heuen there hym selffe ys/ now shall ye goe with me./ Tunc ibit angelus adducens ennok et helyam ad celum cantans Gaudete iusti in domino.

Summary

Speculation about the end of the world is a common human activity, and medieval English literature abounds with the fruits of such labors. St. Michael's legendary roles at the end of Time are manifold. Not only will he announce the end with a blast from his trumpet, but he will also slay Antichrist and supervise the weighing of all souls at the Final Judgment. Although not all medieval writers were in agreement over the archangel's role in the death of Antichrist, his stature as a hero whose efficacy transcends human history was universally accepted. In addition to his role as weigher of souls, St. Michael also commanded a measure of respect as a powerful intercessor on behalf of the faithful at judgment. These vivid and often lurid descriptions of doom preserve a vital image of St. Michael as an active agent in the events at Doomsday, one whose power in those events, at least in the popular imagination, may even have exceeded that of Christ.

Conclusion

and th' Arch-Angel soon drew nigh,
Not in his shape Celestial, but as Man
Clad to meet Man; over his lucid Arms
A military Vest of purple flow'd
Livelier than *Melibaean*, or the grain
Of *Sarra*, worn by Kings and Heroes of old
In time of Truce; *Iris* had dipt the woof;
His starry Helm unbuckl'd show'd him prime
In Manhood where Youth ended; by his side
As in a glistening *Zodiac* hung the Sword,
Satan's dire dread, and in his hand the Spear.

John Milton, *Paradise Lost*, Book XI, lines 238–48

The legends of St. Michael the archangel were widespread in medieval England. Indeed, it was upon the well-established stock of legends of the archangel as warrior-angel and psychopomp that the poet John Milton relied to create his heroic figure of St. Michael in *Paradise Lost*.

These legends derive their literary impetus from a matrix of references to the archangel in scriptural and apocryphal literature. Part I of this book, "Genesis and Migration of the Legends," presents a historical survey of this body of literature. One of the principal angels venerated by the early Church, St. Michael the archangel appears five times in canonical scripture: three times in the Old Testament and twice in the New Testament. As Chapter One, "Literary Origins of the Archangel's Legendary Roles," makes clear, there was no Michaeline *cultus* to speak of in the biblical era, only a measure of popular appeal, and this appeal was defined largely by the archangel's roles in biblical and extra-biblical literature. St. Michael's popularity was directly related to his literary stature as a heroic martial warrior figure. In the literature of the Old Testament, the archangel is designated "the great prince" of the Hebrews (Daniel 12:1) and a powerful intercessor in their behalf. In the literature of the New Testament, St. Michael becomes a mythic hero whose battle with Lucifer takes on a new eschatological significance. In the Letter of Jude, St. Jude alludes to the apocryphon known as the "Assumption of Moses," in which St. Michael disputes with Satan over the body of Moses. St. Michael also appears in Revelation 12:7–9, where he and his angels fight with the devil in the time-collapsing conflict at the beginning and end of time.

Based largely on these passages from Scripture, Christian tradition assigned St. Michael four offices: to fight against Satan; to protect the souls of the faithful from Satan and his minions, especially at the hour of death; to defend God's chosen people, namely the Jews in the Old Testament and the Christians in the New Testament; and to call away souls from earth and bring them to judgment.

Despite the heroic stature the archangel achieves in this body of literature, the evidence of his intercessory power remains locked in the scriptural and apocryphal tales of his interventions, and is not supported by any physical manifestations of the intercessions, a crucial step in the development of a popular *cultus*. As the occasions of the archangel's earthly visitations increased in the early Christian era, however, a stock of legendary tales began to form. As Chapter Two, "The Archangel's Legendary History," indicates, these legends not only gave rise to an increase in St. Michael's popularity as a heroic figure who interceded on behalf of God's faithful, but they also provided him with a body of physical evidence of his intercessions. Although slight in volume, this evidence (e.g., an altar-cloth and a set of footprints on Monte Gargano, and a miniature sword and shield at Mont-Saint-Michel) guaranteed the establishment and viability of permanent cultic sites by attracting a steady flow of pilgrims.

St. Michael's cult began in the Near East, where he was usually invoked to protect and care for the sick. There were medicinal springs dedicated to St. Michael at Chairotopa near Colossae in Phrygia, at Colossae itself (present-day Khonas, Turkey), and elsewhere across Asia Minor. Without a doubt his most famous shrine in the east was the Michaelion at Sosthenion near Constantinople (present-day Istanbul, Turkey). The archangel is said to have appeared to the Emperor Constantine there and caused a curative spring to spout from a rock.

From its origins in the East, the cult of St. Michael spread through the Roman empire in the third and fourth centuries CE In the Roman calendar, there were originally two feasts for St. Michael: May 8 and September 29. The date May 8 holds special significance for it is allegedly the day marking both the legendary apparition of the archangel on Monte Gargano and his military intervention on behalf of the Sipontans in their victory over their pagan neighbors. In honor of their victory and the archangel, the citizens instituted a special feast which spread over the entire Latin church, but was later abandoned in favor of the feast of September 29. Traditionally, this date commemorated the dedication of a church to the archangel on the Salarian Way, six miles north of Rome. Over time, the various local feasts of St. Michael came to be celebrated on this date.

Perhaps the archangel's most famous sanctuary in the West is Mont-Saint-Michel in Normandy. Tradition has it that St. Michael appeared three times in dreams to St. Aubert, bishop of Avranches, in the year 708, commanding him to build a sanctuary in the archangel's honor on Mont Tombe, a rocky promontory jutting into the sea off the coast of Normandy. From Gaul, the cult of St. Michael spread to Ireland, Scotland, and Wales, where it flourished and eventually spread to England.

Through a close reading of the hagiographical foundation-myths of the three principal Michaeline cultic centers, Chapter Two demonstrates that after a series of apparitions and earthly interventions each of the three great regional powers appropriated St. Michael, commander of the heavenly host in battle, as the patron saint of its imperial ambition. Chapter Two also demonstrates that the hagiographical accounts of St. Michael's legendary apparitions at the three cultic centers had a significant impact on the characterization of the archangel in the medieval English legends examined in Part II.

Many of the legendary texts of Part II, "The Archangel in Medieval English Legend," derive their representations of St. Michael in large measure from the stock of motifs found in the canonical and extra-canonical literature of the Old and New Testament eras. The texts of all three language groups covered in this book, Old English, Anglo-Norman, and Middle English, suggest a level of popular veneration of St. Michael in the principal roles assigned him by Christian tradition: he is a militant protector of the faithful, a benevolent guide of the souls of the dead to heaven, and a fair but stern weigher of souls at judgment. In Chapter Three, "Vernacular Versions of the Hagiographic Foundation-Myth," I examine vernacular texts that adopt the motifs found in the hagiographic foundation myth of Monte Gargano (*BHL* 5948). The sheer number of the vernacular recensions of the myth suggests an abiding interest in the efficacy of the archangel's intervention. Chapter Four, "The Archangel as Guardian and Psychopomp," suggests that the medieval English embraced the archangel in these roles. St. Michael's traditional association with the soul of the Virgin Mary firmly established him in the popular imagination as the psychopomp of preference. As the texts in Chapter Five, "The Archangel and Judgment," indicate, one of St. Michael's most compelling roles, however, is that at Judgment. This chapter explores the English legends of St. Michael's involvement in the individual, post-mortem judgment and the Final Judgment. As the chapters in Part II demonstrate, St. Michael is widely represented in the prose literature of the Anglo-Saxon, Anglo-Norman, and Middle English eras. In these texts, the Archangel is represented performing all four of the offices assigned him by Christian tradition.

The hagiography or legendary history of no other saint offers an analogue for the *vitae* of St. Michael since he cannot participate in the "terrestrial reality" of other saints. And yet the Archangel possesses a rich metaphysical existence, an incorporeal individuality, that invigorates the legendary and apocryphal literature in which he appears. His is a dual character: the ruthless commander of the celestial troops who smites the enemies of the Lord, and the merciful angel who intercedes on our behalf. Given his office, it is little wonder that devotion to St. Michael was widespread in the British Isles, and that by the end of the Middle Ages church dedications to the Archangel were exceeded only by those to the Virgin Mary. In their representations of St. Michael, the legends of the archangel in medieval England have preserved for us an enduring and compelling image of medieval Christianity.

Appendices

Appendix A
De Apparitione Sancti Michaelis (*BHL* 5948)

(Reprinted with permission from MGH SRL,
ed. G. Waitz [Hanover, 1878]: 541–3.)

1. Memoriam beati Michaelis archangeli toto orbe venerandam ipsius et opere condita et consecrata nomine demonstrat ecclesia. Quae non metallorum fulgure, sed privilegio commendata signorum, vili facta scaemate, sed caelesti predita virtute, utpute quam fragilitatis humanae memor archangelus dę celo veniens, ad promerendam ibi mortalibus supernorum sociaetatem, propria manu condere dignatus est. Vertice siquidem montis excelsi posita, de corpore eiusdem saxi speluncae instar precavata ostenditur. Est autem locus in Campaniae finibus, ubi inter sinum Adriaticum et montem Garganum civitas Sepontus posita est, qui a moenibus civitatis ad 12 milia passuum preerectus, in cacumine supremo beati archangeli, quam prefatus sum, gestat ecclesiam. Hanc mortalibus hoc modo cognitam libellus in eadem ecclesia positus indicat.

2. Erat in eadem civitate predives quidam nomine Garganus, qui et ex eventu suo monti vocabulum indidit. Huius dum peccora, quorum infinita multitudine pollebat, passim per divexi montis latera pascerentur, contigit, taurum, armenti congregis consortia spernentem, singularem incedere solitum et extremum, redeunte peccore, domum non esse regressum. Quem dominus, collecta multitudine servorum, per devia quaeque requirens, invenit tandem in vertice montis foribus cuiusdam adsistere speluncae, iraque permotus, cur solivagus incederet, arrepto arcu appetit illum sagitta toxicata. Quae velud venti flamine retorta, eum a quo iecta est mox reversa percussit. Turbati cives et stupefacti, qualiter res fieret effecta – non enim accedere propius audebant –, consulunt episcopum, quid facto opus esset. Qui, indicto ieiunio triduano, a Deo monuit esse quaerendum. Quo peracto, sanctus Domini archangelus episcopum per visionem alloquitur, dicens: "Iam bene fecistis, quod homines latebat a Deo quaerendum; mysterium videlicet hominem suo telo percussit, ut sciatis, hoc mea gestum voluntate. Ego enim sum Michael archangelus, qui in conspectu Domini semper adsisto. Locumque hunc in terra incolasque servare instituens, hoc volui probare inditio omnium quae ibi geruntur ipsiusque loci esse inspectorem atque custodem." Hac revelatione conperta, consuetudinem fecerunt cives hic Dominum sanctumque deposcere Michaelem. Duas quidem ibi ianuas cernentes, quarum australis, quae et maior erat, aliquot gradibus in occasum vergentibus adiri poterat, sed ne ultra cruptam intrare ausi sunt, prae foribus orationi vacabant.

On the Apparition of Saint Michael

1. The feast day of the blessed archangel Michael, which ought to be celebrated throughout the world, marks the commemoration of the church that he founded by his own work and consecrated in his name. Its distinction lies not in the gleam of precious metals but in the privilege bestowed by miracles; though humble in form, it is imbued with heavenly power, inasmuch as the archangel, mindful of the frailty of humankind, came down from heaven and deigned to establish the church with his own hands, there to obtain for mortal men the fellowship of those on high. Indeed, it is situated at the summit of a high mountain, from whose rocky mass the church is revealed to have been hollowed out in the likeness of a cave. On the borders of Campania, where the city of Siponto is situated between an arm of the Adriatic sea and Mount Gargano, twelve miles from the city walls, and on the very summit of the mountain, is the place where the church of the blessed archangel, mentioned earlier, is located. A little book placed in that very church relates that it was revealed to mortal men in the following way.

2. There was in that city a very rich man whose name was Garganus, whose name was given to the mountain as a result of what happened to him there. It happened that while his cattle, whose infinite numbers made him so prosperous, were spread out over all the mountain grazing, a singular bull, despising the company of the herd of cattle, wandered away alone, and at the end of the day, when the cows returned home, he did not come back. The master, who gathered a multitude of slaves, and searching every unfrequented place, at last found the bull standing in front of a cave on the summit of the mountain. Thoroughly enraged that the bull should wander away alone, seizing a bow he shot at the bull with a poisoned arrow. The arrow, as if twisted around by a blast of wind, came straight back and struck him who had just loosed it. Troubled and stupefied as to how such a thing could have been done, the local people – for none dared approach the place – consulted the bishop about what should be done. The bishop, ordering a three-day fast, advised they must seek the answer from God. When this was done, the holy archangel of the Lord spoke to the bishop in a vision, saying: "You have done well in seeking from God the mystery that was concealed from men; that is to say, a man struck by his own weapon. For you should know that this was done by my own will. For I am Michael the archangel, who always stands in contemplation of the Lord. And deciding to guard this place and its inhabitants in this country, I wished to demonstrate by this sign that I am watching over and guarding the place and everything that happens there." When that revelation was told and made known to the citizens they established the custom of praying there to God and St. Michael. They saw that there were two doors in that place, and that the south door, the larger of the two,

3. Haec inter et Neapolitae, paganis adhuc ritibus oberrantes, Sepontinos et Beneventanos, qui 250 milibus a Seponto distant, bello lacessere temptant. Qui antistitis sui monitis edocti, triduo petunt indutias, ut triduano ieiunio liceret eis quasi fideli patrocinio sancti Michaelis implorare presidium. Quo tempore pagani ludis scenicis falsorum invitant auxilia deorum. Ecce autem nocte ipsa quae belli precederet diem adest in visione sanctus Michael antistiti, preces dixit exauditas, spopondit se affuturum, et quarta diei hora bello premonet hostibus occurrendum. Laeti ergo mane et de angelica certi victoria, Neapolitani demoniaco redacti spiritu, obviant christiani paganis, atque in primo belli apparatu Garganus inmenso tremore concutitur; fulgura crebra volant, et caligo tenebrosa totum montis cacumen obduxit, impleta prophetia, quae Dominum laudans dicit: "Qui facit angelos suos spiritus et ministros suos flammam ignis." Fugiunt pagani, partim ferro hostium, partim igniferis inpulsi sagittis, et Neapolim usque sequentibus atque extrema quaeque cedentibus adversariis, moenia tandem suae urbis moribundi subintrant. Qui autem evaserant periculum, comperto, quod angelus Dei in adiutorium venerat christianis – nam et sexcentos ferme suorum fulmine videbant interemptos –, regi regum Christo continuo colla submittentes, armis induuntur fidei. Cumque domum reversi victores vota Domino gratiarum ad templum referebant archangeli, videntes mane iuxta ianuam septemtrionalem, quam predixi, instar posteruli pusilla quasi hominis vestigia marmori artius inpressa, agnoscuntque, beatum Michaelem hoc presentiae suae signum voluisse monstrare. Ubi postea culmen adpositum et altare inpositum, ipsa ecclesia ob signa vestigiorum Apodonia est vocata.

4. Multa interea dubitatio inter Sepontinos erat, quid de loco agerent, et ubi intrari vel dedicari illa debeat ecclesia. Unde conlatione facta, ad orientem loci illius beati Petri apostolorum principis nomine condunt ecclesiam et dedicant. In qua etiam beatae semper virginis Mariae sanctique baptistae Iohannis altaria statuunt. Tandem antistes, salubri reperto consilio, Romanum episcopum, quid de his agendum sit, per nuntios sciscitabatur. Qui tunc forte in monte fere 50 miliario a Romana urbe distante degebat, quem incolae sancti Silvestri cognomine vocant, eo quod et ipse ibi quondam exulaverat et pro fidei persecutione delituerat in Zirapti monte, taliaque mandata remittit: "Si hominis est illam dedicare basylicam, hoc maxime die quo victoria data est fieri oportet; sin autem alias provisori placuerit, eodem precipue die illius in hoc voluntas est quaerenda. Hoc ergo et tempore inminente agamus ambo triduanum cum civibus nostris ieiunium, sanctam Trinitatem rogantes, ut munera, quae per summum suae sedis ministrum conferre dignatus est, ad certum usque finem perducat." Factumque est ut suggesserat antistes. Nocte vero instituti ieiunii supprema angelus Domini Michael episcopo Sepontino per visionem apparens: "Non est vobis," inquit, "opus hanc quam ego edificavi dedicare basylicam. Ipse enim qui condidi etiam dedicavi. Vos tantum intrate et me adstante patrono precibus locum frequentate. Et te quidem cras ibi missas caelebrante, populus iuxta morem

could be approached by some steeply descending steps, but they did not dare go inside any further than the crypt, and so they would devote themselves to prayer outside the doors.

3. Meanwhile the Neapolitans, who, misguided, still practiced the pagan rituals, challenged the Sipontans and Beneventans, who were at 250 miles distance from Siponto, to battle. They, instructed by the admonitions of the bishop, asked for a three-day truce so that, by means of a three-day fast, they might entreat the faithful guardian St. Michael for protection. During this time the pagans summoned the aid of their false gods by devilish illusions. On the night before the day on which the battle was to take place, St. Michael appeared to the bishop in a vision, said that he had heard their prayers, promised his aid, and forewarned them to meet the enemy in battle at the fourth hour of the day. Therefore in the morning, happy and confident that the angel would bring victory, with the Neapolitans reduced by means of a demonic spirit, the Christians encountered the pagans, and as the battle was joined, Mount Gargano was struck by an immense earth tremor; lightning bolts flew, and a dark mist covered the summit of the mountain, in fulfillment of the prophecy which says, praising God, "He who makes his angels spirits, and his ministers a burning fire." [Psalm 103:4] The pagans fled, driven partly by the weapons of their enemies, partly by flaming arrows, and, with their adversaries pursuing them all the way to Naples and slaughtering the stragglers, finally at their last gasp they stole inside the walls of their city. Those who had escaped these perils ascertained that the angel of God had come to the aid of the Christians – for they saw nearly 600 of their own killed by lightning – submitting their necks immediately to the King of Kings, Christ, put on the armor of faith. When the victors returned home, at the shrine of the archangel they gave offerings of thanks to God. They saw in the morning next to the north door, which we mentioned before, the footprints of a man, as it seemed, firmly impressed in the marble; and then they understood that blessed Michael wished to show in this the sign of his presence. When later the roof and the altar had been properly set the church was called Apodonia on account of the signs of the footprints.

4. Meanwhile there was much doubt among the Sipontans, what they should do about the place, whether they should enter or dedicate the church. Making a decision through discussion, they built a church to the east of that place and dedicated it in the name of Saint Peter first among the apostles. And also in that church they placed altars to the Blessed Mary ever-virgin and Saint John the Baptist. At last, the bishop, devising a salutary plan, sent messengers to ask the Bishop of Rome what ought to be done. He happened by chance to be in residence at a mountain nearly 50 miles from the city of Rome, which local inhabitants call by the name of St. Silvester, who himself at one time lived in exile [there] and, persecuted for his faith, hid away on mount Zirapti, and [he] sent back this command: "If it is for men to dedicate the church, then it is most proper it should be done on that day on which victory was given them; but if something else should please the guardian, you should ask his will in this matter on that same day. When therefore that time approaches let both of us with our citizens perform a three-day fast, entreating the Holy Trinity to lead [us] to the proper decision concerning the gifts which He has deigned to bestow through the highest minister of His throne." And it came to pass as the bishop advised. On the night they completed their fast Michael angel of the Lord appeared in a vision to the bishop of Siponto: "It is not," he said, "your work to dedicate the church which I built. For I, who built it, also

communicet; meum autem erit ostendere, quomodo per memet ipsum locum consecraverim illum."

5. At veniunt mane cum oblationibus et magna instantia precum, intrant regiam australem, et ecce longa porticus in aquilonem porrecta atque illam attingens ianuam, extra quam vestigia marmori diximus inpressa; sed priusquam huc pervenias, apparet ad orientem basylica grandis, qua per gradus ascenditur. Haec cum ipso porticu suo quingentos fere homines capere videbatur, altare venerandum rubroque contectum palliolo prope medium parietis meridiani ostendens. Erat autem ipsa domus angulosa, non in morem operis humani parietibus erectis, sed instar speluncae preruptis et sepius eminentibus asperata scopulis, culmine quoque petroso diversae altitudinis, quod hic vertice tangi, alibi manu vix posset adtingi; credo docente archangelo Domini, non ornatus lapidum, sed cordis quaerere et diligere puritatem. Vertex vero montis extrinsecus partim cornea silva tegitur, partim virenti planitiae dilatatur.

6. Missarum itaque caelebratione conpleta, magno attoniti gaudio quique redierunt in sua. Episcopus vero, delegato ministrorum, cantorum sacerdotumque offitio, et mansione constructa, omnem ibidem cotidie psalmorum missarumque cursum congruo precepit ordine celebrari. Nullus autem huic nocturno tempore est ausus ingredi, sed aurora transacta matutinos ibidem cantant ymnos. Ex ipso autem saxo, quo sacra contegitur aedis, ad aquilonem altaris dulcis et nimium lucida guttatim aqua delabitur, quam incolae stillam vocant. Ob hoc et vitreum vas eiusdem receptui preparatum argentea pendit catena suspensum, morisque est populo communicato singulos ad hoc vasculum ascendere per gradus donumque caelestis degustare liquoris. Nam et gustu suavis est et tactu salubris. Denique nonnulli post longas foebrium flammas hac austa stilla celeri confestim refrigerio potiuntur salutis. Innumeris quoque et aliis modis ibi et crebri sanantur aegroti, et multa quae angelicae tantum licet potestati geri miracula conprobantur. Maxima tamen eiusdem die natalis, cum et de provinciis circumpositis plus solito conflua turba recurrat et angelicae virtutis maior quodammodo credatur adesse frequentia, et quod spiritaliter dixit apostolus et corporaliter agi videtur: "Quia angeli sunt administratores spiritus et in ministerium missi propter eos qui hereditatem capiunt salutis." In Christo Ihesu domino nostro, amen.

dedicated it myself. But enter this place, where I am present, as protector, and fill it with prayers. And celebrate mass there tomorrow and let the people take communion in the usual way; it is my prerogative, however, to show in what manner, by myself, I have consecrated that place."

5. They came in the morning with oblations and great earnestness in prayer, they entered the south portico, and behold, there is a long portico stretching north and leading to the door outside of which the footprints we talked about are impressed in the marble; but before you get there, to the east a great basilica appears, which one enters via a stairway. This church with its portico seemed to hold about 500 men; it contains a venerable altar covered with a red altar cloth near the middle of the south wall. That house has lots of corners, for its walls are not straight as is customary with human workmanship but they are rough hewn as in a cave with rugged and often protruding outcroppings of rock, and the rocky ceiling is of varying height, for here the top of your head touches it, but there you can hardly reach it with your fingertips; I believe that the archangel of the Lord would instruct us not to seek beauty in stones but in the heart, and to love purity. As for the exterior of the mountain top, it is partly covered with cornel forest, partly spread with verdant fields.

6. After mass and sacrament were completed, each returned to his own with great joy. To be sure the bishop assigned ministers, singers, and priests, and commanded to be built a dwelling in that place so that they might daily perform the complete sequence of psalms and masses in the proper order. No one dared enter there at night-time, however, but after daybreak in that place they would sing the morning hymns. From the rock which covers the sacred sanctuary, to the north of the altar runs sweet-tasting and exceedingly clear water, which the local inhabitants call "the drip." And on account of this, a glass vessel to receive the liquid is suspended by a silver chain, and it is the custom of the local people after partaking each one of communion to go up by steps to the vessel and taste the gift of heavenly fluid. In fact it is pleasant to taste and salutary to the touch. And thereafter many were restored health, after suffering for a long time the flames of fever were immediately refreshed through the drinking of this drop. Also many people are healed there of innumerable and various ailments, and many miracles are attested there, which could only have been performed through the angel's power. But most [miracles are attested] on his feast day, when a more numerous crowd than usual assembles from the surrounding districts and when it is believed there is somehow present a greater abundance of the angel's power, and that which the apostle said spiritually may be seen to be enacted bodily: "For angels are ministering spirits and sent to minister for them who will receive the inheritance of salvation." [Hebrews 1:14] In Jesus Christ our Lord, amen.

Appendix B
The Michael Inventory

For convenience of reference, I have divided the Inventory into two sections. Section I is a list of the titles of texts with references to St. Michael. Section II contains a fuller description of St. Michael's roles in the texts of the Old and New Testament eras. I have not included detailed descriptions of the Old English, Anglo-Norman, and Middle English texts in section II since many of these texts are discussed at length in the main text. The lists in sections IA, IB, ID, and IE are presented chronologically (according to scholarly consensus as to the dates of the texts). The texts in section IC are listed according to the system established by the *Dictionary of Old English* Project, Centre for Medieval Studies, University of Toronto (i.e., by Cameron number). Most of the texts listed are readily available in translation, and I have provided bibliographic references for many of the texts. The most common sources in translation are referred to according to the Abbreviations page, with the exception of the following works:

Schneemelcher   Wilhelm Schneemelcher, *New Testament Apocrypha*, 2 vols, trans. R. McL. Wilson (Louisville, KY, 1991): [cited by volume and page]

Sparks   H. F. D. Sparks, *The Apocryphal Old Testament* (Oxford, 1992)

Section I. List of Texts

A. Old Testament Texts

1 Enoch (Ethiopic)
Book of Daniel
Testaments of the Twelve Patriarchs: Testament of Naphtali
War Scroll (1QM)
Ascension of Isaiah
Sibylline Oracles
II Enoch (Slavonic)
III Baruch (Greek)
Apocalypse of Abraham
Apocalypse of Elijah
Testament of Abraham
Life of Adam and Eve (Latin)
Revelation/Apocalypse of Moses (Greek)
IV Baruch (Paraleipomena of Jeremiah)
Testament of Solomon
Testament of Isaac

Testament of Jacob
Apocalypse of Sedrach
Apocalypse of Ezra (Greek)
Vision of Esdras (Ezra)
III Enoch (Hebrew)

B. New Testament Texts

The Shepherd of Hermas
Book of Revelation
Epistle of Jude
Epistle of the Apostles
History of Joseph the Carpenter
Acts of Phillip
Slavonic Acts of Andrew and Paul
Acts of Peter and Andrew
Life of Peter
Apocalypse of Paul
Revelation of John the Theologian
Gospel (or Questions) of Bartholomew
Coptic Resurrection of Christ by Bartholomew
Gospel of Nicodemus ("Descensus ad inferos")
Texts of the Assumption of Mary

C. Old English Texts

Anonymous, "Menologium," London, BL, Cotton MS Tiberius B.i: E. V. K. Dobbie, *Anglo-Saxon Minor Poems*, 54 and H. Greeson, "Two Old English Observance Poems," 208–9 (A14)

Ælfric, Homily for September 29, "Dedicatio ecclesiae sancti Michaelis" (B1.1.36)

Ælfric, *Lives of the Saints*, St. Maur: W. W. Skeat, *Lives of the Saints*, I, 148–66 (B1.3.7)

Ælfric, *Lives of the Saints*, St. Martin: W. W. Skeat, *Lives of the Saints*, II, 218–312 (B1.3.30)

"Ælfric," Addition to the *Catholic Homilies* II, no. 36: J. C. Pope, *Homilies of Ælfric: A Supplementary Collection*, II, 775–9 (B1.4.28)

Ælfric, *Grammar*: J. Zupitza, *Ælfrics Grammatik und Glossar* (B1.9.1)

Anonymous, Homily for Third Sunday after Epiphany, CCCC 302: R. Willard, *Two Apocrypha*, 38–56 [partial edition] (B3.2.5)

Anonymous, Homily for Second Sunday in Lent, Oxford, Bodleian Library, MS Hatton 114: A.M.L Fadda, *Nuove Omelie Anglosassoni* (B3.2.12)

Anonymous, Homily for Easter Day, Blickling 7 (B3.2.26)

Anonymous, Homily for Easter Day, CCCC 41: W. H. Hulme, "The Old English Gospel of Nicodemus," 610–14 (B3.2.29; see also B8.5.3.2)

Anonymous, Homily "In Letania maiore," Oxford, Bodleian Library, MS Hatton 114: R. Willard, *Two Apocrypha*, 38–54 (B3.2.31)

Anonymous, Homily "In Letania maiore," Oxford, Bodleian Library, MS Hatton 116: M. Förster, "Der Vercelli-Codex CXVII," 128–37 (B3.2.33)

Anonymous, Homily for Wednesday in Rogationtide, CCCC 162: J. Bazire and J. E. Cross, *Eleven Old English Rogationtide Homilies* (B3.2.44)

Anonymous, Homily on St. Giles, CCCC 303: B. Picard, *Das altenglische Ægidiusleben*, 96–129 (B3.3.9)

Anonymous, Homily on the Assumption of the Virgin Mary, Blickling 13 (B3.3.20)

Anonymous, Homily on the Assumption of the Virgin Mary, CCCC 41: R. J. S. Grant, *Three Homilies*, 13–41 (B3.3.21)

Anonymous, Homily on St. Michael, CCCC 41: R. J. S. Grant, *Three Homilies*, 42–77 (B3.3.24)

Anonymous, Homily on St. Michael, Blickling 16 (B3.3.25)

Anonymous, "De die iudicii" (Apocalypse of Thomas), Vercelli 15: D. Scragg, *The Vercelli Homilies*, 249–65 (B3.4.6)

Anonymous, Apocalypse of Thomas, CCCC 303: R. Willard, *Two Apocrypha*, 4–6 [partial edition] (B3.4.12.2)

Pseudo-Wulfstan, Untitled homily for unspecified occasion: A. Napier, *Wulfstan*, no. 29, 134–43 (B3.4.26)

Pseudo-Wulfstan, "De temporibus antichristi": Napier, no. 42, 191–205 (B3.4.34)

Pseudo-Wulfstan, "Sermonem angelorum nomina": Napier, no. 45, 226–32 (B3.4.36)

Pseudo-Wulfstan, "Larspell": Napier, no. 46, 232–42 (B3.4.37)

Anonymous, Homily, "The Sunday Letter": R. Priebsch, "The Chief Sources of Some Anglo-Saxon Homilies," 129–47 (B3.4.54)

Anonymous, Untitled homily on the functions and duties of priests, CCCC 201: B. Thorpe, *Ancient Laws and Institutions*, II, 394–400 (B3.4.55)

Anonymous, Old English Vision of St. Paul, Oxford, Bodleian Library, MS Junius 85 and 86: A. diP. Healey, *The Old English Vision of St. Paul*, 63–73 (B3.5.1)

Anonymous, Gospel of Nicodemus, Cambridge, University Library, MS Ii.2.11 and London, BL, Cotton MS Vitellius A.xv: Hulme, "The Old English Version of the Gospel of Nicodemus," 471–515 and T. P. Allen, "A Critical Edition of the Old English *Gospel of Nicodemus*" (B8.5.2.1)

Anonymous, Gospel of Nicodemus homily, London, BL, Cotton MS Vespasian D.xiv: Hulme, "The Old English Gospel of Nicodemus," 591–610 (B8.5.3.1)

Anonymous, Homily for Easter Day, CCCC 41: Hulme, "The Old English Gospel of Nicodemus," 610–14 (B8.5.3.2; see also B3.2.29)

Bede, *HE*, V,2 and V,19: Colgrave and Mynors, 456–57 and 526–27 (B9.6.7)

Anonymous, Forms of Confession and Absolution, CCCC 190: Förster, "Zur Liturgik der angelsächsischen Kirche," 14–18 (B11.9.1)

Anonymous, Forms of Confession and Absolution, London, BL, Royal MS 2B.v: Hallander, "Two Old English Confessional Prayers," 100–102 (B11.9.3.1)

Anonymous, Forms of Confession and Absolution, London, BL, Cotton MS Tiberius C.i: Logeman, "Anglo-Saxonica Minora," 101–103 (B11.9.4)

Anonymous, Prayer of confession, London, BL, Cotton MS Galba A.xiv: B. Muir, *A Pre-Conquest English Prayer-Book*, 136 (B12.4.5)

Anonymous, Prayer following translation of Boethius: Sedgefield, *King Alfred's Old English Version of Boethius' De consolatione philosophiae*, 149 (B12.4.7)

Anonymous, Rubrics and Directions for Use of Forms of Service, London, BL, Cotton MS C.viii: Ker, *Catalogue of Manuscripts Containing Anglo-Saxon*, 292 (B12.5.7)

Laws of England, Æthelred (VIIaAtr), CCCC 201: Lieberman, *Die Gesetze der Angelsächsen*, 262 (B14.25)

Law of Excommunication (VII), CCCC 303: Lieberman, 438–9 and E. M. Treharne, "A Unique Old English Formula," 209–10 (B14.42)

Rectitudines, CCCC 383: Lieberman, 444–53 (B14.44)

Charter of King Æthelstan to Milton Abbey: Sawyer, *Anglo-Saxon Charters*, no. 391; Robertson, *Anglo-Saxon Charters*, no. 23 (B15.1.23)

Charter of Bishop Oswald to Ælfhild: Sawyer, no. 1309; Robertson, no. 42 (B15.3.14)

Charter of Bishop Oswald to Æthelweard: Sawyer, no. 1312; Birch, *Cartularium Saxonicum*, no. 1206 (B15.3.16)

Charter of Bishop Oswald to Eadmaer: Sawyer, no. 1313; Birch, nos. 1202–3 (B15.3.17)

Charter of Bishop Oswald to Osulf: Sawyer, no. 1315; Birch, no. 1204 (B15.3.18)

Charter of Bishop Oswald to Æthelweard: Sawyer, no. 1317; Birch, no. 1236 (B15.3.20)

Charter of Bishop Oswald to Brihtmaer: Sawyer, no. 1320; Birch, no. 1241 (B15.3.22)

Charter of Bishop Oswald to Osulf: Sawyer, no. 1326; Robertson, no. 46 (B15.3.23)

Charter of Bishop Oswald to Æthelwold: Sawyer, no. 1332; Robertson, no. 55 (B15.3.25)

Charter of Archbishop Oswald to Æfnoth: Sawyer, no. 1337; Kemble, *Codex Diplomaticus Aevi Saxonici*, no. 620 (B15.3.28)

Charter of Archbishop Oswald to Æthelmund: Sawyer, no. 1338; Kemble, no. 619 (B15.3.29)

Charter Archbishop Oswald to Æthelnoth: Sawyer, no. 1339; Kemble, no. 618 (B15.3.30)

Charter of Archbishop Oswald to Wulfgar: Sawyer, no. 1342; Kemble, no. 627 (B15.3.31)

Charter of Archbishop Oswald to Ælfwine: Sawyer, no. 1355; Kemble, no. 542 (B15.3.33)

Charter of Archbishop Oswald to Goding: Sawyer, no. 1369; Robertson, no. 61 (B15.3.39)

Charter of Archbishop Oswald to Wulfgar: Sawyer, no. 1372; Robertson, no. 58 (B15.3.40)

Charter of Archbishop Oswald to Wulfgeat: Sawyer, no. 1373; Robertson, no. 56 (B15.3.41)

Charter of Archbishop Oswald to Wulfheah: Sawyer, no. 1374; Robertson, no. 57 (B15.3.42)

Record of Dues Rendered to the Church of Lambourn: Robertson, App. I, no. 5 (B15.5.39)

Will of Æthelwyrd: Sawyer, no. 1506; Robertson, no. 32 (B15.6.23)

Bounds: Sawyer, no. 1003; Davidson, "On Some Anglo-Saxon Charters at Exeter," 292–5 (B15.8.511)

Notice of Guild Assembly at Exeter: B. Thorpe, *Diplomatarium Anglicum aevi Saxonici*, 613 (B16.10.3)

List of Relics, Exeter: Förster, *Zur Geschichte des Reliquienkultus in Altengland*, 63–80 (B16.10.8)

Dues, Worcester: Ker, "Hemming's Cartulary," 74 (B16.23.4)

Anglo-Saxon Chronicle, entries for years 759, 1011, 1014, 1052, 1065, 1066, 1086, 1095,

1097, 1098, 1099, 1100, 1001, 1102, 1103, 1106, 1119, 1125, 1126, and 1129 (B17.1; B17.7; B17.8; and B17.9)

Old English Martyrology, entries for May 8, April 24, July 2, July 19, and September 29 (B19.4 and B19.5)

Computistics, "De diebus festis": H. Henel, *Studien zum altenglischen Computus*, 71–73 (B20.18.2)

Caption for illustration of St. Michael, Oxford, Bodleian Library, MS Junius 11 (p. 9): G. P. Krapp, *The Junius Manuscript*, xvii (B27.2.9.1)

Glosses to Latin hymns: J. Stevenson, *Latin Hymns of the Anglo-Saxon Church*, nos. 96 and 97 (C18.2) and H. Gneuss, *Hymnar und Hymnen*, nos. 95, 96, and 97 (C18.3)

Liturgical Texts, Durham Ritual, Durham, Cathedral Library, MS A.v.19: Thompson and Lindelöf, *Rituale Ecclesiae Dunelmensis* and A. Corrêa, *The Durham Collectar*, 193 (C21.1)

Lorica of Gildas, London, BL, MS Harley 585: J. H. C. Grattan and C. Singer, *Anglo-Saxon Magic and Medicine*, 133, no. 7 (C22)

Prayers from London, BL, MS Arundel 155: J. J. Campbell, "Prayers from MS Arundel 155," 82–117 (C23.1)

Latin-Old English Glossaries, CCCC 144: J. H. Hessels, *An Eighth-Century Latin-Anglo-Saxon Glossary*, 200 (D4.1)

D. Anglo-Norman Texts

Adam de Ross, Vision of St. Paul (versified): I. Short, "The Bodleian Fragment," 175–89

Henri d'Arcy, Vision of St. Paul (versified): L. Kastner, "Les versions françaises," 385–95

Anonymous, Eleven Pains of Hell: P. Meyer, "La Descente de Saint Paul en Enfer," 365–75

Anonymous, Translation of Book of Revelation (prose): M. R. James, *The Trinity Apocalypse* and W. O. Hassall, *The Douce Apocalypse*

Anonymous, Translation of Book of Revelation (versified): O. Rhys and J. Fox, *An Anglo-Norman Rhymed Apocalypse* and H. A. Todd, *The Old French Versified Apocalypses*

E. Middle English Texts

John Mirk, Homily on the Assumption of the Virgin Mary: T. Erbe, *Mirk's Festial*, 227–35

John Mirk, Homily on St. Michael: T. Erbe, *Mirk's Festial*, 257–60

Anonymous, Homily on the Assumption of the Virgin Mary: E. Weatherley, *Speculum Sacerdotale*, 182–92

Anonymous, Homily on St. Michael: E. Weatherley, *Speculum Sacerdotale*, 210–15

Anonymous, Gospel of Nicodemus (versified): Hulme, *The Middle English Harrowing of Hell*

Anonymous, "Canticum de Creatione," Oxford, Trinity College, MS 57: C. Horstman, "Canticum de Creatione," 287–331

Anonymous, *Cursor Mundi*: R. Morris, *Cursor Mundi*, III, lines 17928–18389

Anonymous, Legends of the Cross: R. Morris, *Legends of the Holy Rood*, 67–72

Anonymous, Translation of Revelations of Methodius, London, BL, MS Stowe 953: C.
   D'Evelyn, "The Middle English Metrical Version," 181
Anonymous, "The Play of Antichrist," Chester Cycle: W. W. Greg, *The Play of Antichrist*
Anonymous, "The Harrowing of Hell," York Cycle: R. Thomas, *Ten Miracle Plays*,
   130–44

Section II. The Texts

A. Old Testament Texts

1. I Enoch (Ethiopic; Second century BCE – First century CE)
EDITIONS/TRANSLATIONS
AOT, 170–319.
APOT, II, 163–277.
OTP, I, 5–89.
REFERENCES
1. Book of Watchers (Chapters 1–36)
a. Chapter 9:1: **Michael**, Gabriel, Suriel, and Uriel ask the Lord what to do with souls
clamoring at the gates of heaven to escape the iniquity that the fallen angels are perpe-
trating on earth.
b. Chapter 10:11: **Michael** to bind Samyaza, leader of angels who debauched themselves with women, and his followers for 70 generations until Judgment.
c. Chapter 20: **Michael** put in charge of best part of mankind, the nation (most likely,
of Israel), and chaos.
d. Chapters 24–25: **Michael** in charge of mountains and trees where the throne of
Eternal King at Judgment is to be found.
2. Book of Parables (Chapters 37–71)
a. First Parable (Chapters 38–44): In Chapter 40, **Michael** identified to Enoch as first of
the four figures standing around the Lord. **Michael** is designated the merciful and
long-suffering, and he blesses the Lord for ever and ever.
b. Second Parable (Chapters 45–57): At Judgment, **Michael** with Gabriel, Raphael,
and Phanuel will throw host of Azazel into the furnace of burning fire as vengeance for
the iniquity they practiced on earth (54:6).
c. Third Parable (Chapters 58–69): In Chapter 60, **Michael** describes the Day of Judgment to Enoch. Lord promises that **Michael**, who is in command of the waters, will be
the judge of fallen angels and evil kings (67:12). **Michael** and Raphael discuss severity
of the judgment of the fallen angels (68:2–5). **Michael** can't understand why the fear of
such a judgment would not compel one to renounce evil. In chapter 69, **Michael** is said
to be in possession of the secret oath of creation, Akae.
d. Chapter 71: **Michael** shows Enoch all the secrets of mercy and righteousness.

2. Book of Daniel (Second century BCE)
REFERENCES
a. Chapter 10: **Michael** is said to come to the aid of Gabriel, who is struggling with the
kings of Persia (10:13). He is also designated prince of the Israelites (10:21).

b. Chapter 12: **Michael** is again described as the great prince and protector of the Israelites (12:1).

3. Testaments of the Twelve Patriarchs (Second century BCE)
EDITIONS/TRANSLATIONS
Sparks, 505–600.
APOT, II, 282–367.
OTP, I, 775–828.
REFERENCES
Charles would identify **Michael** as the "angel of peace" in the Testaments of Levi (5:1–7), Dan (6:5 *et passim*), Asher (6:6), and Benjamin (6:1).
a. Late Hebrew Testament of Naphtali, son of Jacob (*APOT*, I, 361–63): In Chapter 9, **Michael** takes a message from the Lord individually to all seventy nations. Each nation defies the Lord and chooses its own angel. When **Michael** speaks to Abraham, the patriarch of Israel chooses to accept **Michael** as the angel of Israel and to worship the Lord. The Lord then disperses all the nations.

4. War Scroll (First century BCE – First century CE)
EDITIONS/TRANSLATIONS
Yadin, Yigael, *The Scroll of the War of the Sons of Light against the Sons of Darkness* (Oxford, 1962).
REFERENCES
a. Throughout the text, **Michael** is designated as the "Angel/Prince of Light" who will fight against Belial, the angel of darkness, and his forces.

5. Ascension of Isaiah (Second century BCE – Fourth century CE)
EDITIONS/TRANSLATIONS
AOT, 775–812.
OTP, II, 143–76.
REFERENCES
a. Chapter 3: Gabriel, angel of the Holy Spirit, and **Michael**, prince of the holy angels, open the tomb of Christ and bring Him forth sitting on their shoulder to send the twelve disciples to teach all nations about the resurrection.
b. Chapter 9: At verse 21, the "more glorious angel" holding the book of deeds of the sons of Israel is identified with **Michael** in the Slavonic text (A. N. Popov, *Opisanie rukopisei*, 414–19) and in the Latin text (C. F. A. Dillmann, *Ascensio Isaiae*; and R. H. Charles, *The Ascension of Isaiah*). In both the Slavonic and Latin, **Michael** is said worship the Lord with all angels (9:29) and sing His praises (9:41).

6. Syblline Oracles (Second century BCE – Seventh century CE)
EDITIONS/TRANSLATIONS
OTP, I, 317–472.
REFERENCES
a. Book 2, lines 215–20: **Michael**, with Gabriel, Raphael, and Uriel, lead souls of men to judgment.

7. II Enoch (Slavonic; Late First century CE)

EDITIONS/TRANSLATIONS

AOT, 321–62.

APOT, II, 425–69.

OTP, I, 91–221.

REFERENCES

a. Chapter 9: **Michael** brings Enoch into the presence of the Lord, who commands **Michael** to remove Enoch's earthly garments, anoint him with good oil, and clothe him in glorious garments. Enoch looks like of the "glorious ones" (i.e., angels).

b. Chapter 11: The Lord reveals the secrets of creation to Enoch and dedicates **Michael**, "Prince of my hosts" to Enoch as intercessor.

c. Chapter 23: In "The Tale of Melchizadek," **Michael** is substituted for Gabriel in some manuscripts. In these versions, **Michael** is sent by the Lord to get the infant Melchizadek from Nir's house (23:33) and transport the child on his wings to Paradise (23:28).

8. III Baruch (Greek; First – Third centuries CE)

EDITIONS/TRANSLATIONS

AOT, 897–914.

APOT, II, 527–41.

OTP, I, 653–79 (where Greek and Slavonic versions are on facing pages).

REFERENCES

a. Chapter 11: **Michael** is in the fifth heaven and holds the keys to the kingdom of heaven. Prince **Michael** receives prayers of men. He collects the merits of the righteous in an enormous bowl to be brought before the Lord (2–9).

b. Chapter 12: The angels who watch over the righteous arrive with baskets full of flowers which represent the merits of the righteous. They give the baskets to **Michael**, who rejoices. Some angels arrive with bowls which are neither full nor empty, and **Michael** laments with them because they did not fill the bowls.

c. Chapter 13: The angels who are over evil men lament their fate and ask **Michael** to be transferred from their duties. **Michael** tells them to await the instructions he will receive from the Lord.

d. Chapter 14: **Michael** leaves. A loud noise like thunder indicates that he is presenting the merits of men to the Lord.

e. Chapter 15: **Michael** returns with oil for the angels of the righteous, telling them to reward their charges a hundred times over. To the angels whose baskets were only half full, he tells them that their charges will receive the same reward of oil according to their merits.

f. Chapter 16: **Michael** tells the angels appointed over wicked men not to be sad, but to provoke their charges to jealousy and anger. He also commands them to send caterpillars, locusts, rust, grasshoppers, and hail with lightning and fury against the wicked. Since these evil men did not heed the Lord's advice or observe his commandments, **Michael** says they should be punished "with the sword and death, and their children with demons" (3).

9. Apocalypse of Abraham (First – Second centuries CE)
EDITIONS/TRANSLATIONS
OTP, I, 681–705.
REFERENCES
a. Chapter 10: The angel Iloil, in the appearance of a man, reports to Abraham that **Michael** sends his blessing of eternal happiness.

10. Hebrew Apocalypse of Elijah (First – Fourth centuries CE)
EDITIONS/TRANSLATIONS
M. Buttenwieser, *Die hebräische Elias-Apokalypse und ihre Stellung in der apokalyptischen Litteratur des rabbinischen Schrifttums und der Kirche* (Leipzig, 1897).
REFERENCES
a. Chapter 2: **Michael**, the Great Prince, appears to Elijah on Mount Carmel and reveals to him a vision concerning the times of the End.

11. Testament of Abraham (First – Second centuries CE)
EDITIONS/TRANSLATIONS
AOT, 393–421.
OTP, I, 871–902.
REFERENCES
a. Chapter 1: **Michael** is sent to inform Abraham of his imminent death.
b. Chapter 2: At the oak of Mamre, Abraham greets **Michael** who has taken on the appearance of a soldier. **Michael** says that he has come from a great city and sent by a great king to arrange for the departure of a great friend of his. **Michael** reveals that he does not ride horses, so **Michael** and Abraham walk together back to Abraham's house.
c. Chapter 3: Isaac recognizes **Michael** as not of the human race and greets him respectfully. Abraham, who washes **Michael**'s feet, is moved by the stranger and begins to cry, which sets the whole household to crying. **Michael** also cries, and his tears turn into precious stones as they fall into a basin of water.
d. Chapter 4: Abraham puts on a feast for **Michael**, who sneaks up to heaven and tells God that he cannot bring himself to mention Abraham's death to the patriarch. The Lord tells **Michael** to eat with Abraham and that He will put in Isaac's mind the thought of death so that he will see his father's death in a dream. **Michael** inquires of the Lord how he, as an incorporeal being, possibly eat human food. The Lord tells him that He will send a devouring spirit in **Michael** to eat the food and instructs him to interpret Isaac's dream for him so Abraham can begin settling his earthly affairs before death.
e. Chapter 5: The Lord puts the dream in Isaac's head during a nap. Isaac awakes frightened, runs to find his father weeping and hugs him. **Michael** also weeps and Sarah comes to inquire as to the cause of the weeping.
f. Chapter 6: Recognizing **Michael** as an angel of the Lord, Sarah takes Abraham aside and tells him that **Michael** is an angel. She recognizes him as one of the three guests at the oak of Mamre when the slaughtered and eaten calf rose again after the meal. Abraham shows her the stones he took from the water basin, and Sarah tells him that they can expect some great revelation from the angel.
g. Chapter 7: Isaac tells the assembled group of his dream, in which a brilliant shining

man comes twice and deprives Isaac first of the sun and then of the moon. **Michael** interprets the dream as the Lord's taking away of Abraham first and then Sarah. **Michael** reveals himself to Abraham and Isaac as the one who will convey Abraham's soul to heaven. Abraham says he will not follow **Michael**, but that the angel should do whatever the Lord commanded.

h. Chapter 8: **Michael** immediately disappears and stands before the Lord. The Lord tells him to go down and promise Abraham infinite blessings on his family and make him aware that all men must eventually die.

i. Chapter 9: **Michael** returns and relates all the Lord said to Abraham, who implores him to tell the Lord that he would while still in his body see the whole earth and all created things. He promises he will leave the earth after such a journey. **Michael** appears before the Lord who grants the patriarch's wish.

j. Chapter 10: In the course of their travels, **Michael** and Abraham see humans involved in all manner of activities. When they see thieves, Abraham bids that wild beasts devour the thieves and it is done; when they see a couple fornicating, Abraham bids fire consume the couple and it is done. The Lord tells **Michael** to bring the tour to an end as Abraham is likely to destroy the whole earth. The Lord instructs **Michael** to take him to the first gate of heaven to witness the post-mortem judgment and retribution, so that he might repent for the souls he has destroyed.

k. Chapter 11: At the first gate, they witness Adam rejoicing for the souls who pass through the narrow gate of righteousness and lamenting for the souls who pass through the gate of sin. Abraham worries that he will not fit through the narrow gate of righteousness, but **Michael** reassures him that he will.

l. Chapter 12: **Michael** and Abraham go through the gate of destruction and witness the judgment and retribution of a soul whose good and bad deeds are evenly balanced. **Michael** and Abraham go up to the judgment place and witness the judgment and retribution of an evil soul.

m. Chapter 13: **Michael** tells Abraham that the man on the seat of judgment is Abel. There are two angels who flank him to either side. The angel on the right records the good deeds and the angel on the left the sins. The deeds of all men are subjected to two tests: one by the angel Dokiel who balances the good and evil deeds in his scales, and the angel Pyruel who tests the deeds by fire. Enoch, the teacher of heaven and earth, and the scribe of righteousness, is the one who presents the souls before Abel and records their judgment.

n. Chapter 14: Abraham asks **Michael** about the soul whose deeds were evenly balanced (see chapter 12). **Michael** tells him that the soul is set in the middle, in neither punishment or salvation. Abraham asks **Michael** to intercede with him on behalf of this soul. The Lord grants the intercession. Abraham then asks **Michael** to intercede with him on behalf of the souls he cursed during their tour of the world, since it was a sin on Abraham's part to have judged the souls. The Lord forgives Abraham and the souls are returned to life.

o. Chapter 15: God commands **Michael** to take Abraham back to earth to get his affairs in order. When Abraham and **Michael** return, everyone hugs Abraham as they thought he had been taken from them. **Michael** tells Abraham to put his earthly matters in order since God has commanded that he should come with **Michael** to heaven. Abraham again refuses. **Michael** goes before the Lord to seek further instruction.

p. Chapter 16: God tells **Michael** to call Death to Him. God commands Death to put on a fair face and bring Abraham to heaven, but not to frighten him. Death goes to Abraham who does not believe him that he is death. Death tells him he has come for his soul, but Abraham says he will not follow him.

q. Chapter 19: After a harrowing experience with Death, in which Death reveals his true appearance and all of Abraham's household dies and is restored, Abraham says he will only depart with **Michael**.

r. Chapter 20: After several more attempts to stall by Abraham, Death tricks Abraham into kissing his ring, promising that joy and life and power would come to him. Abraham's soul sticks to Death's ring and immediately **Michael** and a host of angels appears to convey the patriarch's soul to heaven. **Michael** wraps Abraham's soul in sheet of divinely woven cloth, and the angels tend his body for three days when they bury his body at the oak of Mamre. The angels escort Abraham's soul to Paradise.

12. Life of Adam and Eve (Latin; First century CE)
EDITIONS/TRANSLATIONS
AOT, 141–67.
OTP, II, 249–95 (Latin text printed on facing pages with Greek text of "Revelation/Apocalypse of Moses").
APOT, II, 123–54.
REFERENCES
a. Chapters 13–14: Satan tells Adam the story of how **Michael** brought Adam before the angels of heaven to be worshipped. **Michael** was the first angel to worship Adam.

b. Chapter 21: **Michael** sent to help Eve give birth to Cain.

c. Chapter 22: The Lord sends **Michael** with seeds to Adam. **Michael** show Adam how to work the land.

d. Chapters 25–29: Adam tells Seth the story of the fall and in particular of a vision in which **Michael** takes him to Paradise where he sees the Lord. Michael leads Adam out of Paradise by freezing the waters of the river which surround it and returns Adam to where the vision came upon him.

e. Chapters 30–48: These chapters tell the story of Seth's quest for the Oil of Mercy. **Michael** appears in Chapters 41–42 at the gates of Paradise to tell Seth not to weep or pray for the Oil of Mercy and to inform him that Adam would die in six days (cf. **Michael**'s speech in the Latin A version of the Gospel of Nicodemus). In Chapter 48, **Michael** and Uriel bury Adam.

f. Chapter 51: **Michael** tells Seth not to mourn for more than six days because the seventh day is the day of resurrection and happiness.

13. Revelation/Apocalypse of Moses (Greek; First – Third centuries CE)
EDITIONS/TRANSLATIONS
OTP, II, 249–95 (Translation of Greek text printed on facing pages with translation of Latin text of "Life of Adam and Eve").
A. Walker, *Apocryphal Gospels, Acts, and Revelations* (Edinburgh, 1870): 454–67.
REFERENCES
a. Preface (a later addition to the Greek text): The text is an account of the life of Adam and Eve are revealed to Moses by **Michael** when he received the tables of the Law of the Covenant.

b. Chapter 3: The murder of Abel by Cain is revealed to Eve in a dream. The Lord commands **Michael** to tell Adam not to reveal that he and Eve know of the murder for He will them another son. Adam and Eve go to find Abel murdered by Cain and grieve for him. Eve soon has another son, Seth.

c. Chapter 13: **Michael** is sent by the Lord to tell Seth not to weary himself praying for the oil of mercy since it will not be made available to him until the last days. **Michael** tells Eve and Seth of Judgment Day and bids them return to Adam who will die in three days.

d. Chapters 15–30: Upon their return, Adam commands Eve to tell the story of their transgression in Paradise. In Chapter 22, Eve describes how **Michael** sounded his trumpet in Paradise to assemble all the angels so that they would witness the Lord's sentencing of Adam and Eve.

e. Chapter 37: After Adam's death, Eve sees the heavens open and witnesses the procession of Adam's soul to heaven. Adam is cleansed in the Acherousian lake and is handed over to **Michael**, who anoints Adam and leads him to the third heaven where he is to await Judgment Day.

f. Chapter 38: The Lords instructs **Michael** about Adam's funeral, for which all the angels are assembled.

g. Chapter 40: Adam's body is laid to rest in Paradise. The Lord commands **Michael** to bring cloths of fine linen and silk, and **Michael**, Gabriel, Uriel, and Raphael cover Adam's body with the cloth and anoint him with sweet-scented olive oil in preparation for burial. The same treatment is given Abel's body, which is retrieved from where Cain had hidden it. The bodies are put in separate tombs, and God seals Adam's tomb.

h. Chapter 43: Eve dies within six days of Adam, and **Michael** stands beside her at the hour of death. Eve is buried by three angels in the same tomb as Abel. **Michael** instructs Seth to bury all humans in this same fashion until the day of resurrection. **Michael** also tells Seth not to mourn more than six days and to rejoice in rest on the seventh day, since this is the way the angels' rejoice when a righteous soul is received in heaven. **Michael** returns to heaven.

14. IV Baruch (Paraleipomena of Jeremiah; First – Second centuries CE)

EDITIONS/TRANSLATIONS

OTP, II, 413–25.

AOT, 813–33 (where it is entitled "The Paraleipomena of Jeremiah").

REFERENCES

a. Chapter 9: In prayer, Jeremiah invokes **Michael** as the angel of righteousness (Ethiopic version adds the detail that **Michael** is skilled in song) who holds open the gates of heaven for the righteous.

15. Testament of Solomon (First – Third centuries CE)

EDITIONS/TRANSLATIONS

AOT, 733–51.

OTP, I, 935–87.

REFERENCES

a. Chapter 1: **Michael** gives Solomon is given a little ring with a seal of God carved upon it and tells him that the ring will give him the power to control demons who will then build the temple at Jerusalem. Solomon then commands that each demon be brought before him for interrogation. Unable to withstand his power, the demons reveal to him which angel is able to mitigate their evil. Thus, Uriel is said to control the chief demon, Ornias, and is charged with supervising the demon's work on the Temple. Other angels are mentioned in connection with specific demons: Raphael inhibits Asmodeus; Patike/ Emmanuel/Eloi has control over Beelzebub; Azael over Lix Tetrax; Bazazath over Winged Serpent; Rathanael over Enepsigus; and Iameth over Cynopegus.

16. Testament of Isaac (Second century CE)
EDITIONS/TRANSLATIONS
AOT, 423–39.
OTP, I, 903–11.
REFERENCES
a. Chapter 2: God sends an angel in the form of Abraham to Isaac on his deathbed. In Bohairic version, this angel is **Michael**.
b. Chapter 3: Isaac laments that after his death his son Jacob may be harmed by Esau. The angel tells him that he need not worry since Jacob has been blessed by the Father, Son, and Holy Spirit, to which **Michael**, Gabriel and all angels answer "Amen."

17. Testament of Jacob (Second – Third centuries CE)
EDITIONS/TRANSLATIONS
AOT, 441–52.
OTP, I, 913–18.
REFERENCES
a. Chapter 1: When Jacob is near the time of his death, the Lord sends **Michael** to him. **Michael** appears in the form of Isaac and tells Jacob to write his testament for his sons and to put his earthly affairs in order.
b. Chapter 3: Michael tells Jacob not to fret over his imminent death. He tells Jacob that he is the angel who has been with Jacob since birth; who chose Jacob to receive his father's blessing; who is with him, Israel, in everything he does; who delivered Jacob from Laban when he possess Jacob; who blessed Jacob, all his sons, wives, and cattle; who rescued Jacob from Esau; who brought Jacob into the land of Egypt; and who has spread Jacob's wealth far and wide. Michael blesses Jacob, Abraham, Isaac, and all his descendants, and any who might emulate Jacob's life and death.

18. Apocalypse of Sedrach (Second – Fifth centuries CE)
EDITIONS/TRANSLATIONS
AOT, 953–66.
OTP, I, 605–13.
REFERENCES
a. Chapter 14: After postponing his own death through tears and lamentations, and by getting Christ to make concessions on behalf of repentant sinners, Sedrach beseeches **Michael** as an intercessor before the Lord on behalf of the world.

19. Apocalypse of Ezra (Greek; Second – Ninth centuries CE)

EDITIONS/TRANSLATIONS

AOT, 927–41 (where it is entitled "The Apocalypse of Esdras").

OTP, I, 561–79.

REFERENCES

a. Chapter 1: **Michael** answers Ezra's prayer to see the mysteries of the Lord by telling him to fast for seventy days. Raphael comes and gives him a stick of incense while he fasts.

b. Chapter 2: **Michael**, Gabriel, and all the apostles appear as Ezra is talking to the Lord.

c. Chapter 4: **Michael**, Gabriel, and thirty-four other angels are commanded by the Lord to take Ezra to see the lower part of Tartarus. **Michael** answers Ezra's questions about the sinners he sees in Tartarus, including Antichrist.

d. Chapter 6: The Lord tells Ezra the names of the angels at the consummation: **Michael**, Gabriel, Uriel, Raphael, Gabuthelon, Aker, Arphugitonos, Beburos, and Zebulon.

20. The Vision of Ezra (Greek; Fourth – Seventh centuries CE)

EDITIONS/TRANSLATIONS

AOT, 943–51 (where it is entitled "The Vision of Esdras").

OTP, I, 581–91.

REFERENCES

a. Verse 56: **Michael** and Gabriel come to lead Ezra to heaven, but he refuses to join them until he sees all the judgments of the sinners. They lead him further into the nether regions. After he has seen the judgments, he is taken up to heaven (presumably by **Michael** and Gabriel).

21. III Enoch (Hebrew; Fifth – Sixth centuries CE)

EDITIONS/TRANSLATIONS

OTP, I, 223–315.

REFERENCES

a. Chapter 17: **Michael** is described as the Great Prince in charge of the seventh and highest heaven.

b. Chapter 44: **Michael** laments the Lord's unwillingness to save His people.

B. New Testament Texts

1. The Shepherd of Hermas (Second century CE)

EDITIONS/TRANSLATIONS

A. Roberts and J. Donaldson, eds., "The Pastor of Hermas," in *Ante-Nicene Christian Library*, vol. 1 (Grand Rapids, 1950–52).

Graydon F. Snyder, "The Shepherd of Hermas," in *Apostolic Fathers*, vol. 6 (Camden, NJ, 1968).

J. B. Lightfoot and J. R. Harmer, eds. and trans., "The Shepherd of Hermas," edited and revised Michael W. Holmes, *The Apostolic Fathers: Greek Texts and English Translations of their Writings*, 2nd ed. (Grand Rapids, MI, 1992).

REFERENCES

a. Book Three: Parables: In Chapter Three of the Eighth Parable, **Michael** is the "great and glorious" angel who has charge over the believers and guides them. **Michael** puts the law into the hearts of the faithful and keeps a close eye on them to determine whether they observe the law.

2. Book of Revelation (First century CE)
REFERENCES

a. Chapter 12: **Michael** appears in the context of the heavenly contest between the forces of good and the forces of evil. In verses 7–9, **Michael** and his angels are said to battle against and defeat the old serpent, the devil who is Satan.

3. Epistle of Jude (First century CE)
REFERENCES

a. Verse 9: To illustrate a model of restraint worthy of emulation by his audience, Jude refers to a Jewish apocryphal tradition in which **Michael** contends with Satan over the body of Moses. Jude declares that **Michael** showed considerable restraint in his ancient contest by refraining from judging Satan harshly for his impudence.

4. Epistle of the Apostles (Second century CE)
EDITIONS/TRANSLATIONS

Elliott, *ANT*, 515–18 (Coptic text and Latin fragment of an Ethiopic version of Greek original).

REFERENCES

a. Chapter 13: Christ tells apostles of how he descended from heaven in the form of one of the archangels. **Michael**, Gabriel, Raphael, and Uriel follow him until the fifth firmament of heaven, where Christ gives them the voice with which they are to praise and serve the Father until He should return to them. In the next chapter, Christ tells the apostles that He took the form of the archangel Gabriel at the annunciation.

5. History of Joseph the Carpenter (Fourth – Fifth centuries CE)
EDITIONS/TRANSLATIONS

Elliott, *ANT*, 111–17.

Schneemelcher, I, 483–85.

F. Robinson, *Coptic Apocryphal Gospels* (Cambridge, 1896): 130–59, 220–35.

REFERENCES

a. Chapter 23: **Michael** and Gabriel come for Joseph's soul and wrap it in a shining cloth. Angels protect his soul from demons of darkness and praise God as they conduct the soul to heaven.

6. Acts of Phillip (Fourth – Fifth centuries CE)
EDITIONS/TRANSLATIONS

Elliott, *ANT*, 512–18 (summary and translation of Act VIII).

James, *ANT*, 439–53 (summary).

REFERENCES

a. Chapter 15: Accused of sorcery, Phillip and Bartholomew are punished. John arrives and addresses the crowd. Unable to endure the pain of his punishment, Phillip ignores the advice of John and invokes the Lord to open up the earth and swallow the crowd of some seven thousand men. Jesus appears and rebukes Phillip, who defends himself. Jesus tells Phillip that he will die in glory and be taken to Paradise by angels, but that he will remain outside the gates of Paradise for forty days in fear of the flaming sword as punishment for having been so unforgiving. After forty days, Jesus promises He will send **Michael** to open the gates of Paradise for Phillip.

7. Coptic Acts of Andrew and Paul (Eighth – Ninth centuries CE)
EDITIONS/TRANSLATIONS
Elliott, *ANT*, 301–302 (summary).
James, *ANT*, 472–75 (summary).
REFERENCES
a. Paul has dived into the sea to visit the underworld but is returned through the prayers of Andrew. He tells Andrew that he has seen Judas and heard his story. Judas had repented, given back the money, and pleaded for forgiveness from Jesus. Jesus sent him to the desert to repent, telling him to fear no one but God. Satan appears to Judas, who was afraid and worshipped him. Judas seeks Jesus again to plead for pardon, but cannot find him and so resolves to hang himself and meet Jesus in Amente. Jesus comes to Amente and retrieves all the souls but Judas's. Satan boasts that he is stronger than Jesus since one soul was left in Amente. Jesus orders **Michael** to take away Judas's soul also in order to prove Satan's boast vain.

8. Acts of Peter and Andrew (possibly Third – Fifth centuries CE)
EDITIONS/TRANSLATIONS
Elliott, *ANT*, 299–301 (summary).
James, *ANT*, 458–60 (summary).
A. Walker, *Apocryphal Gospels, Acts, and Revelations* (Edinburgh, 1870): 368–73.
REFERENCES
a. The men of a particular city attempt to deny Andrew and Peter entry to their city by placing a naked woman at the gates. The apostles perceive the snare and pray. **Michael** is sent to grasp the woman by the hair and hold her up until the apostles had passed into the city. The woman then hurls abuse at the elders of the city and prays for pardon. Many believe as a result of her word and worship the apostles who perform many cures in the city.

9. Slavonic Life of Peter (possibly Fifth – Sixth centuries CE)
EDITIONS/TRANSLATIONS
James, *ANT*, 474 (summary).
Schneemelcher, II, 438–39 (summary).
Elliott, *ANT*, 430.
REFERENCES
a. Jesus comes to Peter in the form of a Child and tells him to travel by sea to Rome. Peter comes to a boat in the harbor, whose captain, **Michael**, pretends not to wish to take Peter on board because he is a disciple of Christ. Michel relents and the voyage begins. During the voyage, Peter calms a violent storm, converts and baptizes the captain, **Michael**. **Michael** then sells him the Child. In Rome, Nero arrests Peter, and the Child rebukes Nero. The councilor Cato hits the Child behind the ear and is

withered up. The city shakes violently and the dead arise, believing it to be the Day of Judgment. The Child tells the dead to return to their resting places until **Michael** raises them on that final day.

10. Apocalypse of Paul (Third – Sixth centuries CE)
EDITIONS/TRANSLATIONS
Elliott, *ANT*, 616–44.
James, *ANT*, 526–55.
REFERENCES
a. Chapter 14: **Michael** and angelic host praise and adore God, telling a good soul that God is the God of all things and is the God who made man in his own image. God is pleased with the good soul and commands that it be handed over to **Michael**, "the angel of the covenant," to be led into Paradise.
b. Chapter 25: **Michael** is said to lead the souls of those who have subjected their own will to the will of God into the city of Prophets by the river of honey, where the souls are met by Isaiah, Jermiah, Ezekiel, Amos, Micah and Zechariah.
c. Chapter 26: **Michael** is said to lead the souls of those who preserved their chastity and purity to the river of milk where they will inherit the promises of God and where they are greeted by the whom Herod slew.
d. Chapter 27: **Michael** is charged with leading the souls of those who have given hospitality to strangers to the river of wine where they are greeted by Abraham, Isaac, Jacob, Lot, and Job.
e. Chapter 43: The sinners whom Christ did not raise from the dead (in Chapter 42) cry out for mercy. **Michael** and the angelic host descend from heaven. The sinners appeal for mercy directly to **Michael**, who rebukes them and all humans for having squandered their time on earth in self-indulgent pursuits. **Michael** represents himself to sinners as one who always stands in presence of the Lord and who prays incessantly for human race. Nevertheless, **Michael** pities the souls and vows to intercede on behalf of any who may have done good while on earth. He also says that he will pray that God send rain and dew upon the earth and that the earth might therefore produce its fruits. Paul joins **Michael** in beseeching the Lord to have mercy on the sinners.
f. Chapter 44: Christ descends from heaven. Although he rebukes the sinners for their previous lack of repentance, he ultimately grants the intercession for the sake of **Michael**, the archangel of the Lord's covenant, and for Paul the well-beloved. Christ grants the grace of one day and one night's refreshment on the Lord's Day forever.
g. Chapter 48: Paul sees Moses, the law-giver, weeping. Moses tells Paul that he is weeping for all the Israelites who hanged Jesus. In his speech, Moses mentions **Michael** as one of the blessed and righteous who wept for the Son of God hanging on the cross.
h. Chapter 49: Isaiah, Jeremiah, and Ezekiel each tell Paul of his death at the hands of the children of Israel. In Ezekiel's story, **Michael** comes to retrieve Ezekiel while he is praying for his persecutors.

11. Revelation of John the Theologian (Fifth century CE)
EDITIONS/TRANSLATIONS
A. Roberts and J. Donaldson, *Ante-Nicene Fathers*, vol. 8 (New York, 1903): 582–86.
A. Walker, *Apocryphal Gospels, Acts, and Revelations* (Edinburgh, 1870): 493–503.

[Greek text in C. Tischendorf, *Apocalypses Apocryphae* (Leipzig, 1866; repr. Hildesheim, 1966): 70–94.]

REFERENCES

a. After the description of Antichrist, Tischendorf's MS E claims that Antichrist's appearance is due to his capture by **Michael**, who stripped him of his divinity (in Roberts, ANF 8, at 582, n. 9).

b. **Michael** and Gabriel are said to announce the day of Judgment by blowing ram's horns.

c. At the very end of the text in Tischendorf's MS E, the Lord will send **Michael** after the Judgment to seal up the pit of lamentation into which all the sinners will have been thrown (in Roberts, ANF 8, at 586, n. 7).

12. Gospel (Questions) of Bartholomew (Second – Sixth centuries CE)

EDITIONS/TRANSLATIONS

Elliott, *ANT*, 652–68.

James, *ANT*, 166–81.

Schneemelcher, I, 537–57.

REFERENCES

a. Chapter 12: Jesus beckons **Michael** to sound the trumpet in the height of the heavens to summon the demon Beliar (Satan, the Devil) from beneath the earth that Bartholomew may question him as to his powers.

b. Chapters 28–29: Beliar describes the order in which God created the angels. Beliar was created first, **Michael** second, Gabriel third, then variously Raphael or Uriel fourth and fifth, and sixth Nathanael, Xathanael, or Zathael.

c. Chapters 53–55: **Michael** helps God create Adam with clods from the four corners of the earth and water from the four rivers of Paradise. **Michael** shows reverence for God's creation Adam and commands Beliar to do so as well. Beliar refuses and provokes God's wrath. No mention here of **Michael**'s role in casting Beliar out of heaven.

13. Coptic Resurrection of Jesus Christ by Bartholomew the Apostle (Fifth – Sixth centuries CE)

EDITIONS/TRANSLATIONS

Elliott, *ANT*, 668–72.

E. A. Wallis Budge, *Coptic Apocrypha in the Dialect of Upper Egypt* (London, 1913): 1–48, 179–230.

REFERENCES

a. **Michael** is said to have brought Adam and Eve, who were 80 and 50 cubits high respectively, before the Father upon their reception in heaven.

b. Thomas raises his son Siophanes (possibly Theopanes?) from the dead in the name of Jesus Christ after seven days. Siophanes tells his father how his soul sprang from his body into the hands of **Michael**, who wrapped the soul in fine linen. Siophanes was washed three times in the Acherusian lake and taken to heaven.

14. Gospel of Nicodemus (Fifth – Sixth centuries CE)

EDITIONS/TRANSLATIONS

Elliott, *ANT*, 164–225.

James, *ANT*, 94–146.

REFERENCES

1. Christ's Descent into Hell (Greek A):

a. Chapter 9 (25): Christ leads Adam into Paradise, and hands him and all the righteous over to **Michael**.

b. Chapter 10 (26): **Michael** meets the thief crucified with Christ at the gates to paradise, tells him to wait a short while as Adam also was soon to arrive with the rest of the righteous. The implication seems to be that the thief arrives even as the Harrowing was taking place, but before the righteous had arrived in heaven.

c. Chapter 11 (27): Two brothers, Karinus and Leucius, ostensible authors of the Descent although they are not mentioned by name in Greek A, are sent by **Michael** the archangel to preach the resurrection of the Lord. First they must go to the Jordan and be baptized.

2. Christ's Descent into Hell (Latin A):

a. Chapter 3 (19): Seth and Oil of Mercy: Adam tells Seth to tell the assembled patriarchs and prophets what he (Seth) had heard from **Michael** when Adam had sent Seth to procure the oil of the tree of mercy to anoint Adam's body with. **Michael** met Seth at the gates of Paradise and tells him not to pray for the oil of the tree of mercy to anoint his father Adam for the pain of his body. Michael tells him that he will not be able to receive it except in the last days and times, some five thousand five hundred years in the future. Then the Son of God will raise the body of Adam and the bodies of the dead.

b. Chapter 9 (25): Jesus delivers Adam to **Michael**, and followed by all the saints, **Michael** leads them into the glorious grace of paradise.

c. Chapter 11 (27): Karinus and Leucius aver that **Michael** had forbidden them to say more than what they had just uttered. They also say that **Michael** had ordered them to cross the Jordan and go to Jerusalem where they were allowed to keep Passover with their kindred.

3. Christ's Descent into Hell (Latin B):

a. Chapter 4 (20) 3: Seth and the Oil of Mercy: At the gates of paradise Seth prays, entreats the Lord, and calls upon the guardian of paradise to give the oil of mercy to him. **Michael** appears to Seth and tells him that he will not receive the oil until the last days.

15. Texts of the Assumption of the Virgin Mary

The Assumption is also known as the Dormition, Falling Asleep, Passing Away, Transitus, or Obsequies of Mary.

EDITIONS/TRANSLATIONS

Elliott, *ANT*, 691–723.

James, *ANT*, 194–227.

Forbes Robinson, *Coptic Apocryphal Gospels* (Cambridge, 1896): 66–89.

[Latin text of Transitus Mariae B² in Monika Haibach-Reinisch, *Ein Neuer "Transitus Mariae" de Pseudo-Melito* (Rome, 1962): 63–87.]

[Latin text of Transitus Mariae C in A. Wilmart, *Analecta Reginensia* (Vatican, 1933): 325–57.]

W. Wright, *Contributions to the Apocryphal Literature of the New Testament* (London, 1865): 10–51.

REFERENCES

A. Coptic Text:

1. Bohairic Account of the Falling Asleep of Mary attributed to Evodius, Archbishop of Rome (Robinson):

a. Chapter 12: Mary's soul, which is as white as snow, is wrapped in garments of fine linen and given to **Michael** who bares it on his wings of light until Jesus appoints a place for her holy body.

B. Latin Accounts:

1. The recensions of the Narrative of Pseudo-Melito:

a. Transitus Mariae B (Elliott, *ANT*, 708–14):

i. Chapter 9: Jesus delivers soul of Mary to **Michael**, guardian of Paradise and Prince of the Jews.

ii. Chapter 17: The apostles have just told Jesus that they believe it right that He raise up the body of Mary and take her with Him into Heaven. Jesus commands **Michael** to bring the soul of Mary. **Michael** then rolls away the stone from the door of the sepulchre where Mary's body has been since Jesus commanded that her soul be taken to heaven. Jesus commands Mary to rise up and she does.

b. Transitus Mariae B² (Haibach-Reinisch):

i. Chapter 8: Jesus passes Mary's soul in to charge of **Michael**, guardian of Paradise and Prince of the Hebrew people.

ii. Chapter 16: **Michael** is commanded to bring the soul of Mary before Jesus.

iii. Chapter 17: **Michael** conveys the Virgin Mary to Paradise with the angelic host.

c. Transitus Mariae C (Wilmart):

i. Chapter 24: **Michael**, the prince of the angels, sings hymns with all the angels.

ii. Chapter 26: Mary's soul is entrusted to **Michael**.

iii. Chapter 48: **Michael** conveys Mary's body to Paradise.

C. Syriac Accounts:

1. Fragment i (Wright, 10–15): Jesus appears to Mary. She speaks her last words and dies. Her soul is delivered to **Michael**.

2. Fragments of the Obsequies of the Holy Virgin (Wright, 42–51):

a. Fragment i (46–48): Jesus bids **Michael** bring forth the body of Mary from the tomb and carry it into the clouds. The apostles gathered at the tomb are all carried to paradise, where they ask the Lord to show them the place of torment, reminding Him of His promise that on the day of the departure of Mary they should see it. They are all taken on a cloud to the west. The Lord speaks to the angels of the pit, and the earth springs upwards and they see the pit. The lost souls see **Michael** and beg for respite. Mary and the apostles fall down and intercede for them. **Michael** speaks to them, telling them that all twelve hours of the day and of the night the angels intercede for creation. The fragment ends.

b. Fragment ii (48–50): This fragment is narrated by **Michael** to Mary about the concealing of the bones of Joseph in the Nile by Pharaoh and their discovery by Moses. It would seem that this passage must have been in response to some inquiry of Mary's about her own body, and therefore it should perhaps be placed earlier in order of the fragments.

16. Apocalypse of the Holy Mother of God Concerning the Chastisements (Ninth century CE)

EDITIONS/TRANSLATIONS

R. Rutherford, in A. Menzies, ed., *Ante-Nicene Fathers*, vol. 9 (Edinburgh, 1897): 169–74.

James, *ANT*, 563 (summary).

REFERENCES

a. Chapter 1: **Michael** descends to the Virgin Mary, who has prayed to God that Gabriel should tell her about the punishments of the sinful and about all things in heaven and on earth. The Virgin hails **Michael** in a series of praise-epithets: he is commander-in-chief; minister of the invisible Father; associate of Mary's son, Jesus Christ; most dread of the six-winged; he who rules through all things and is alone worthy to stand before the throne of the Lord; he who will sound the trumpet to awaken the dead; and first of all before the throne of the Lord. For the rest of the text, **Michael** serves as the Virgin's guide to the punishments of Hell.

b. Chapters 2–29 (*passim*): **Michael** shows Mary in turn the punishment of those who did not worship the Lord; those who did not believe in the Father, Son, and Holy Spirit, and did not believe that Jesus Christ was born to Mary; those who inherited the curses of their fathers and mothers; those who ate the flesh of men; those who swore on the cross falsehoods to be true; those who committed usury; those who spoke ill of neighbors in order to sow strife; those who sleep on the morning of Lord's day; one who did not honor the presbyter when they enter a church; those who are perjurers, blasphemers, and slanderers; priests who practiced iniquity; readers in church who did not act according to the precepts of the Gospels; those who on earth were patriarchs and bishops but were not worthy of the title; the wife of a presybter who took another husband after the death of the presbyter; an archdeaconess who defiled her body in fornication; those who did not perform the will of God and loved money in excess; those who refused holy baptism; those who committed fornication and sin within the bonds of marriage; those who debauched their daughters; those who slay others with poison or the sword; women who strangle their offspring; and finally those Christians who worked the works of the devil and squandered their lives without repenting of their sins. At the sight of the suffering Christians, the Virgin Mary wishes to be chastised with the children of her son Jesus Christ. Mary prays that **Michael** might command the angelic host to lead her into the presence of the Lord. Immediately Mary is transported before the undefiled throne of the invisible Father where she prays for the relief of the Christians. The Lord grants that any sinner who invokes the name of the Holy Virgin will not be forsaken by the Lord. **Michael** and all the angels, Moses, John, and Paul, and all the saints join the Virgin Mary in supplicating the Lord for mercy on the Christians. Finally the Lord is moved by the appeal and descends before the chastised and rebukes them for their sins. The Lord grants the sinners rest on the day of Pentecost to glorify the Father, Son, and Holy Ghost because of the prayers of Mary, **Michael**, and all the saints.

Appendix C
The Motif Index

This list is limited to the roles of St. Michael in scriptural, apocryphal, and pseudepigraphal texts. It is meant to serve as a convenient index of the variety of the archangel's roles in that body of literature. I have deliberately left out the medieval English materials since the organization of Part II is based on a full discussion of those roles. Cross-referencing titles of texts in this list with those in the "Inventory," which has a fuller bibliographic apparatus, should facilitate sourcing materials mentioned in this list.

I. Roles in Creation and Procreation
1. Gospel (Questions) of Bartholomew (53): Michael helps God in creation, bringing him a clod of dirt from the four corners of the earth, and water out of the four rivers of paradise.
2. Life of Adam and Eve/Revelation of Moses: Michael helps Eve give birth to Cain.
3. I Enoch (Ethiopic) 69: Michael is in charge of secret oath of creation, Akae.

II. Psychopomp
1. II Enoch (Slavonic).
2. Syblline Oracles
3. Greek Revelation/Apocalypse of Moses.
4. Life of Adam and Eve/Revelation of Moses (where he also buries Adam, Abel, and Eve).
5. IV Baruch (Paraleipomena of Jeremiah).
6. Apocalypse of Sedrach.
7. Vision of Esdras (Ezra).
8. Testament of Abraham.
9. Testament of Isaac.
10. Testament of Jacob.
11. Apocalypse of Ezra (Greek).
12. Apocalypse of Paul.
13. Acts of Andrew and Paul.
14. Coptic Resurrection of Christ by Bartholomew.
15. Christ's Descent into Hell ("Oil of Mercy" exemplum in Gospel of Nicodemus).
16. History of Joseph the Carpenter
17. Acts of Phillip.
18. Texts of Assumption of Mary.

III. Rule over Humankind

1.   Apocalypse of Moses (32:6).
2.   Shepherd of Hermas
3.   Latin A version of Christ's Descent into Hell (19:1).

IV. Associated with Water

1.   Life of Adam and Eve/Apocalypse of Moses, where he casts Adam from paradise and freezes the water for him to walk upon.
2.   I Enoch (Ethiopic): God promises Noah that Michael, who is in charge of the waters, will judge the evil angels and kings.
3.   Apocalypse of Paul: Michael prays for dew and rain so that the earth may bear fruit.
4.   Testament of Abraham: Michael's tears turn into semi-precious stones when they fall into a bucket of water.

V. Associated with Agriculture

1.   Life of Adam and Eve/Revelation of Moses: Michael teaches Adam to farm, and also provides Adam with seeds and instructs him in the ways of agriculture.
2.   I Enoch (Ethiopic): Michael is in charge of the Tree of Life.

VI. Blowing of Horn or Trumpet at Judgment

1.   Revelation of St. John the Theologian (accompanied by Gabriel).
2.   Greek Revelation/Apocalypse of Moses: Michael blows his trumpet to call the angels together to hear the judgment of the Lord against Adam and Eve.
3.   Gospel (Questions) of Bartholomew: Michael sounds the "trumpet in the height of heavens" to summon the demon Beliar from beneath the earth so that Bartholomew may question him as to his powers.

VII. Intercessor/Protector of the Lord's Chosen People

1.   Daniel 10:13, 21 and 12:1.
2.   I Enoch 20:5–7.
3.   II Enoch (Slavonic) 11.
4.   Greek Revelation/Apocalypse of Moses.
5.   Life of Adam and Eve/Revelation of Moses.
6.   III Baruch 11:4.
7.   IV Baruch (Paraleipomena of Jeremiah).
8.   Testament of Levi (5:6ff.): Michael is the angel who intercedes for Israel and all the righteous.
9.   Testament of Dan (6:2): Michael is a mediator between God and man.
10. Testament of Abraham (14): Michael and Abraham intercede successfully on behalf of a sinful soul.
11. In the Latin and Slavonic versions of the Ascension of Isaiah (9:23): Michael is the "magnus angelus deprecans sempre pro humanitate."
12. Apocalypse of Sedrach.
13. Vision of Esdras.
14. Latin A version of Christ's "Descent into Hell" ("Oil of Mercy" exemplum): Michael tells Seth that he is set over the human race as protector.

15. Apocalypse of Paul: In a speech to sinful souls who beg him to intercede on their behalf, Michael acknowledges his role as intercessor before the Lord.
16. Michael is also regarded as a powerful intercessor in many versions of the Assumption of Mary texts.

VIII. Fall of the Angels
1. Life of Adam and Eve/Revelation of Moses.
2. Questions of Bartholomew.
3. I Enoch (Ethiopic) 6–16.

IX. Guardian/Custodian of Paradise
1. III Baruch: Michael holds keys to heaven.
2. Epistle of Jude.

X. Messenger of the Lord
Instances of Michael in this role are numerous; only a representative sample is listed.
1. Book of Daniel 10.
2. Revelation of Moses: Michael is sent to talk to Seth about the death of his father Adam.
3. I Enoch (Slavonic) 22:6–9.
4. Testament of Abraham: Michael is sent to inform Abraham of his imminent death.
5. Hebrew Apocalypse of Elijah.
6. Apocalypse of Ezra.
7. Vision of Ezra.

XI. Involved with the Burial of Humans
1. Life of Adam and Eve/Revelation of Moses.
2. Epistle of Jude.

XII. Association with Animals
1. III Baruch 16: Michael commands the angels appointed over wicked men to send caterpillars, locusts, rust, grasshoppers, and hail with lightning against them as punishment.
2. Testament of Abraham: Michael does not ride horses.

Appendix D
Saint Michael in Medieval English Iconography

Much has been written about the pictorial traditions of St. Michael.[1] This Appendix is meant to present the reader with a glimpse of these rich and manifold traditions of representation. There are two principal thematic types of representations of the archangel associated with scriptural passages mentioning St. Michael. The references to the archangel in the Book of Daniel (10:13, 21 and 12:1) depict him as a "great prince" of the Hebrews.[2] These references gave rise to a pictorial tradition, principally early Christian and Byzantine, in which St. Michael is depicted as a singular, princely individual. In this tradition, he is nimbed and dressed in a long, flowing tunic or occasionally the royal mantle of the Byzantine imperial court. He holds, most often in his right hand, a staff, scepter, or occasionally a sword,[3] and in his left hand a globe topped by a cross. Less frequently, he is represented in the company of his fellow archangel Gabriel and/or other unidentified angels.

The other iconographic tradition derives from the Epistle of Jude 9 and the Book of Revelation 12:7–9.[4] This tradition, found exclusively in the west, depicts St. Michael in his militant role fighting the devil and represents in a general sense the triumph of good over evil.[5] These scenes depict the archangel atop the devil, who is represented

---

1 Principal among the works on the iconography of St. Michael are F. Wiegand, *Der Erzengel Michael in der bilden Kunst* (1886); A. Renner, *Der Erzengel Michael in der Geistes- und Kunstgeschichte* (1927); E. Mâle, *L'Art religieux du XIIe siècle en France* (1928): 257–62; M. de Fraipont, "Les origines occidentales du type de Saint Michel debout sur le dragon," *Revue Belge d'Archéologie et d'Histoire de l'Art 7* (1927): 289–301; R. Janin, "Les sanctuaires byzantins de Saint Michel," *Échos d'Orient* (1938): 28–52; M. Laurent, "Le Bas-relief de Saint Michel à l'abbaye de Maredsous," *Revue Belge d'Archéologie et d'Histoire de l'Art 8* (1938): 337–48; P. G. de Jerphanion, "L'Origine copte du type de Saint Michel debout sur le dragon," *Académie des Inscriptions et Belles-lettres, Comptes Rendues* (1938): 367–81; Louis Réau, *Iconographie de L'Art Chrétien* (Paris, 1956): vol. 2, 44–51; J. J. G. Alexander, *Norman Illumination at Mont St Michel 966–1100* (Oxford, 1970): 86ff.; Maria Grazia Mara, "Iconografia" under "Michele, arcangelo, santo" in *Bibliotheca Sanctorum*, vol. 9 (Rome, 1962): 410–46 at 438–46; Martha Abbott Lawrenz, "The Cult of Saint Michael the Archangel as Expressed in the Art of Western Europe from the Ninth through the Twelfth Centuries," unpublished Honors Thesis, Smith College, 1962; Pina Belli D'Elia and Immacolata Aulisa, *L'angelo la montagna il pellegrino: Monte Sant'Angelo e il santuario di San Michele del Gargano: archeologia, arte, culto, devozione dalle origini ai nostri giorni* (Foggia, 1999); and Glenn Peers, *Subtle Bodies: Representing Angels in Byzantium* (Berkeley, 2001).
2 On the characterization of St. Michael in the Book of Daniel, see Chapter One, 14–16.
3 On the eastern iconographic traditions, see P. G. de Jerphanion, "L'Origine copte du type de Saint Michel debout sur le dragon," 368–370, and G. Peers, *Subtle Bodies*.
4 For a discussion of St. Michael in these texts, see Chapter One.
5 M. Laurent has argued that this scene is a type of the triumph of good over evil and that it may derive from the iconographic tradition of representing the image of "Christus super aspidem" in Psalm 90:13 ("Le Bas-relief de Saint Michel à l'abbaye de Maredsous," 292).

variously as a human or a dragon, and thrusting a sword or spear into his mouth.[6] Most often in this pictorial tradition, St. Michael holds a spear/sword in his right hand and a shield in his left. There are two types of this scene: in the first, and more static, type, St. Michael transfixes the devil vertically beneath him, thrusting the spear straight into the devil's mouth. In the second type, the archangel appears to engage in the struggle more actively, thrusting the spear diagonally across the front of his body at the devil (the cross-lance motif).

Less common, and without scriptural source, is the iconographic motif of the archangel bearing the scales of judgment. Although they are by far the fewest in number, the images of St. Michael as weigher of souls constitute an intriguing dimension of Christian eschatology.[7] While there are references in the Old Testament Book of Job, and in the writings of St. Augustine and St. John Chrysostom to a post-mortem weighing of good and evil deeds, the most likely line of tradition leads back to Egypt where the weighing of the heart of the deceased is found in graphic detail in *The Book of Dead*.[8] Although most of the medieval English representations of St. Michael as the weigher of souls are later than the Anglo-Saxon period, there are several striking examples from this earlier period.

This essay examines a representative number of medieval English iconographic images of St. Michael in these roles. The representations of the archangel were created as a means of rendering the bodiless and immaterial archangel apprehensible, an important step in establishing devotions to St. Michael. These images, however, reveal a relationship between man and angel which exceeds the traditional roles assigned to St. Michael in scripture and patristic thought on the role of angels and archangels. In fact, it would seem that devotions to and representations of St. Michael in Anglo-Saxon and later medieval England derive largely from apocryphal sources. The iconographic representations of the archangel examined here range in date from the late seventh century to the early twelfth and include carvings (in wood or stone) and manuscript drawings (dry-point or pigment).

Anglo-Saxon iconographic representations of St. Michael fall into two broad categories: St. Michael with the archangel Gabriel and occasionally with other angels; and St. Michael acting alone in his various traditional roles. The archangel's two principal roles in the iconography are fighting the Dragon of Revelation 12:7–9, and participating in scenes of Judgment, in which he is often depicted with a pair of scales.

---

[6] It is interesting to note that from the reign of Edward IV (starting from about 1470) through the reign of Charles I (to 1649) gold coins denominated as the "angel" and "half-angel" were minted with the image of St. Michael piercing the dragon with his spear. See Herbert A. Grueber, *Handbook of the Coins of Great Britain and Ireland in the British Museum* (London, 1899; repr. 1970).

[7] For a discussion of St. Michael as weigher of souls, see Chapter Five, 87–88.

[8] Either painted on the walls of the tomb or buried on papyrus with the deceased, this book related all the necessary travel information for a successful voyage to the next world. In the scene of post-mortem judgment, the deceased is brought before the jackal-headed Anubis who is assisted by the falcon-headed Horus. The heart of the deceased is weighed against a feather symbolizing truth. To pass the judgment successfully, the two should balance each other. In Egyptian iconographic tradition, the ibis-headed Thoth the scribe stands to the left of the scales and records the verdict of the judgment. On the Egyptian scene of judgment in particular and the psychostasis in general, see E. A. W. Budge, *The Book of the Dead: The Papyrus of Ani*, 3 vols. (London and New York, 1913); T. G. Allen, *The Egyptian Book of the Dead* (Chicago, 1960); and S. G. F. Brandon, *The Judgment of the Dead: A Historical and Comparative Study* (New York, 1967).

In the earliest representations of the archangel, he is depicted with his fellow arch-angel Gabriel. Both St. Cuthbert's coffin-reliquary, from the late seventh century, and the Mortain casket, from the eighth century, have Irish connections. The third repre-sentation is in an Insular Gospel Book of the eighth century.

The very earliest Insular representation of the archangel is carved on St. Cuthbert's coffin-reliquary, most likely constructed at Lindisfarne at the time of his death (ca. 698).[9] Michael and Gabriel are depicted by name on one of the end-walls of the coffin. On one of the side-walls of the coffin-reliquary, a group of five archangels is carved. The full names of only the first two, Raphael and Uriel, survive. The four letters UMIA can be seen above a third angel. E. Kitzinger has argued that these letters probably formed part of the name of the archangel Rumiel (1 Enoch).[10] Since the spelling of the indi-vidual names of the archangels vary considerably in early sources, Kitzinger's assertion is likely correct. Taken together, then, figures carved on the end panel and the long side panel of the coffin-reliquary represent the seven archangels.

If, in fact, the third name can reliably be assumed to be Rumiel, the list of seven archangels is most likely derived from Irish sources. Lists including the name Rumiel (or a similar name) exist in many insular texts. M. R. James first drew attention to lists of archangels in Anglo-Saxon sources.[11] The only Anglo-Saxon list which includes the name Rumiel occurs in a prayer found in both the Irish-influenced *Book of Cerne*,[12] and in the so-called *Collectanea* of Pseudo-Bede,[13] a compilation ascribed to an Irish author. Thus, it is not surprising that most often the lists of archangels which include Rumiel are Irish in origin. Elsewhere, the name Rumiel occurs in an Irish prayer to the seven archangels for each day of the week;[14] in the lists of archangels found in the Liber de numeris;[15] the "Imchlód Aingel";[16] the *Saltair na Rann*;[17] and the *Tenga Bithnua*,

---

9   For a full discussion of St. Cuthbert's coffin-reliquary and for illustrations of the four panels and lid, see E. Kitzinger, "The Coffin-Reliquary," in *The Relics of St. Cuthbert*, ed. C. F. Battiscombe (Oxford, 1956): 202–304. See also Elisabeth Okasha, *Hand-List of Anglo-Saxon Non-Runic Inscriptions* (Cambridge, 1971): 67–69. In his eleventh-century Chronicle, Jocelin of Brakelond describes an image of St. Michael carved on the lid of St. Edmund's coffin: "Over the Martyr's breast, fixed to the outside of the coffin, was an angel of gold, about the length of a man's foot, having a sword of gold in one hand and a banner in the other; . . . And above the angel was written this verse: 'Lo! Michael's image guards the holy corpse.' And at the ends of the coffin were iron rings, after the fashion of a Norse chest" (H. E. Butler, *The Chronicle of Jocelin of Brakelond* [London, 1949; repr. 1962]: 112–13). Whether the carving was made at the time of St. Edmund's martyrdom (869), at the time of his first translation (ca. 915) to Beadericesworth (later Bury St. Edmunds), or either of his subsequent transla-tions (1032 and 1095) remains uncertain. For a full discussion of the coffin and St. Edmund's various translations, see Antonia Gransden, "The Alleged Incorruption of the Body of St. Edmund, King and Martyr," *Antiquaries Journal* 74 (1994): 135–68.

10   *Ibid.*, 276.

11   M. R. James, "Names of Angels in Anglo-Saxon and Other Documents," *JTS* 11 (1909/10): 569–71.

12   A. B. Kuypers, *The Book of Cerne*, 153. Michelle Brown, however, notes that the knowledge of apoc-rypha in this prayer (Cerne 54) is of a general character and need not necessarily suggest an Irish affiliation (*The Book of Cerne*, 138).

13   *PL* 94: 561–62. For the Irish authorship of this text, see Michael Lapidge and Richard Sharpe, *Bibliog-raphy of Celtic-Latin Literature* (Dublin, 1985).

14   T. P. O'Nowlan, "A Prayer to the Archangels for each Day of the Week," *Ériu* 2 (1905): 92–94.

15   R. E. McNally, *Der irische Liber de numeris*, 127.

16   Thomas P. O'Nolan, "Imchlód Aingel," in *Miscellany Presented to Kuno Meyer*, ed. Osborn Bergin and Carl Marstrander (Halle, 1912): 253–57 at 255.

17   W. Stokes, *The Saltair Na Rann* (Oxford, 1883): 12 at line 796.

Recension III.[18] Thus, the fact that the occurrence of the name Rumiel on St. Cuthbert's coffin is paralleled in Irish texts (or texts found in manuscripts known to have been composed in an Irish literary milieu) suggests the possibility that Irish influence is responsible for the carvings of the archangels on St. Cuthbert's coffin.

Another early representation of St. Michael with Gabriel is found on the Mortain Casket from the cathedral of Notre Dame de Mortain, France.[19] Thought to have been constructed in the late eighth century, the small house-shaped reliquary (12 x 13.5 x 5 cm) is made of wood covered with copper. On one side the copper plate contains an etching of Christ flanked by St. Michael and his fellow archangel Gabriel. The archangels are identified in Latin script: "SCS MIH" and "SCS GAB."[20] On the other side there is an inscription in Old English runes which reads, "Good Helpe: Ædan þiiosne ciismeel ge<w>arahtæ" (May God help Ædan [who] made this casket).[21] Since the name of the creator of the casket, "Ædan," is most likely Irish, the insular origins of the casket are not in doubt. How and when the casket made its way to Mortain, however, is not known, but its presence in France suggests interaction between Ireland and the continent in the early ninth century.

St. Michael is also represented with his fellow archangel Gabriel in an eighth-century insular Gospel Book, Trier, Domschatz Codex 61 (Bibliotheksnummer 134).[22] The Gospel Book was written by two scribes, one of whom was Anglo-Saxon.[23] The archangels appear in a miniature holding a plaque with the incipit of St. Matthew's Gospel (fol. 9r).[24] They are inscribed Scs Michael and Scs Gabriel and appear in mirror image of each other surrounded by a frame with corners of interlace. They are nimbed and winged, and dressed in flowing robes; each archangel holds a staff. The classic dress and pose suggests to Alexander that they are based on an early Christian prototype.[25]

The two archangels Michael and Gabriel are also thought to be represented adoring the Virgin and Child over one of the Canon tables in the tenth-century Arenberg Gospels (New York, Pierpont Morgan Library, MS 869, fol. 11r).[26] In her unpublished dissertation, Jane Rosenthal argues that the scene is a novel depiction of the Incarnation of Christ.[27] The image of an angel over another Canon table (fol. 10r) in this manuscript has also been interpreted as representing St. Michael, nimbed and wielding two sticks over his head, flanked by two anonymous angels, who hold open rolls and palm fronds before them.[28] Rosenthal argues that the three angels represent

[18] G. Dottin, "Une rédaction moderne du Tenga Bithnua," RC 28 (1907): 277–307 at 299.

[19] Okasha, Hand-List, 102, ill. 93 (of non-runic side). Okasha also prints an extensive bibliography for this reliquary.

[20] Ibid.

[21] A photograph of the runic inscription can be found in James Campbell, The Anglo-Saxons (Harmondsworth, 1982): 114.

[22] J. J. G. Alexander, Insular Manuscripts: 6th to the 9th Century (London, 1978): 52–54, ill. 109.

[23] Ibid., 53.

[24] Alexander reproduces the miniature as illustration 109 (Insular Manuscripts).

[25] Ibid., 53.

[26] For a discussion and reproduction of this Canon Table, see Thomas Ohlgren, Anglo-Saxon Textual Illustration (Kalamazoo, MI, 1992): 57 and 334.

[27] Jane E. Rosenthal, "The Historiated Canon Tables of the Arenberg Gsopels" (unpublished Ph.D. dissertation, Columbia University, 1974): 200–218.

[28] Ohlgren, Anglo-Saxon Textual Illustration, 56 and 332.

the future triumph of the cross. She claims that the sticks St. Michael holds above his head are two branches which serve as an iconographic prefiguration of the cross.[29]

The second category of iconographic representations of St. Michael consists of the archangel performing the various roles assigned to him in the vast literature of the Old and New Testament eras. Although St. Michael's two principal roles in the iconography are in scenes of combat and in scenes of Judgment, he is also represented in two other roles clearly derived from apocryphal sources: overseeing God's creation of Eve and teaching Adam and Eve how to till the earth.

A crude representation of St. Michael's battle with the Dragon is found in an eleventh-century carving on the Caen stone (53.3 x 86.4 x 15.2 cm) from St. Nicholas's Church, Ipswich.[30] It is possible that the carving was part of a more extensive frieze depicting the events of the Last Days. The stone is inscribed in Old English, "Her S[an]c[t]e Mihael feht <w>ið dane draca[n]" (Here St. Michael fights [possibly "fought"] against the dragon).[31] A similar image, but without inscription, depicting the archangel skewering the dragon is carved into a stone slab which is thought to belong to the eleventh century.[32]

Images of St. Michael in his struggle with the dragon are also found in various Anglo-Saxon manuscripts. St. Michael is depicted fighting the dragon in an eleventh-century Psalter produced in Winchester (London, BL, Cotton MS Tiberius C vi, fol. 16r).[33] Part of a cycle of illustrations opening the Psalter, the representation of St. Michael depicts the archangel moving toward a seated dragon with his lance aimed at the beast's mouth (the cross-lance motif).[34] F. Wormald considers the illustrations in this manuscript as being related in style to the late tenth-century Ramsey Psalter (London, BL, Harley MS 2904).[35] Alexander points out that if Wormald's assertion is true, then the cross-lance motif "would have been current in the last quarter of the tenth century in England."[36] Wormald has also noted that an illustration of St. Michael is likely to have been in the Benedictional of St. Æthelwold (London, BL, Additional MS 49598).[37]

In the Tiberius Psalter, the St. Michael image is found between a representation of the descent of the Holy Spirit and a section of illustrations on musical instruments.[38] In another illustration of the theme of the archangel's battle with the devil, the image of

---

29 Rosenthal, "The Historiated Canon Tables," 169–71.

30 Okasha, Hand-List, 82–83, ill. 58. Campbell also reproduces a photograph of the carving (The Anglo-Saxons, 195).

31 Okasha, Hand-List, 83.

32 A. Gardner, English Medieval Sculpture (1951): ill. 66 (cited in Alexander, Norman Illuminations, 92, n. 1).

33 Campbell reproduces a photograph of this image (The Anglo-Saxons, 228).

34 The image is reproduced in Kathleen Openshaw, "Weapons in the Daily Battle: Images of the Conquest of Evil in the Early Medieval Psalter," The Art Bulletin 75.1 (1993): 17–38.

35 F. Wormald, "An English Eleventh-century Psalter with Pictures," Walpole Society 38 (1960–62): 1–13.

36 Alexander, Norman Illumination, 91–92.

37 Wormald, "An English Eleventh-century Psalter," 5. See also Robert Deshman, The Benedictional of Æthelwold, Studies in Manuscript Illumination 9 (Princeton, 1995): 259.

38 For the fullest and most recent discussion of the cycle of illustrations in the Tiberius Psalter, see Kathleen Openshaw, "Images, Texts and Contexts: The Iconography of the Tiberius Psalter, London, British Library, Cotton MS Tiberius C. VI" (unpublished Ph.D. dissertation, University of Toronto, 1990).

St. Michael straddling the dragon forms the initial **L** of the phrase "Liber de generationis" opening the Book of Matthew in the eleventh-century Carilef Bible (Durham, Cathedral Library, MS A. II. 4, fol. 87v).[39]

St. Michael is thought to be represented battling the dragon in a large, paneled initial **Q** in the eleventh-century Crowland Psalter (Oxford, Bodleian Library MS Douce 296, fol. 40v).[40] In the bowl of the **Q**, a figure in chain mail, armed with a sword and shed, fights a dragon which forms the tail of the letter. A similar wingless figure has been uncovered by Thomas Ohlgren in the Junius manuscript (Oxford, Bodleian Library MS Junius 11, page 12). Using ultraviolet light, Ohlgren discovered five metalpoint sketches in the manuscript. One of these, he argues, is an unfinished preliminary sketch of St. Michael.[41] The sketch of the archangel is a "metalpoint outline of a standing male figure with a round shield in his left hand and the fragment of a lance in his upraised right hand."[42] Ohlgren believes that this outline complements thematically the other two drawings of St. Michael on pages 2 and 9 of the manuscript.[43]

Perhaps one of the most unusual representations of St. Michael fighting the Dragon, however, is carved on an altar or processional cross of wood and bronze (Copenhagen, Nationalmuseet, D894).[44] The wooden cross is Anglo-Saxon, from the third quarter of eleventh century, the bronze work Scandinavian and possibly contemporary with the cross. The image of St. Michael is carved on the back of the cross. The archangel is depicted with four wings which spread into the arms of the cross. He is nimbed and carries a shield and lance, which he plunges into the gaping mouth of the dragon below him. The dragon's tail is coiled and ends in the head of another beast. In a brief description of the cross, Leslie Webster has noted similarities between the iconography of the Arundel Psalter (London, BL, Arundel MS 60) and the Tiberius Psalter (on which see above) and the carving of St. Michael on this cross.[45] Webster suggests influence of the Winchester style, a hypothesis which is made plausible by an inscription which indicates the cross was either made or commissioned by an Anglo-Saxon: "AILMAR / F[...]T.PA[..]A / RE.CRUCE / M[..]NMI[...] /" (Ailmar [Æthelmar] had the cross of the Lord prepared).[46]

Two other images of St. Michael portray the archangel in roles associated with him only in apocryphal sources. In a drawing in the late tenth-century Junius manuscript,

---

[39] The image is reproduced in R. A. B. Mynors, *Durham Cathedral Manuscripts to the End of the Twelfth Century* (Oxford, 1939): no. 30.

[40] E. Temple, *Anglo-Saxon Manuscripts*, 96–97, ill. 260.

[41] Thomas Ohlgren, "Five New Drawings in the *MS Junius 11*: Their Iconography and Thematic Significance," *Speculum* 47 (1972): 227–33 at 227–30 and Fig. 1.

[42] *Ibid.*, 227.

[43] The angel in the drawing on page 2 is not identified as St. Michael. Ohlgren identifies him as the archangel based on his interpretation of the scene as it relates to the accompanying poetic text of *Genesis* (lines 20b to 46) in the manuscript, which describes the rebellion of Lucifer and the expulsion of the angels from heaven. Although St. Michael is often associated with the expulsion of the rebellious angels from heaven, Ohlgren's identification of St. Michael as the angel on page 2 is tenuous. On the representation of St. Michael on page 9 of the manuscript, see below.

[44] Janet Backhouse, D. H. Turner, and Leslie Webster, eds. *The Golden Age of Anglo-Saxon Art 966–1066* (Bloomington, 1984): 204–206.

[45] *Ibid.*, 204.

[46] *Ibid.*

St. Michael surveys a scene depicting God's creation of Eve from Adam's rib (Oxford, Bodleian Library, MS Junius 11).[47] Flanked by several unidentified angels, St. Michael stands in the gates of heaven at the top of a ladder descending into a tripartite scene in which God puts Adam to sleep, removes a rib with which to create Eve, and awakens Eve. The inscription above the heavenly choir reads, "Her godes engles astigan of heovenam mid paradisum" (Here God's angels descend from heaven). St. Michael is the only identified figure; his name appears above his figure. The ultimate source for the archangel's implicit participation in an act of creation lies in the apocryphal Gospel (or Questions) of Bartholomew 53 (RBMA 135).[48] The apocryphal Bartholomew has been cited by some critics as the possible source text for several motifs in Anglo-Saxon and early Irish literature.[49] Since most of the Anglo-Saxon texts in which these motifs occur are from the tenth century, it is possible that the Gospel of Bartholomew is the source for the identification of St. Michael as the angel witnessing the creation of Eve in the Junius manuscript.

Almost certainly from another apocryphal source, St. Michael is depicted instructing Adam and Eve in the skill of agriculture in a miniature found in the early eleventh-century Old English Bible paraphrase known as Ælfric's Hexateuch (British Library, Cotton MS Claudius B iv, fol. 7v).[50] Otto Pächt first identified St. Michael as the angel guiding Adam and Eve in tilling the earth and suggested that the source for this scene must be the apocryphal Life of Adam and Eve (Vita Adae et Evae; RBMA 74).[51] It has also been suggested that this apocryphon is the source for two distinct motifs in the tenth-century Old English poems Guthlac A and Christ and Satan, and thus Pächt's identification of St. Michael based on this apocryphon is plausible.[52]

The third category of representations depict the archangel in scenes of judgment, often implicitly as the weigher of souls at the individual, post-mortem judgment (as opposed to his role at the Final Judgment). In many renditions of the psychostasis, St. Michael appears not as the impartial weigher of souls, as was Anubis in the Egyptian post-mortem judgment scene, but as the champion of man against the Devil.[53]

Although representations of the full drama of the psychostasis are found only in later sources, St. Michael can be found in two Anglo-Saxon manuscripts holding a pair of scales, an iconographic emblem of the psychostasis. In the tenth-century Salisbury Psalter (Salisbury, Cathedral Library, MS 150, fol. 7r), there occurs a sketch of a winged and helmeted man holding a pair of scales. Since the illustration occurs in the right margin of a calendar for September, it is likely that the figure is meant to be St.

---

[47] The drawing is reproduced in Israel Gollancz's facsimile edition, The Caedmon Manuscript of Anglo-Saxon Biblical Poetry (Oxford, 1927): 9.

[48] The apocryphal Gospel of Bartholomew is printed in Elliot, ANT, 652–72. See also Appendices B and C.

[49] For a discussion of Anglo-Saxon knowledge of this text, see C. D. Wright, "Questions of Bartholomew" in SASLC: Trial, 35–36.

[50] The manuscript has appeared in a facsimile edition as EEMF 18. The illumination of Michael instructing Adam and Eve is discussed on pages 19 and 65.

[51] Otto Pächt, "A Cycle of English Frescoes in Spain," The Burlington Magazine 103 (1974): 169. Pächt also argues that the appearance of this scene among a series of thirteenth-century frescoes at the Convent of Sigena in Spain suggests that the artist of the frescoes was English.

[52] For a discussion of Anglo-Saxon knowledge of this text, see Frederick M. Biggs, "Life of Adam and Eve," in SASLC: Trial, 23–24. See also Appendices B and C.

[53] See Chapter Five, 89–96.

Michael. The entry for September 29 in this calendar is marked by a marginal cross and reads, "Dedicatio sancte, Michaelis archangeli." Another figure with scales and what appears to be a rod has been interpreted as St. Michael in a Canon table in Cambridge, Pembroke College, MS 301 (fol. 3r).[54]

Perhaps the most significant representation of St. Michael in a scene of Judgment, however, occurs in several line drawings in the eleventh-century New Minster *Liber Vitae* (British Library, Stowe MS 944, fols. 6v and 7r).[55] Although he is not represented holding a pair of scales, the archangel's role in the scene in keeping with his traditional mission as protector of the souls of the faithful. The *Liber Vitae* scene unfolds over two folios. At the top of folio 6v, two groups of figures, the saints and martyrs wearing the nimbus and the blessed without nimbus, are guided by a pair of angels. In the top register of folio 7r, St. Peter beckons to the assembled group on folio 6v to enter the gates of Heaven where Christ sits in majesty. Just below this scene, a soul awaits judgment in the middle of the second register. He looks imploringly to his right at St. Peter, who strikes a devil over the head with his double-warded keys. The devil is holding an open book, presumably a book recording the evil deeds of the souls awaiting judgment. An angel stands behind St. Peter inspecting a book recording the good deeds of the soul. In the bottom register, an angel locks the gates of hell and throws the key back over his shoulder into hell. In recent research, David F. Johnson has considered these four scenes and argues that the angel is likely to be St. Michael.[56] Johnson reviews a large body of visionary literature containing similar motifs, including the *Visio Sancti Pauli*, Vercelli 15, Pseudo-Wulfstan 29, and *Christ III*, and concludes that the *Liber Vitae* scenes represent the particular judgment of souls, and not the Final Judgment. In the context of the particular judgment, St. Michael can be fairly safely identified as the angel with the open book and the key.

As a martial figure representing the powers of good, St. Michael enjoyed considerable popularity among the Normans.[57] The archangel can be found fighting the dragon in the tympanum of the twelfth-century Norman Church of St. Michael, Moreton Valence, Gloucestershire.[58] St. Michael is similarly depicted in a thirteenth-century Apocalypse Picture Book in the collection of the Pierpoint Morgan Library. Produced around 1250, this book employs the apocalyptic imagery of Abbot Joachim of Fiore's *Book of Figures*. The great seven-headed dragon of the twelfth chapter of the Apocalypse

[54] Ohlgren, *Anglo-Saxon Textual Illustraton*, 66 and 396.
[55] This manuscript has been reproduced as Volume 26 of the EEMF series, ed. Simon Keynes, *The Liber Vitae of the New Minster and Hyde Abbey, Winchester, British Library Stowe 944* (Copenhagen, 1996).
[56] David F. Johnson reached these conclusions in an unpublished article, "Guardian Angel, Attendant Demon: Spiritual Conflict in Anglo-Saxon Art and Literature," which was first read as a paper at the Twenty-First Annual Meeting of SEMA, College of Charleston, Charleston, South Carolina, October 5–7, 1995 and then presented in a slightly different form as a lecture at Loyola University, Chicago, March, 1996. I would like to thank Dr. Johnson for sending me an early draft of his work on these scenes. Catherine E. Karkov has reached these same conclusions in "Judgement and Salvation in the New Minster Liber Vitae," in *Apocryphal Texts and Traditions in Anglo-Saxon England*, ed. D. Scragg and K. Powell (Cambridge, 2003): 151–63.
[57] For a discussion of the iconography of St. Michael in Norman manuscripts at Mont-Saint-Michel, see J. J. G. Alexander, *Norman Illumination at Mont St. Michel 966–1100* (Oxford, 1970): especially 85–183.
[58] G. H. Cook, *The English Medieval Parish Church* (London, 1954): ill. 120.

is the image in which the abbot sees the whole history of the Church's persecutions, past, present, and future, revealed to the believer.

In an allegorical wall painting of the Ladder of Salvation in the Church of Saints Peter and Paul, Chaldon (Surrey), the archangel's role in the horrific drama of Judgment is depicted.[59] Painted at the end of the twelfth century, the design of this particular composition is divided horizontally by wavy lines and vertically by the Ladder of Salvation which extends from the depths of Hell to highest Heaven. In the upper right-hand panel, Christ is seen harrowing Hell and skewering Satan, who seems to be manacled, symbolic of his eternal bondage. On the opposite side of the Ladder, in the upper left-hand panel, St. Michael is seen weighing souls. To the left of the scales a demon awaits the condemned. With one of his hands, he is weighing down the scale of sin in an attempt to gain possession of the soul being judged. This trickery, however, proves unsuccessful and the innocent souls are conducted by angels up the final rungs of the Ladder.

Other later representations of St. Michael with scales include a wall painting from the fifteenth century in the Church of St. James, South Leigh (Oxfordshire).[60] Here St. Michael is dressed in full military armor to symbolize the eternal battle he wages against Satan and his minions. Once again, in this painting, demons are trying to tip the scales in favor of sin, while the poor beleaguered soul sits praying in the opposite scale, mostly likely to the Virgin Mary, who stands beside the archangel. To secure this naked soul, St. Michael wields his sword in a threatening gesture above the interfering demons teeming from the jaws of Hell. The Virgin Mary and St. Michael appear together in a grille of Henry the Seventh's monument in the Abbey at Westminster (fourteenth century).[61] Here St. Michael holds the scale while trampling on the human-like figure of Satan, whose dragon tail tries to tip the scale. The Virgin Mary gently cradles the figure of a small child, most likely a representation of the soul to be judged.

From this brief survey of iconographic representations of St. Michael, it seems clear that in medieval England there existed a striking belief in the efficacy of angels and their intercession. Among angels, the roles assigned to St. Michael are remarkable, but they had been anticipated in Jewish apocalyptic and Christian apocryphal literatures. St. Michael's prowess against the Devil led to his invocation in times of crisis, and at the moment of death his succor was especially sought. The early English iconography of St. Michael constitutes an important collection of representations which underscore the devotional appeal of the archangel for the English in the medieval period.

[59] Ibid., ill. 107.
[60] F. Bond, Dedications and Patron Saints of English Churches (Oxford, 1914): 35.
[61] Ibid., 39.

Bibliography

Alexander, J. J. G. *Norman Illumination at Mont St. Michel 966–1100*. Oxford: Clarendon Press, 1970.

———. *Insular Manuscripts: 6th to the 9th Century*. London: Harvey Miller, 1978.

Alexander, Paul J. *The Byzantine Apocalyptic Tradition*. Ed. Dorothy deF. Abrahamse. Berkeley: University of California Press, 1985.

Anderson, Alan Orr and Marjorie Ogilivie Anderson. *Adomnán's Life of Columba*. New York: Thomas Nelson and Sons Ltd., 1961.

Anderson, Lewis O. "The Michael figure in the book of Daniel." Unpublished Th.D. thesis, Andrew's University, Seventh-Day Adventist Theological Seminary, 1997.

Anderson, M. D. *History and Imagery of British Churches*. Edinburgh: John Murray, 1971.

Arcamore, Maria Giovanna. "Le iscrizioni runiche di Monte Sant' Angelo sul Gargano." *Vetera Christianorum* 18:1 (1981): 157–72.

———. "Una nuova iscrizione runica da Monte Sant'Angelo." In *Culto e Insediamenti*. Eds. C. Carletti and G. Otranto. Bari: Edipuglia, 1994: 185–89.

Arnold, John Charles. "*Ego Sum Michael*: The Origin and Diffusion of the Christian Cult of St. Michael the Archangel." Unpublished Ph.D. Dissertation. University of Arkansas-Fayetteville, 1997.

———. "Arcadia becomes Jerusalem: Angelic Caverns and Shrine Conversion at Monte Gargano." *Speculum* 75 (2000): 567–88.

Arnold-Foster, F. *Studies in Church Dedications*. 3 vols. London: Skeffington and Son, 1899.

Atkins, Ivor. "An Investigation of Two Anglo-Saxon Kalendars." *Archæologia* 78 (1928): 219–54.

Atkinson, Robert. *The Passions and the Homilies from Leabhar Breac*. Dublin: Royal Irish Academy, 1887.

Babcock, Robert G. "Astrology and Pagan Gods in Carolingian 'Vitæ' of St. Lambert." *Traditio* 42 (1986): 95–113.

Bachmann, J. *Aethiopische Lesestücke*. Leipzig, 1893.

Banting, H. M. J. *Two Anglo-Saxon Pontificals*. HBS 104. London, 1989.

Barker, Margaret. *The Older Testament*. London: SPCK, 1987.

———. *The Lost Prophet*. London: SPCK, 1988.

———. *The Great Angel: A Study of Israel's Second God*. London: SPCK, 1992.

Barlow, Frank. *The Feudal Kingdom of England: 1042–1216*. London: Longman, 1988.

Bately, Janet. *Anonymous Old English Homilies: A Preliminary Bibliography of Source Studies*. Binghamton: SUNY Press, 1993.

Battiscombe, C. F. *The Relics of St. Cuthbert*. Oxford: Oxford University Press, 1956.

Baumstark, A. *Comparative Liturgy*. London: A. R. Mowbray, 1958.

Baxter, James H. "An Index of British and Irish Latin Writers: 400–1520." *Archivum Latinitatis Medii Aevi*, vol. 7. Paris, 1932: 110–219.

Bazire, J. and J. E. Cross. *Eleven Old English Rogationtide Homilies*. London: Kings College, 1990.

Belli, D'Elia, Pina. *L'angelo, la montagna, il pellegrino: Monte Sant'Angelo e il santuario di San Michele del Gargano: archeologia, arte, culto, devozione dalle origini ai nostri giorni*. Foggia: C. Grenzi, 1999.

Berger, Samuel. *La Bible Française au Moyen Age*. Paris, 1884. rpt. Geneva: Slatkine Reprints, 1967.

———. *Histoire de la Vulgate pendant les premiers siècles du moyen âge*. Paris: Hachette, 1893.

Bernard, J. H. and Robert Atkinson. *The Irish Liber Hymnorum*. HBS 13 and 14. London, 1898.

Bestul, Thomas. *A Durham Book of Devotions*. Toronto Medieval Latin Texts 18. Toronto: Pontifical Institute of Mediaeval Studies, 1987.

Bethurum, Dorothy. *The Homilies of Wulfstan*. Oxford: Oxford University Press, 1957.

Bettochi, Silvia. "La diffusione del culto micaelico in Puglia tra XI e XII secolo." *Vetera Christianorum* 33 (1996): 133–62.

Bevan, Edwyn. *Holy Images: An Inquiry into Idolatry and Image-Worship in Ancient Paganism and Christianity*. London: Allen & Unwin, 1940.

Bialas, Andrew. *The Patronage of Saint Michael the Archangel*. Chicago: Clerics of St. Viator, 1954.

Bibliotheca Sanctorum. 13 vols. Rome: Instituto Giovanni XXIII della pontifica universita Lateranense, Citta Nuova editrice, 1961–1970.

Biggs, Frederick M., Thomas D. Hill, and Paul E. Szarmach, eds. *Sources of Anglo-Saxon Literary Culture: A Trial Version*. Binghamton, NY: SUNY Press, 1990.

———. Thomas D. Hill, Paul E. Szarmach, and E. Gordon Whatley, eds. *Sources of Anglo-Saxon Literary Culture*. Volume 1: Abbo of Fleury, Abbo of Saint-Germain-des-Prés, and *Acta Sanctorum*. Kalamazoo, MI: Medieval Institute Publications, 2001.

Binns, Alison. *Dedications of Monastic Houses in England and Wales: 1066–1216*. Woodbridge: Boydell, 1989.

Birch, Walter de Gray. *Cartularium Saxonicum*. 3 vols. London, 1885.

———. *An Ancient Manuscript of the Eighth or Ninth Century Formerly Belonging to St. Mary's Abbey or Nunnaminster, Winchester*. London and Winchester: Hampshire Record Society, 1889.

Bishop, Edmund and F. A. Gasquet. *The Bosworth Psalter*. London: G. Bell and Sons, 1908.

Black, Matthew, ed. *The Book of Enoch or 1 Enoch: A New English Edition*. SVTP 7. Leiden, 1985.

Blume, Clemens. *Die Hymnen des Thesaurus Hymnologicus H. A. Daniels*. Analecta Hymnica Medii Aevi 51. Leipzig, 1908; repr. 1961.

Bognetti, G. P. *L'Età Longobarda*. 3 vols. Milan: Giuffrè, 1967.

Bond, F. *Dedications and Patron Saints of English Churches*. Oxford: Oxford University Press, 1914.

Bonnet, Max. *Narratio de miraculo a Michaele archangelo Chonis patrato*. Paris: Hachette, 1890.

———. "Narratio de miraculo a Michaele archangelo Chonis patrato." *AB* 9 (1890): 202–203.

Bosworth, Joseph and T. Northcote Toller. *An Anglo-Saxon Dictionary.* Oxford: Oxford University Press, 1898; repr. 1929, 1954.

Bozic, Ivan. "Le culte de Saint Michel sur les deux cotes de l'Adriatique." *Rivista storica del Mezzogiorno* 11–12 (1976–7): 17–30.

Bradshaw, Paul F. *The Search for the Origins of Christian Worship.* Oxford: Oxford University Press, 1992.

Brandon, S. G. F. *The Judgement of the Dead: An Historical and comparative Study of the Idea of a Post-Mortem Judgement in the Major Religions.* London: Weidenfeld and Nicolson, 1967

——. *Religion in Ancient History.* New York: Charles Scribner's Son, 1969.

——. "The Idea of the Judgement of the Dead in the Ancient Near East." in *Mithraic Studies,* ed. J. Hinnells. Manchester: Manchester University Press, 1975.

Brett, M. *The English Church under Henry I.* Oxford: Oxford University Press, 1975.

Bronzini, Giovanni Battista. "Culto garganico di san Michele." *Lares* 54:3 (1988): 307–66.

——. "Culto garganico di san Michele (parte secondo)." *Lares* 54:4 (1988): 463–521.

——. "Testi Latini delle apparizioni di San Michele." *Lares* 54:4 (1988): 555–92.

Brooke, Christopher and W. Swaan. *The Monastic World.* London, 1974.

Brooke, Z. N. *The English Church and the Papacy from the Conquest to the Reign of John.* Cambridge: Cambridge University Press, 1952.

Brown, Michelle P. *The Book of Cerne: Prayer, Patronage and Power in Ninth-Century England.* London and Toronto: British Library and University of Toronto Press, 1996.

Brown, Peter. *The Cult of the Saints: Its Rise and Function in Latin Christianity.* Chicago: University of Chicago Press, 1981.

Budge, E. A. Wallis. *Saint Michael the Archangel: Three Encomiums.* London: Kegan Paul, Trench, Trübner, 1894.

——. *Coptic Apocrypha in the Dialect of Upper Egypt.* London: British Museum, 1913.

——. *Miscellaneous Coptic Texts in the Dialect of Upper Egypt.* London: Longmans, 1915.

——. *The Book of Saints of the Ethiopian Church.* 6 vols. Cambridge: Cambridge University Press, 1928.

Butler, H. E. *The Chronicle of Jocelin of Brakelond.* London: Thomas Nelson, 1949; repr. 1962.

Buttenweiser, M. *Die hebräische Elias-Apokalypse und ihre Stellung in der apokalyptischen Litteratur des rabbinischen Schrifttums und der Kirche* (Leipzig, 1897).

Cagiano de Azevedo, Michelangelo. "Memorie della vittoria sul Gargano e del culto di S. Michele a Milano." *Il Santuario di S. Michele sul Gargano* [Coll. P.] 503–12.

Callison, T. C. "An Edition of Previously Unpublished Anglo-Saxon Homilies in MSS CCCC 302 and Cotton Faustina A. ix." Unpublished Ph.D. Dissertation, University of Wisconsin, 1973.

Cameron, A., Ashely C. Amos, A. diP. Healey, *et al.* eds. *The Dictionary of Old English: A-F.* CD-ROM. Version 1.0. Toronto: University of Toronto, 2003.

Campbell, Alistair. *Æthelwulf, De Abbatibus.* Oxford: Oxford University Press, 1967.

Campbell, Jackson J. "Prayers from MS Arundel 155." *Anglia* 81 (1963): 82–117.

——. "To Hell and Back: Latin Tradition and Literary Use of the 'Descensus ad Inferos' in Old English." *Viator* 13 (1982): 107–152.

Campbell, James. *The Anglo-Saxons.* Harmondsworth: Penguin Books, 1982.

Campione, A. "Storia e santità nelle due Vitae di Lorenzo vescovo di Siponto." *Vetera Christianorum* 29 (1992): 169–213.

Canivet, P. "Le Michaélion de Huarte (Ve s.) et le culte syrien des anges." *Byzantion* 50 (1980): 85–117.

Carletti, Carlo "Le iscrizioni murali." In *Il Santuario di S. Michele sul Gargano*. Eds. C. Carletti and G. Otranto. Bari: Edipuglia, 1980: 7–160.

———. "I graffiti sull'affresco di S. Luca nel Cimitero di commodilla: Addenda et Corrigenda." *Rendiconti della Pontificia Academia Romana di Archeologia* 57 (1984–85): 129–43.

——— and Giorgio Otranto. *Il Santuario di S. Michele sul Gargano dal VI al IX secolo. Contributo alla storia della Langobardia meridionale*. Atti del convegno tenuto a Monte Sant'Angleo il 9–10 decembre 1978. Bari: Edipuglia, 1980.

———. and Giorgio Otranto. *Culto e Insediamenti Micaelici nell'Italia meridionale fra tarda antichità e medioevo*. Atti del Convegno Internazionale Monte Sant'Angelo 18–21 novembre 1992. Bari: Edipuglia, 1994.

Ceccaroni, Sandro and Giovanni Antonelli. *Il culto di S. Michele Arcangelo nella religiosità mediovale del territorio spoletino*. Spoleto: Edizioni dell'Accadmia spoletina, 1993.

Chadwick, O. "The Evidence of Dedications in the Early History of the Welsh Church." In *Studies in Early British History*. Eds. H. M. and Nora Chadwick. Cambridge: Cambridge University Press, 1959.

Chaîne, M. "Apocalypsis seu Visio Mariae Virginis." In *Apocrypha de Beata Maria Virgine: Scriptores Aethiopici*. Series 1. Vol. 7 (Rome, 1909): 43–68.

Charles, R. H. *The Assumption of Moses*. London: Black, 1897.

———. *The Ascension of Isaiah*. London: SPCK, 1918.

——— et al., eds. *The Apocrypha and Pseudepigrapha of the Old Testament in English*. 2 vols. Oxford: Oxford University Press, 1913.

——— and W. R. Morfill. *The Book of the Secrets of Enoch*. Oxford: Oxford University Press, 1896.

Charlesworth, James H., ed. *The Old Testament Pseudepigrapha*. 2 vols. New York: Doubleday & Company, Inc., 1983–85.

Chibnall, Marjorie. *Anglo-Norman England: 1066–1166*. Oxford: Basil Blackwell, 1986.

Ciccarese, Maria Pia. "Le visioni di S. Fursa." *Romanobarbarica* 8 (1984–85): 231–303.

Clanchy, M. T. *England and its Rulers: 1066–1272*. New York: Barnes and Noble Books, 1983.

Clayton, Mary. "Delivering the Damned: A Motif in Old English Homiletic Prose." *MÆ* 55 (1986): 92–102.

———. "Blickling Homily XIII Reconsidered." *Leeds Studies in English* 17 (1986): 25–40.

———. "The Assumption Homily in CCCC 41." *N&Q*, September, 1989: 293–95.

———. *The Cult of the Virgin Mary in Anglo-Saxon England*. CSASE 2. Cambridge: Cambridge University Press, 1990.

———. *The Apocryphal Gospels of Mary in Anglo-Saxon England*. CSASE 26. Cambridge: Cambridge University Press, 1998.

Clemoes, Peter. *Ælfric's Catholic Homilies: The First Series*. EETS SS 17. Oxford: Oxford University Press, 1997.

Colchester, Leo. S. "Dragons, Serpents, and Saint Michael." *Friends of Wells Cathedral Reports* (1984): 18–23.

Colgrave, Bertram. *The Life of Bishop Wilfrid by Eddius Stephanus*. Cambridge: Cambridge University Press, 1927.

Colgrave, Bertram and R. A. B. Mynors. *Bede's The Ecclesiastical History of the English People*. Oxford: Oxford University Press, 1969.

Collins, Adela Yarbro. *The Combat Myth in the Book of Revelation*. Missoula, MT: Scholars Press, 1976.

———. "Early Christian Apocalypses." *Semeia* 14 (1979): 70–72.

Collins, John J. "The Mythology of Holy War in Daniel and the War Scroll." *Vetus Testamentum* 25 (1975): 596–612.

———. *The Apocalyptic Vision of the Book of Daniel*. Missoula, MT: Scholars Press, 1977.

———. "Pseudonymity, Historical Review, and the Genre of the Revelation of John." *Catholic Biblical Quarterly* 39 (1977): 329–343.

———. "The Jewish Apoclaypses." *Apocalypse: The Morphology of a Genre. Semeia* 14 (1979): 30–31.

———. *The Apocalyptic Imagination*. New York: Crossroad, 1984.

Collins, Rowland. "Six Words in the Blickling Homilies." In *Philological Essays: Studies in Old and Middle English Language and Literature in Honor of Herbert Dean Merritt*. Ed. James L. Rosier. The Hague: Mouton, 1970: 137–141.

———. "Blickling Homily XVI and the Dating of Beowulf." In *Medieval Studies Conference, Aachen 1983*. Ed. Wolf-Dietrich Bald and Horst Weinstock. Frankfurt, 1984: 61–69.

Cook. G. H. *The English Mediaeval Parish Church*. London: Readers Union, 1954.

Corrêa, Alicia. *The Durham Collectar*. HBS 107. London, 1992.

Cross, F. M. *The Ancient Library of Qumran*. Garden City, NY: Doubleday, 1961.

———. *Canaanite Myth and Hebrew Epic*. Cambridge: Harvard University Press, 1973.

———, Werner E. Lemke, and Patrick D. Miller, Jr., eds. *Magnalia Dei: The Mighty Acts of God*. Garden City, NY: Doubleday, 1976.

Cross, James E. "An Unrecorded Tradition of St. Michael in Old English Texts." *N&Q* n.s. 28, no. 1 (1981): 11–13.

———. "The Influence of Irish Texts and Traditions on the Old English Martyrology." *PRIA* 81C (1981): 173–92.

———. "The Latinity of the Ninth-Century Old English Martyrologist." In *Studies in Earlier Old English Prose*. Ed. Paul Szarmach. Binghamton: SUNY Press, 1982: 275–99.

———. "Source, Lexis, and Edition." In *Medieval Studies Conference, Aachen 1983*. Eds. Wolf-Dietrich Bald and Horst Weinstock. Frankfurt, 1984.

———. "An Unpublished story of Michael the Archangel and its connections." In *Magister Regis: Studies in Honor of Robert Earl Kaske*. Ed. Arthur Groos. New York: Fordham University Press, 1986: 23–35.

———. and Thomas N. Hall. "The Fragments of Homiliaries in Canterbury Cathedral Library MS Addit. 127/1 and in Kent, County Archives Office, Maidstone, MS PRC 49/2." *Scriptorium* 47 (1993): 186–192.

———, ed. *Two Old English Apocrypha and their Manuscript Source: The Gospel of Nichodemus and The Avenging of the Saviour*. Cambridge: Cambridge University Press, 1996.

——— and C. J. Tuplin. "An Unrecorded Variant of the 'Passio S. Christinae' and the Old English Martyrology." *Traditio* 36 (1980): 161–75

Cutforth, Sarah. "Delivering the Damned in Old English Homilies: An Additonal Note." *N&Q* 40 (1993): 435–37.

Dahlof, Tordis. "Det ar inte saker att sjalva vintern borjar med 'forste vinterdan': Nagra tankar kring folklig tradition och kalendarisk kunskap." *Svenksa Landsmal och Svenskt Folkliv* vol. 112(315), 1989: 36–44.

Dalton, O. M. *The History of the Franks by Gregory of Tours*. 2 vols. Oxford: Clarendon Press, 1927.

Daniell, Christopher. *Death and Burial in Medieval England: 1066–1550*. London: Routledge, 1997.

Danielou, Jean. *Les Anges et leur Mission*. Chevetogne, Belgium: Editions de Chevetogne, 1963.

David-Roy, Marguerite. "A l'époque romans chapelles hautes dédiées à Saint Michel." *Archéologia* (Paris) 106 (1977) 49–57.

Davidson, Maxwell J. *Angels at Qumran*. Sheffield Academic Press, 1992.

Davies, P. R. *1QM, The War Scroll from Qumran*. Rome: Biblical Institute Press, 1977.

Davis, P. G. "Divine Agents, Mediators, and New Testament Christology," *JTS* 45 (1994): 479–503.

Davril, A. *The Winchcombe Sacramentary*. HBS 109. London, 1995.

Debary, Michel. "Les origines du culte de Saint Michel en Bretagne." *Mémoires de la Société d'Histoire et d'Archéologie de Bretagne* (Rennes) 46 (1966): 47–65.

De Bruyne, D. "Fragments retrouvés d'apocryphes priscillianistes." *RB* 24 (1907): 318–25.

de Fraipont, M. "Les origines occidentales du type de Saint Michael debout sur le dragon." *Revue Belge d'Archéologie et d'Histoire de l'Art* 7 (1927): 289–301.

Dekkers, E. *Clavis Patrum Latinorum*. Turnhout: Brepols, 1995.

de Jerphanion, J. P. "L'origine copte du type de Saint Michel debout sur le dragon." *Comptes rendu des séances de l'Académie des Inscriptions* (1938): 367–81.

Delaruelle, Étienne. *La Piété Populaire au Moyen Age*. Torino: Bottega d'Erasmo, 1975.

Delehaye, Hippolyte. *Les Legendes hagiographiques*. Brussels, 1905. Translated as *The Legends of the Saints* by Donald Atwater. New York: Fordham University Press, 1962.

———. *Les Légendes Grecques des Saints Militaires*. New York: Arno Press, 1975.

Derolez, R. and U. Schwab. "The Runic Inscriptions of Monte S. Angelo (Gargano)," *Academiæ Analecta* (Mededelingen Letteren) 45 (1983): 97–130.

Derolez, R. "Anglo-Saxons in Rome." *Nytt om Runer* 2 (1987): 14–15.

——— and U. Schwab. "More Runes at Monte Sant'Angelo." *Nytt om Runer* 9 (1994): 18–19.

de Rossi, G. B. "Epitome libri de locis sanctorum martyrum." *Bulletino di Archeologia* 2 (1871): 88–101.

Deshman, Robert. "The Leofric Missal and English Art." *ASE* 6 (1977): 144–13.

———. *The Benedictional of Æthelwold*. Studies in Manuscript Illumination 9. Princeton: Princeton University Press, 1995.

Dewick, E. S. *The Leofric Collectar*. Vol. 1. HBS 45. London, 1914.

———. and W. H. Frere. *The Leofric Collectar*. Vol. 2. HBS 56. London, 1921.

Didion, Adolphe Napoleon. *Christian Iconography*. London, 1891.

Dix, G. H. "The Seven Archangels and the Seven Spirits: A Study in the Origin, Development, and Messianic Associations of the Two Themes." *JTS* 28 (1927): 233–53.

Dobbie, E. V. K. *The Anglo-Saxon Minor Poems*. ASPR 6. New York: Columbia University Press, 1942.

Dobiache-Rojdestvensky, Olga A. *Kult sv. Michaila v latinskom Srednovekovi*. Petrograd, 1917. Translated as *Le culte de Saint Michel et le moyen âge latin*. Paris: Auguste Picard, 1922.

Doble, G. H. "Hagiography and Folklore." *Folklore* 54 (1943).

Donahue, Charles. *The Testament of Mary*. New York: Fordham University Press, 1942.

Dubois, Dom Jacques. *Le Martyrologe d'Usuard*. Subsidia Hagiographica 40. Brussels: Société des Bollandistes, 1965.

——— and Genevieve Renaud. *Edition Pratique des Martyrologes de Bède, de l'Anonyme Lyonnais et de Florus*. Paris: Editions du Centre National de la Recherche Scientifique, 1976.

———. *Les Martyrologes du Moyen Âge Latin*. Turnhout: Brepols, 1978.

Duchesne, L. *Le Liber Pontificalis*. 2 vols. Paris: Ernst Thorin, 1886.

Dudley, Louise. *The Egyptian Elements in the Legend of the Body and Soul*. Baltimore, 1911.

Dumézil, Georges. *Naissance D'Archanges: Essai sur la formation de la théologie zoroastrienne*. Paris: Gallimard, 1945.

Dumville, David N. "Liturgical Drama and Panegyric Responsory from the Eighth Century: A Re-examination of the origin and contents of the Ninth-Century Book of Cerne." *JTS* n.s. 28 (1972): 374–406.

———. "Biblical Apocrypha and the Early Irish: A Preliminary Investigation." *PRIA* 73C (1973): 299–338.

———. *Liturgy and the Ecclesiastical History of Late Anglo-Saxon England*. Woodbridge: Boydell Press, 1992.

Düwel, Klaus. "Die Runenarbeit am Seminar für deutsche Philologie (Arbeitsstelle: Germanische Altertumskunde), Göttingen," *Nytt om Runer* 10 (1995/1996): 9.

Dwyer, M. E. "An Unstudied Redaction of the *Visio Pauli*." *Manuscripta* 32 (1988): 121–38.

Dyer, Joseph. "The Singing of Psalms in the Early-Medieval Office." *Speculum* 64 (1989): 535–78.

Eiximenis, Francesco. *De sant Miguel arcàngel: el quint tractat del "Libre dels àngels."* Ed. Curt J. Wittlin. Barcelona: Curial, 1983.

Eliason, Norman and Peter Clemoes, eds. *Ælfric's First Series of Catholic Homilies*. Vol. 13. Early English Manuscripts in Facsimile. Copenhagen: Roskilde and Bagger, 1966.

Elliott, J. K. *The Apocryphal New Testament*. Oxford: Clarendon Press, 1993.

Elliott, R. W. V. *Runes: An Introduction*. 2nd ed. New York: St. Martin's Press, 1989.

Erbe, Theodore. *Mirk's Festial: A Collection of Homilies*. EETS ES 96. London, 1905; repr. 1987.

van Esbroeck, Michel. "Les Textes Littéraires sur l'Assomption avant le Xe Siècle." In *Les Actes Apocryphes des Apôtres: Christianisme et Monde Païen*. Ed. François Bovon *et al.* Publications de la Faculté de Théologie de l'Université de Genève. Geneva: Labor et Fies, 1981, 265–85.

Evans, J. Daryll. "St. Michael in Gwent." *Gwent Local History* 70 (1991): 10–14.

Fadda, A. M. L. *Nuove omelie anglosassoni della rinascenza benedettina*. Florence: F. LeMonnier, 1977.

Farmer, David Hugh. *The Oxford Dictionary of Saints*. 3rd ed. Oxford: Oxford University Press, 1992.

Faure, Phillippe. "L'age du haut Moyen Age occidental (IVe–IXe siècles): creation ou tradition." *Médiévales* 15 (1988): 31–49

Finberg, H. P. R. *Early Charters of Wessex*. Leicester: Leicester University Press, 1964.

Fletcher, J. R. *Short History of Saint Michael's Mount*. St. Michael's Mount, Cornwall, 1951.

Focillon, H. *The Art of the West in the Middle Ages*. 2 vols. London, 1963.

Förster, Max. *Über die Quellen von Aelfrics Homiliae Catholicae, I Legenden*. Berlin, 1892.

———. "Über die Quellen von Aelfrics exegetischen Homiliae Catholicae." *Anglia* 16 (1894): 1–61.

———. "Altenglische Predigtquellen, I." *Archiv* 116 (1906): 301–307.

———. "Zur Liturgik der angelsächsischen Kirche." *Anglia* 66 (1942): 1–51.

———. "A New Version of the Apocalypse of Thomas in Old English." *Anglia* 73 (1955): 17–27.

Foulke, W. D., trans. *The History of the Langobards*. Philadelphia, 1907.

Frank, Roberta and Angus Cameron, eds. *A Plan for the Dictionary of Old English*. Toronto: University of Toronto Press, 1973.

Fros, Henry, ed. *Bibliotheca Hagiographica Latina, Novum Supplementum*. Brussels, 1986.

Gale, Tara Leigh. "In praise of the archangel Michael: piety and political accommodation in 11th-century England." Unpublished M.A. thesis, University of Alberta, 2002.

Garmonsway, G. N. *The Anglo-Saxon Chronicle*. London: Dent, 1953; repr. 1984.

Gaston, Lloyd. "Angels and Gentiles in early Judaism and in Paul." *Studies in Religion* 11 (1982): 65–75.

Gatch, Milton McC. "Eschatology in the Anonymous Old English Homilies." *Traditio* 21 (1965): 117–65.

———. *Preaching and Theology in Anglo-Saxon England*. Toronto: Toronto University Press, 1977.

Gentz, Günter. *Die Kirchen Geschichte des Nicephorus Callistus Zanthapulus und ihre Quellen*. Ed. Friedhelm Winkelmann. Texte und Untersuchungen 98. Berlin, 1966.

Gibbs, Nancy. "Angels Among Us." *Time* December 27, 1993: 46–53.

Gneuss, Helmut. *Hymnar und Hymnen im englischen Mittelalter*. Tübingen, 1968.

———. *Handlist of Anglo-Saxon Manuscripts: A List of Manuscripts and Manuscript Fragments Written or Owned in England up to 1100*. Medieval & Renaissance Texts & Studies 241. Tempe, AZ, 2001.

——— and Michael Lapidge, eds. *Learning and Literature in Anglo-Saxon England, Studies Presented to Peter Clemoes on the Occasion of his Sixty-fifth Birthday*. Cambridge: Cambridge University Press, 1985.

Godden, Malcolm. *Ælfric's Catholic Homilies, The Second Series*. EETS 5. London: Oxford University Press, 1979.

Godman, Peter. *Alcuin, The Bishops, Kings and Saints of York*. Oxford: Oxford University Press, 1982.

Gollancz, Israel. *The Caedmon Manuscript of Anglo-Saxon Biblical Poetry*. Oxford: Oxford University Press, 1927.

Gothein, E. *Die Kulturenwicklung Süd-Italiens in Einzel-Darstellungen*. Breslau: Wilhelm Koebner, 1886.

Gransden, Antonia. *The Customary of the Benedictine Abbey of Bury St. Edmunds in Suffolk.* HBS 99. London: Harrison and Sons, 1973.

———. "The Question of the Consecration of St. Edmund's Church." In *Church and Chronicle in the Middle Ages: Essays Presented to John Taylor.* Ed. Ian Wood and G. A. Loud. London and Rio Grande: Hambledon Press, 1991: 59–86.

———. "The Alleged Incorruption of the Body of St. Edmund, King and Martyr." *Antiquaries Journal* 74 (1994): 135–68.

Gransden, K. W. *Aeneid: Book XI.* Cambridge: Cambridge University Press, 1991.

Grant, Raymond J. S. *Cambridge, Corpus Christi College 41: The Loricas and the Missal.* Amsterdam: Rodopoi, 1978.

———. *Three Homilies from Cambridge, Corpus Christi College 41.* Ottawa: Tecumseh Press, 1982.

———. "Cambridge, Corpus Christi College, MS 41." Unpublished Description of the Manuscript, 1995.

Grant, R. M. "The Shepherd of Hermas." *Apostolic Fathers* vol. 6. Camden, NJ: T. Nelson, 1968.

Grattan, J. H. G. and C. Singer. *Anglo-Saxon Magic and Medicine.* London, 1952.

Greeson, Hoyt St. Clair Jr. "Two Old English Observance Poems: *Season for Fasting* and *The Menolgoium*—An Edition." Unpublished Ph.D. dissertation, University of Oregon, 1970.

Greer, Rowan A. and Leo Dupuydt. *Homiletica from the Pierpoint Morgan library: Seven Coptic Homilies Attributed to Basil the Great, John Chrysostom, and Euodius of Rome.* Lovanii: E. Peters, 1991.

Grogan, Brian O'Dwyer. "The Eschatology of the Early Irish Church." Unpublished Ph.D. dissertation, Fordham University, 1973.

———. "Eschatological Teaching in the Early Irish Church." In *Biblical Studies: The Medieval Irish Contribution.* Ed. Martin McNamara. Dublin: Dominican Publications, 1976: 46–58.

Gummes, Erik. "Ad St. Mikaels Kirker." *Maddelalderforum- Forum medievale* 1 (1982): 33.

Günzel, Beate. *Ælfwine's Prayerbook.* HBS 108. London: Boydell and Brewer, 1993.

Hiabach-Reinisch, M. *Ein neuer 'Transitus Mariae' des Pseudo-Melito.* Rome, 1962.

Hall, Thomas N. "The Evangelium Nichodemi and Vindicta Salvatoirs in Anglo-Saxon England." In *Two Old English Apocrypha and their Manuscript Source.* Ed. James E. Cross and Thomas N. Hall. Cambridge: Cambridge University Press, 1996: 36–81.

Hallander, L.-G. "Two Old English Confessional Prayers." *Stockholm Studies in Modern Philology* n.s. 3: 87–110.

Hamilton, N. *Wilhelmi Malmesbiriensis Monachi Gesta Pontificum Anglorum.* London: Longman, 1870.

Hampson, R. T. *Medii Ævi Kalendarium or Dates, Charters, and Customs of the Middle Ages with Kalendars from the Tenth to the Fifteenth Century.* 2 vols. London: Henry Kent Causton, 1841.

Handley, Rima. "British Museum MS Cotton Vespasian D. xiv." *N&Q* n.s. 21 (1974): 243–50.

Hannah, Darrell D. *Michael and Christ: Michael traditions and angel Christology in early Christianity.* Tübingen: Mohr Siebeck, 1992.

Hanson, Paul D. "Rebellion in Heaven, Azazel and Euhemeristic Heroes in 1 Enoch 6–11." *JBL* 96 (1977): 195–233.

Harper-Bill, Christopher. *The Anglo-Norman Church*. Bangor, Gwynedd: Headstart History, 1992.

Healey, Antonette diPaolo. *The Old English Vision of St. Paul*. Cambridge, MA: The Medieval Academy of America, 1978.

Heffernan, Thomas. *Sacred Biography: Saints and their Biographers in the Middle Ages*. Oxford: Oxford University Press, 1988.

Heidt, William George. *Angelology of the Old Testament*. Washington, D.C.: Catholic University of America Press, 1949.

Heist, William W. *The Fifteen Signs before Doomsday*. East Lansing: Michigan State College Press, 1952.

Heitz, Carol. "Autels et fêtes des saints (VIIe–XIe siécle)." *Cahiers de St.-Michel-de-Cruxa* 13 (1982) 75–98.

Hellholm, David. "The Problem of Apocalyptic Genre and the Apocalypse of John." In *The Society of Biblical Literature Seminar Papers*. Ed. Kent H. Richard. Missoula, MT: Scholars Press, 1982.

———. *Apocalypticism in the Mediterranean world and the Near East*. Proceedings of the International Colloquium on Apocalypticism, Uppsala, Sweden, August 12–17, 1979. Tübingen: Mohr, 1982.

Henel, H. *Studien zum altenglischen Computus*. Beiträge zur englischen Philologie 26. Leipzig, 1934; repr. 1967.

Hennig, J. "Studies in the Literary Tradition of the 'Martyrologium Poeticum.' " *PRIA* 56C (1954): 197–226.

Herbert, Máire and Martin McNamara. *Irish Biblical Apocrypha*. Edinburgh: T. and T. Clark, 1989.

Herren, Michael. "The Authorship, Date of Composition and Provenance of the so-called *Lorica Gildae*." *Ériu* 24 (1973): 35–51.

Herzfeld, George. *An Old English Martyrology*. EETS 116. London: Oxford University Press, 1900.

Hessels, J. H. *An Eighth-Century Latin-Anglo-Saxon Glossary*. Cambridge: Cambridge University Press, 1890.

Hickes, G. *Thesaurus Grammatico-Criticus et Archaeologicus*. Oxford: Oxford University Press, 1705; repr. New York, 1970.

Hill, G. F. "Apollo and St. Michael: Some Analogies." *Journal of Hellenic Studies* 36 (1916): 134–62.

Hill, Joyce. "Reform and Resistance: Preaching Styles in Late Anglo-Saxon England" in *De l'homélie au sermon: histoire de la prédication médievale*, ed. Jacqueline Hamesse and Xavier Hermand, Publications de l'Iinstitut d'Études Médiévale: Texts, Études, Congrès 14 (Louvain-la-Neuve, 1993): 15–46.

Hill, Thomas D. "Invocation of the Trinity and the Tradition of the *Lorica* in Old English Poetry." *Speculum* 56 (1981): 259–67.

——— "Delivering the Damned in Old English Anonymous Homilies and Jón Arason's 'Ljómur.' " *MÆ* 61 (1992): 75–82.

Hills, Gordon M. "The Antiquities of Bury St. Edmunds." *Journal of the British Archaeological Association* 21 (1865): 32–56.

Hohler, Christopher. "Some Service-books of the Later Saxon Church." *Tenth-Century Studies*. Chichester, 1975.

Hone, William. *The Every-Day Book or Everlasting Calendar of Popular Amusements, Sports, Pastimes, Ceremonies, Manners, Customs, and Events, Incident to Each of the Three Hundred and Sixty-five days, in Past and Present Times*. 2 vols. London, 1827.

Hope, D. M. *The Leonine Sacramentary*. Oxford: Oxford University Press, 1971.

Hughes, Andrew. *Medieval Manuscripts for Mass and Office: A guide to their organization and terminology*. Toronto: University of Toronto Press, 1982.

Hughes, Anselm. *The Portiforium of Saint Wulstan*. 2 vols. HBS 89 and 90. London: Harrison and Sons, 1958–60.

———. *The Bec Missal*. HBS 94. London: Harrison and Sons, 1961.

Hughes, Kathleen. "On an Irish Litany of Pilgrim Saints Compiled. c. 800." *AB* 77 (1959): 305–31.

Hull, P. L. *The Cartulary of St. Michael's Mount*. Devon and Cornwall Record Society, 1962.

Hulme, W. H. "The Old English Version of the Gospel of Nicodemus." *PMLA* 13 (1898): 457–542.

———. "The Old English Gospel of Nicodemus." *Modern Philology* 1 (1903–4): 579–614.

Hurst, David. *Gregory the Great: Forty Homilies on the Gospel*. Kalamazoo, MI: Cistercian Publications, 1990.

Hutton, Ronald. *The Pagan Religions of the Ancient British Isles: Their Nature and Legacy*. Oxford: Blackwell, 1991.

Jackson, Peter and Michael Lapidge. "The Contents of the Cotton-Corpus Legendary." In *Holy Men and Holy Women*. Ed. Paul Szarmach. Albany: SUNY Press, 1996: 131–146/

James, M. R. *The Testament of Abraham*. Text & Studies 2. Cambridge: Cambridge University Press, 1892.

———. *Apocrypha Anecdota: A Collection of 13 Apocryphal Bodies and Fragments*. Text & Studies 2, no. 3. Cambridge: Cambridge University Press, 1893.

———. *Apocrypha Anecdota*. 2 vols. Cambridge: Cambridge University Press, 1897–98.

———. "Names of Angels in Anglo-Saxon and other Documents." *JTS* 11 (1909/10): 569–571.

———. *A Descriptive Catalogue of the Manuscripts in the Library of Cambridge, Corpus Christi College*. 2 vols. Cambridge: Cambridge University Press, 1912.

———. *The Lost Apocrypha of the Old Testament*. London: SPCK, 1920.

———. *The Apocryphal New Testament*. Oxford: Clarendon Press, 1924.

Jameson, Anna Brownell. *Sacred and Legendary Art*. Boston: Houghton, Mifflin & Co., 1885.

Janin, R. "Les sanctuaires byzantins de Saint Michel." *Échos d'Orient* (1938): 28–52.

Johnson, David F. "The Book of Life and the Keys to Hell: Vision, Prayer, and Judgment in Late Anglo-Saxon England." Guest Lecture in series Popular Piety: Prayer, Devotion, and Cult. Loyola University, Chicago. November 22, 1996.

Johnson, Richard F. "The Cult of Saint Michael the Archangel in Anglo-Saxon England." Unpublished Ph.D. dissertation. Northwestern University, 1998.

———. "Archangel in the Margins: St. Michael in the Homilies of Cambridge, Corpus Christi College 41." *Traditio* 53 (1998): 63–91.

————. "Feasts of Saint Michael the Archangel in the Liturgy of the Early Anglo-Saxon Church: Evidence from the Eighth and Ninth Centuries." *Leeds Studies in English* n.s. 31 (2000): 55–79.

Jolly, Karen Louise, *Popular Religion in Late Saxon England: Elf Charms in Context*. Chapel Hill: The University of North Carolina Press, 1996.

Jones, Charles W. *Saints' Lives and Chronicles in Early England*. Ithaca: Cornell University Press, 1947.

Jones, H. L. *Strabo. Geography*. 3 vols. Cambridge: Harvard University Press, 1967.

Kantorowicz, Ernst. *Laudes Regiae: A Study in Liturgical Acclamations and Medieval Ruler Worship*. Berkeley: University of California Press,1958.

Keck, David. *Angels and Angelology in the Middle Ages*. Oxford: Oxford University Press, 1998.

Keefer, Sarah Larratt, "Margin as Archive: The Liturgical Marginalia of a Manuscript of the Old English Bede." *Traditio* 51 (1996): 147–77.

Kenney, James. *The Sources for the Early History of Ireland: Ecclesiastical*. New York: Octagon Books, 1966.

Ker, Neil R. "Membra Disiecta, Second Series," *British Museum Quarterly* 14 (1939–40): 82–83.

————. "Hemming's Cartulary: A Description of the Two Worcester Cartularies in Cotton Tiberius A.XIII" in *Studies in Medieval History Presented to F. M. Powicke*. Ed. R. W. Hunt, W. A. Pantin, and R. W. Southern. Oxford: Oxford University Press, 1948: 49–75.

————. *Catalogue of Manuscripts Containing Anglo-Saxon*. Oxford: Clarendon Press, 1957.

Kitzinger, E. "The Coffin-Reliquary." In *The Relics of St. Cuthbert*. Ed. C. F. Battiscombe. Oxford, 1956: 202–34.

Klee, Vincent. *Les Plus Beaux Textes sur les Saints Anges*. 2 volumes. Collection Angelologia. Paris: Nouvelles Editions Latines, 1984.

Knibb, Michael A. *The Ethiopic Book of Enoch*. 2 vols. Oxford: Oxford University Press, 1978.

————. "The Date of the Parables of Enoch: A Critical Review." *New Testament Studies* 25 (1979): 245–59.

Kolenkow, A. B. "The Genre Testament and the Testament of Abraham." In *Studies on the Testament of Abraham*. Ed. G. E. W. Nickelsburg. Missoula, MT: Scholars Press, 1976: 139–52.

Korpela, Jukka. "Mikkeli – muisto keskiaikaisesta P. Mikaelim kultista" (St. Michael – a reminiscence of the worship of St. Michael). *Historiallinen Aikakauskirja* 87:2 (1989): 83–100.

Kotzor, G. *Das altenglische Martyrologium*. 2 vols. Abhandlungen der Bayerischen Akademie der Wissenschaften, phil.-hist. Kl., n.s. 88.1–2. Munich, 1981.

Krapp, G. P. *The Junius Manuscript*. Anglo-Saxon Poetic Records 1. New York: Columbia University Press, 1931.

Kuhn, Harold. B. "The Angelology of the Non-Canonical Jewish Apocalypses." *JBL* 67 (1948): 217–32.

Kuypers, A. B. *The Prayer Book of Aedeluald the Bishop, commonly called the Book of Cerne*. Cambridge: Cambridge University Press, 1902.

Labande, Edmond-René. *Spiritualité et vie littéraire de l'Occident, Xe–XIVe s.* London: Variorum Reprints, 1974.

Lacocque, André. *The Book of Daniel.* Atlanta: John Knox, 1979.

Lapidge, Michael. "A Tenth-Century Metrical Calendar from Ramsey." *RB* 94 (1984): 326–69.

——— and Richard Sharpe. *A Bibliography of Celtic-Latin Literature: 400–1200.* Dublin: Royal Irish Academy, 1985.

———, ed. *The Anglo-Saxon Litanies of the Saints.* HBS 106. London, 1991.

———and Michael Winterbottom. *Wulfstan of Winchester: The Life of St. Æthelwold.* Oxford: Oxford University Press, 1991.

LaPorte, J., et al., eds. *Millénaire Monastique du Mont Saint-Michel.* 6 vols. Paris: Bibliothèque d'histoire et d'archéologie chrétiennes, 1965–1972 .

Laurent, M. "Le Bas-relief de Saint Michel à l'abbaye de Mardesous." *Revue Belge d'Archéologie et d'Histoire de l'Art* 8 (1938): 337–48.

Lawlor, H. J. *The Psalter and Martyrology of Ricemarch.* HBS 47. London: Harrison and Sons, 1914.

Lawrenz, Martha Abbott. "The Cult of St. Michael the Archangel as Expressed in the Art of Western Europe from the Ninth through the Twelfth centuries." Unpublished Honors Thesis, Smith College, 1962.

Leclercq, J. "Tables pour l'inventaire des homiliaires manuscrits." *Scriptorium* 2 (1948): 195–214.

———. "The 'Sunday Letter' and the 'Sunday Lists.' " *ASE* 14 (1985): 129–51.

———. "Theme and Echo in an Anonymous Old English Homily for Easter." *Traditio* 42 (1986): 115–42.

Leuken, Wilhelm. *Michael. Eine Darstellung und Vergleichung der jüdischen und der morgenländisch-christlichen Tradition von Erzengel Michael.* Göttingen: Vandenhoeck and Ruprecht, 1898.

Levison, Wilhelm. "Conspectus codicum hagiographiorum." *MGH SRM* 7 (1920): 529–706.

———. *England and the Continent in the Eighth Century.* Oxford: Oxford University Press, 1946.

Lieberman, F. *Die Gesetze der Angelsächsen.* Halle, 1903–16.

Lightfoot, J. B. *Saint Paul's Epistles to the Colossians and to Philemon.* New York: Macmillan, 1900.

Lindsay, W. M. *Isidori Hispalensis Episcopi, Etymologiarum sive Originum Libri XX.* 2 vols. Oxford: Clarendon Press, 1911.

Lögeman, H. "Anglo-Saxonica Minora." *Anglia* 11 (1889): 97–120.

Love, Rosalind. *Three Eleventh Century Anglo-Latin Saints' Lives: Vita S. Birini, vita et miracula S. Kenelmi, and Vita S. Rumwoldi.* Oxford: Clarendon Press, 1996.

Lowe, E. A. *The Bobbio Missal, A Gallican Mass-Book.* HBS 58. London: Harrison and Sons, 1920.

———, Dom André Wilmart, and H. A. Wilson. *The Bobbio Missal, Notes and Studies.* HBS 61. London, 1924.

Machielsen, J. *Clavis Patristica Pseudepigraphorum Medii Aevi. Opera Homiletica.* 2 vols. Turnhout: Brepols, 1995.

Mair, G. R. *Callimachus, Lycophron, Aratus.* Cambridge: Harvard University Press, 1940.

Mâle, E. *L'art religieux du XIIe siècle en France.* Paris: Armand Cohn, 1928.

Mango, Cyril. "St. Michael and Attis." *Deltion tês Christiankês Archaiologikês Hetaireia* 12 (1984–86): 39–62.

———. "The Pilgrimage Centre of St. Michael at Germia." *Jahrbuch der Österreichischen Byzantinistik* 36 (1986): 119–24.

Marsden, Richard. *The Text of the Old Testament in Anglo-Saxon England.* Cambridge: Cambridge University Press, 1995.

Mayr-Harting, Henry. *The Coming of Christianity to Anglo-Saxon England.* 3rd ed. University Park, PA: Pennsylvania State University Press, 1991.

McGinn, Bernard. "Early Apocalypticism: the ongoing debate." In The *Apocalypse in English Renaissance thought and literature.* Eds. C. A. Patrides and Joseph Wittreich. Ithaca: Cornell University Press, 1984: 2–39.

McGurk, Patrick. "The Metrical Calendar of Hampson." *AB* 104 (1986): 79–125.

McNally, R. E. "Der irische Liber de numeris." Unpublished Ph.D. dissertation, Munich, 1957.

Meinardus, O. F. A. "Der Erzengel Michael als Psychompompus." *Oriens Christianus* 62 (1978).

Meissner, John L. Gough. *The Celtic Church in England after the Synod of Whitby.* M.A. Thesis, Queen's University, Belfast, 1927.

Meroney, Howard. "Irish in the Old English Charms." *Speculum* 20 (1945): 172–82.

Milful, Inge B. *The Hymns of the Anglo-Saxon Church: A Study and Edition of the "Durham Hymnal."* Cambridge: Cambridge University Press, 1996.

Milik, J. T. *The Books of Enoch.* Oxford: Clarendon Press, 1976.

Miller, Thomas. *The Old English Version of Bede's Eccclesiastical History of the English People.* EETS 95 and 96. London: Oxford University Press, 1890–91.

Mills, Ludo J. R. *Angelic Monks and Earthly Men.* Woodbridge, Suffolk: Boydell Press, 1992.

Mimouni, Simon Claude. *Dormition et Assomption de Marie: Histoire des Traditions Anciennes.* Théologie Historique 98. Paris: Beauchesne, 1996.

Mombritius, B. *Sanctuarium seu Vitae Sanctorum,* 2nd ed., 2 vols. Paris, 1910.

Moore, Albert C. *Iconography of Religions.* Philadelphia: Fortress Press, 1977.

Morin, G. "La liturgie de Naples au temps du saint Grégoire d'après deux évangéliaires du septième siècle." *RB* 11 (1891): 481–93.

Morris, R. *The Blickling Homilies.* EETS 58, 63, 73. London: Oxford University Press, 1874–80.

———. *Cursor Mundi: A Northumbrian Poem of the XIVth Century.* 6 vols. London, 1874–93.

Muir, Bernard James. *A Pre-Conquest English Prayer-Book.* HBS 103. London: Harrison and Sons, 1988.

Mynors, R. A. B. *Durham Cathedral Manuscripts to the End of the Twelfth Century.* Oxford: Oxford University Press, 1939.

Napier, Arthur, ed. *Wulfstan. Sammlung der ihm zugeschriebenen Homilien nebst Untersuchungen über ihre Echtheit. I. Text und Varianten.* Berlin, 1883; repr. with appendix by K. Ostheeren, 1967.

Nau, F. and J. Bousquet. "Miracle de S. Michel à Colosses." *PO* 4 (1907): 547–62.

Nicholson, Lewis, ed. *The Vercelli Book Homilies: Translations from the Anglo-Saxon.* Lanham, MD: University Press of America, 1991.

Nickelsburg, George E. W., ed. *Studies on the Testament of Abraham*. Missoula, MT: Scholars Press, 1976.

———. "Eschatology in the Testament of Abraham: A Study of the Judgment Scenes in the Two Recensions." In *Studies on the Testament of Abraham*. Ed. G. E. W. Nickelsburg. Missoula, MT: Scholars Press, 1976: 23–64.

———. "Apocalyptic and Myth in 1 Enoch 6–11." *JBL* 96 (1977): 383–405.

Ohlgren, Thomas. "Five New Drawings in the MS *Junius 11*: Their Iconography and Thematic Significance." *Speculum* 47 (1972): 227–33.

———. *Anglo-Saxon Textual Illustration*. Kalamazoo, MI: Medieval Institute Publications, 1992.

Okasha, Elisabeth. *Hand-List of Anglo-Saxon Non-Runic Inscriptions*. Cambridge University Press, 1971.

O'Keeffe, Katherine O'Brien. *Visible Song: Transitional Literacy in Old English Verse*. CSASE Cambridge: Cambridge University Press, 1990.

Olsan, Lea. "Latin Charms of Medieval England: Verbal Healing in a Christian Oral Tradition." *Oral Tradition* 7/1 (1992): 116–42.

Openshaw, Kathleen. "Images, Texts and Contexts: The Iconography of the Tiberius Psalter, London, British Library, Cotton MS Tiberius C. VI." Unpublished Ph.D. dissertation, University of Toronto, 1990.

———. "Weapons in the Daily Battle: Images of the conquest of Evil in the Early Medieval Psalter." *The Art Bulletin* 75 (1993): 17–38.

Orchard, Andy. *Pride and Prodigies: Studies in the Monsters of the Beowulf-Manuscript*. Cambridge: D. S. Brewer, 1995.

Ortenberg, Veronica. *The English Church and the Continent in the Tenth and Eleventh Centuries*. Oxford: Clarendon Press, 1992.

Osten-Sacken, P. von der. *Gott und Belial*. Göttingen: Vandenhoeck and Ruprecht, 1969.

Otranto, Giorgio. "Il 'Liber de apparitione' e il culto di San Michele sul Gargano nella documentazione liturgica altomedievale." *Vetera Christianorum* 18:2 (1981) 423–42.

———. "Il 'Liber de Apparitione,' il santuario di san Michele sul Gargano e i Longobardi del Ducato di Benevento." In *Santuari e politica nel mondo antico*. Milan: Università Cattolica del Sacro Cuore, 1983: 210–45.

———. "Per una metodologia della ricerca storico-agiografica, il santuario micaelico del Gargano tra Bizantini e Langobardi." *Vetera Christianorum* 25 (1988): 381–405.

———and Carlo Carletti. *Il Santuario di S. Michele Archangelo sul Gargano: dalle origini al X secolo*. Bari: Edipuglia, 1990.

Owen, A. E. B. "Carlton, Reston, and Saint Michael: A Reconsideration." *Nomina: A Journal of Name Studies Relating to Great Britain and Ireland* vol. 12 (1988–1989): 105–111.

Paasche, Fredrik. "St. Michael og Hans Engle." *Edda* (1914): pp. 33–74.

Pächt, Otto. *An Introduction to English Runes*. London, 1963.

———. "A Cycle of English Frescoes in Spain." *The Burlington Magazine* 103 (1974).

———. "English Runes Imported into the Continent." In *Runische Schriftkultur in kontinental-skandinavischer und -angelsächsischer Wechselbeziehung*. Ed. Klaus Düwel. Berlin and New York: Walter de Gruyter, 1994: 181–82.

Parkes, M. B. "The Scriptorium of Wearmouth-Jarrow." Jarrow Lecture, 1982. Jarrow, 1983.

Peers, Glenn. "Holy Man, Supplicant, and Donor: On Representations of the Miracle of Michael the Archangel at Chonae." *Mediaeval Studies* 59 (1997): 173–82.

———. "Hagiographic Models of Worship of Images of Angels." *Byzantion* 67 (1997): 407–40.

———. *Subtle Bodies: Representing Angels in Byzantium* (Berkeley: University of California Press, 2001).

Percer, Leo R. "The War in Heaven: Michael and Messiah in Revelation 12." Unpublished Ph.D. dissertation, Baylor University, 1999.

Perry, M. P. "On the Psychostasis in Christian Art." *The Burlington Magazine* 22 (1912–13).

Petrucci, Armand. "Aspetti del culto e del pellegrinaggiio di S. Michele sul Monte Gargano." In *Pellegrinaggi e culto dei santi in Europa fino all prima crociata*. Atti del IV Convegno di Studi. Todi, 1963: 147–80.

Pfaff, Richard. *The Liturgical Books of Anglo-Saxon England. Old English Newsletter*, Subsidia vol. 23. Kalamazoo, MI: Medieval Institute Publications, 1995.

Picard, B. *Das altenglische Ægidiusleben in MS CCCC 303: Textedition*. Hochschulsammlung Philosophie, Literaturwissenschaft 7. Freiburg: Hochschulverlag, 1980.

Pigeon, Michel. "Le culte liturgique de St. Michel et des Saints-Anges dans l'ordre de Cîteaux." *Annuales du Mont Saint Michel* 108:4 (1982) 62–64.

Poncelet, A. *Bibliotheca Hagiographica Latina*. 2 vols. Brussels: Bollandists, 1898–1901.

Pope, John C. *Homilies of Ælfric: A Supplementary Collection*. 2 vols. EETS 260. London: Oxford University Press, 1968.

Pretucci, Armando. "Aspetti del culto e del pellegrinaggio di S. Michele sul Monte Gargano." *Pellegrinaggi e culto dei santi in Europa fino la la Crociata*. Todi, 1963.

Priebsch, Robert. "The Chief Sources of some Anglo-Saxon Homilies." *Otia Merseiana* vol. 1 (1899): 129–47.

———. *Letter from Heaven on the Observance of the Lord's Day*. Oxford: Basil Blackwell, 1936.

Pulsiano, Phillip. *An Annotated Bibliography of North American Doctoral Dissertations on Old English Language and Literature*. East Lansing, MI: Colleagues Press, 1988.

——— and Joseph McGowan. "Four Unedtied Prayers in London, British Library, Cotton Tiberius A. iii." *Mediaeval Studies* 56 (1994): 189–216.

———. "The originality of the Old English gloss of the *Vespasian Psalter* and its relation to the gloss of the *Junius Psalter*." *ASE* 25 (1996): 37–62.

Quacquarelli, Antonio. "Gli apocrifi nei riflessi di un graffito del calvario e il 'Liber de Apparitione.'" In *Il Santuario di S. Michele sul Gargano*. Eds. C. Carletti and G. Otranto. Bari: Edipuglia, 1980: 209–239.

Quasten, Johannes. "Oriental Influence in the Gallican Liturgy." *Traditio* 1 (1943): 55–78.

Quentin, H. *Les Martyrologes historiques du Moyen Âge. Étude sur la formation du martyrologe romain*. Paris, 1908.

Quinn, Esther Casier. *The Quest of Seth for the Oil of Life*. Chicago: University of Chicago Press, 1962.

Radozycka-Paoletti, Maria. "Poczatki kultu sw Michala wsrod Longobardow" (The beginning of the cult of St. Michael among the Lombards). *Kwartalnik Historyczny* 94:2 (1988): 17–28.

Raine, James. *The Historians of the Church of York and Its Archbishops*. London: Longman, 1879.

Rauer, C. "The Sources of St. Christina (Cameron B.19.130)." 2000. *Fontes Anglo-Saxonici World Wide Web Register*. http://fontes.english.ox.ac.uk. Accessed June 2004.

Rauer, C. "The Sources of St. Erasmus (Cameron B.19.097)." 2000. *Fontes Anglo-Saxonici World Wide Web Register*. http://fontes.english.ox.ac.uk. Accessed June 2004.

Rauer, Christine. *Beowulf and the Dragon: Parallels and Analogues*. Cambridge: D. S. Brewer, 2000.

———. "The Sources of the *Old English Martyrology*." ASE 32 (2003): 89–109.

Reames, Sherry L. *The Legenda aurea, A Reexamination of its Paradoxical History*. Madison: University of Wisconsin Press, 1985.

Renner, A. *Der Erzengel Michael in der Geistes- und Kunstgeschichte* (1927).

Rice, D. Talbot. *The Beginnings of Christian Art*. London, 1957.

Rickert, M. *Painting in Britain: The Middle Ages*. London: Harmondsworth, 1954.

Ringot, René. *Saint Michel: Très Glorieux Prince des Archanges* Arras, 1951.

von Rintelen, Wolfgang. *Kultgeographische Studien in der Italia byzantine*. Archiv für vergleichende Kulturwissenschaft 3 (Meisenheim am Glan: Anton Hain, 1968).

Robb, Alan P. "The History of the Holy Rood-Tree: Four Anglo-Saxon Homilies." Unpublsihed Ph.D. Dissertation, University of Illinois at Urbana-Champaign, 1975.

Robertson, A. J. *Anglo-Saxon Charters*. 2nd ed. Cambridge: Cambridge University Press, 1956.

Robinson, Forbes. *Coptic Apocryphal Gospels*. Cambridge: Cambridge University Press, 1896.

Rodgers, Barbara Saylor. "Constantine's Pagan Vision." *Byzantion* 50 (1980): 259–78.

Rohland, J. P. *Der Erzengel Michael: Arzt und Feldherr. Zwei Aspekte des vor- und frühbyzantinischen Michaelskultes*. Leiden: E. J. Brill, 1977.

Rosenthal, Jane E. "The Historiated Canon Tables of the Arenberg Gospels." Unpublished Ph.D. dissertation, Columbia University, 1974.

de Rossi, G. B. "Epitome libri de locis sanctorum martyrum." *Bulletino di Archeologia* 2 (1871).

Rost, L. "Zum Buch der Kriege der Söhne des Lichts gegen die Söhne der Finsternis." *Theologische Literaturzeitung* 80 (1955).

Rousseau, Philip. "The Spiritual Authority of the 'Monk-Bishop': Eastern Elements in some Western hagiography of the Fourth and Fifth Centuries." *JTS* n.s. 23 (1971): 380–419.

Rowell, Geoffrey. *The Liturgy of Christian Burial*. London: SPCK, 1977.

Rudolph, Kurt. *Gnosis: The Nature and History of Gnosticism*. San Francisco: Harper & Row, 1987.

Ruggerini, M. E. "L'eroe germanico contro avversi mostruosi: tra testo e iconografia." *La funzione dell'eroe germanico: storicità, metafora, paradigma*. Ed. T. Pàroli. (Rome, 1995): 201–57.

———. "St. Michael in the *Old English Martyrology*." *Studi e materiali di Storia del'le Religioni* 65 (1999): 181–97.

Rule, Martin. *The Missal of St. Augustine's Abbey, Canterbury*. Cambridge: Cambridge University Press, 1896.

Rushing, Dorothy. "The St. Michael legends in Anglo-Saxon and Middle English."

Unpublsihed Ph.D. dissertation, University of Illinois at Urbana-Champaign, 1949.

Rutherford, R. "The Apocalypse of the Virgin, or the Apocalypse of the Holy Mother of God concerning the Chastisements." In *Ante-Nicene Fathers*, vol. 9. Ed. A. Menzies. New York, 1903, 169–74.

Ryan, Granger and Helmut Ripperger. *The Golden Legend of Jacobus de Voragine*. New York: Arno Press, 1969.

Sadlek, Gregory M. "The Archangel and the Cosmos: The Inner Logic of the South English Legendary's 'St. Michael'." *Studies in Philology* 85 (1988): 177–91.

Sawyer, P. H. *Anglo-Saxon Charters: An Annotated List and Bibliography*. London, 1968.

Saxer, Victor. "Jalons pour servir a l'histoire du culte de l'archange saint Michel en orient jusqu'a l'iconoclasme." *Noscere Sancta: Misellanea in memroia di Agostino Amore*. Rome, 1985.

Schiller, Gertrud. *Iconography of Christian Art*. London: Lund Humphries, 1971.

Schipper, J. *König Alfreds Übersetzung von Bedas Kirchengeschichte*. Bibliothek der angelsächsischen Prosa 4. Leipzig 1897.

Schroff, Lois. *The Archangel Michael*. Herndon, VA: Newlight Books, 1990.

Schwab, U. "More Anglo-Saxon Runic Graffitti in Roman Catacombs," *Old English Newsletter* 37.1 (2003): 36–39.

Scragg, Donald. "Vernacular Homilies and Prose Saints' Lives before Ælfric." *ASE* 8 (1979): 223–77.

———. *The Vercelli Homilies*. EETS 300. Oxford: Oxford University Press, 1992.

——— and Kathryn Powell, eds. *Apocryphal Texts and Traditions in Anglo-Saxon England*. Cambridge: D. S. Brewer, 2003.

Serpilli, Bonifacio M. *L'Offertorio della Messa dei defunti*. Rome: Tipografia Agostiniana, 1946.

Sheldon, Suzanne Eastman. "Middle English and Latin Charms, Amulets, and Talismans from Vernacular Manuscripts." Unpublished Ph.D. dissertation, Tulane University, 1978.

Silverstein, Theodore. *Visio Sancti Pauli*. Studies and Documents 4. London, 1935.

———. "The Vision of St. Paul: New Links and Patterns in the Western Tradition." *Archives d'histoire doctrinale et littéraire du moyen âge* 26 (1959): 199–248.

———. "The Date of the 'Apocalypse of Paul.' " *Mediæval Studies* 24 (1962): 335–348.

——— and A. Hilhorst. *Apocalypse of Paul: A New Critical Edition of Three Long Latin Versions*. Cahiers d'Orientalisme 21. Geneva, 1997.

Simon, Jean. "Homélie copte inédite sur S. Michel et le Bon Larron, attribuée à S. Jean Chrysostome." *Orientalia* 3 (1934): 217–22.

———. "Homélie copte inédite sur S. Michel et le Bon Larron, attribuée à S. Jean Chrysostome." *Orientalia* 4 (1935): 222–34.

Sims-Williams, Patrick. *Religion and Literature in Western England 600–800*. CSASE Cambridge: Cambridge University Press, 1990.

Sisam, Kenneth. *Studies in the History of Old English Literature*. Oxford: Oxford University Press, 1953.

Sivo, Vito. "Ricerche sulla tradizione manoscritta e sul testo dell'Apparitio latina." In *Culto e Insediamenti*. Eds. C. Carletti and G. Otranto. Bari: Edipuglia, 1994: 95–106.

Skeat, W. W. *Ælfric's Lives of Saints*. 4 vols. EETS 76, 82, 94, 114. London, 1881–1900; repr. in 2 vols. 1966.

Smetana, Cyril. "Aelfric and the Early Medieval Homiliary." *Traditio* 15 (1959): 163–204.

———. "Aelfric and the Homiliary of Haymo of Halberstadt." *Traditio* 17 (1961): 457–69.

Sparks, H. F. D. *The Apocryphal Old Testament.* Oxford: Clarendon Press, 1992.

Stegmüller, F. *Repertorium Biblicum Medii Aevi.* 11 vols. Madrid, 1950– .

Stevenson, J. *The Latin Hymns of the Anglo-Saxon Church.* Durham, 1851.

Stokes, Whitley, ed. *Félire Óengusso Céli Dé, or The Martyrology of Œngus the Culdee.* HBS 29. London, 1905.

Stone, L. *Sculpture in Britain: The Middle Ages.* Penguin, 1955.

Stone, M. E. "Lists of Revealed Things in the Apocalyptic Literature." In *Magnalia Dei: The Mighty Acts of God.* Eds. F. M. Cross *et al.* Doubleday, 1976: 414–52.

Suter, D. W. "Fallen Angel, Fallen Priest: The Problem of Family Purity in 1 Enoch 6–16." *Hebrew Union College Annual* 50 (1979): 115–35.

———. "Weighed in the Balance: The Similitudes of Enoch in Recent Discussion." *Religious Studies Review* 7 (1981): 217–21.

Szarmach, Paul. *Vercelli Homilies IX–XXIII.* Toronto: Toronto University Press, 1981.

——— and V. D. Oggins. *Sources of Anglo-Saxon Culture.* Studies in Medieval Culture 20. Kalamazoo, MI: Medieval Institute Publications, 1986.

———, ed. *Studies in Earlier Old English Prose.* Binghamton: SUNY Press, 1986.

———, ed. *Holy Men and Holy Women: Old English Prose Saints' Lives and Their Contexts.* Binghamton: SUNY Press, 1996.

Szöverffy, J. *Latin Hymns.* Turnhout: Brepols, 1989.

Temple, Elzbieta. *Anglo-Saxon Manuscripts: 900–1066.* London: Harvey Miller, 1976.

Thompson, E. A. *Romans and Barbarians.* Madison: University of Wisconsin Press, 1982.

Thorpe, Benjamin. *Ancient Laws and Institutes of England.* 2 vols. London, 1840.

———. *The Homilies of the Anglo-Saxon Church: The First Part, Containing the Sermones Catholici, or Homilies of Ælfric.* London: The Ælfric Society, 1844–46.

———. *Diplomatarium Anglicum aevi Saxonici.* London, 1865.

Tischendorf, Constantin. *Apocalypses Apocryphae Mosis, Esdrae, Pauli, Iohannis item Mariae Dormitio.* Leipzig: Herman Mendelssohn, 1866.

Trigg, J. W. "The Angel of Great Counsel: Christ and the Angelic Hierarchy in Origen's Theology." *JTS* 42 (1991): 35–51.

Tristram, H. L. C. *Vier altenglische Predigten aus der heterodoxen Tradition, mit Kommentar, Übersetzung und Glossar sowie drei weiteren Texten im Anhang.* Freiburg, 1970.

Tromp, Johannes. *The Assumption of Moses: A Critical Edition with Commentary.* SVTP 10. Leiden, 1993.

Trotta, Marco. "I luoghi del Liber de Apparitione. Il santuario di S. michele dal V all'VIII secolo." In *Culto e Insediamenti.* Eds. C. Carletti and G. Otranto. Bari: Edipuglia, 1994: 125–66.

Turmel, J. "Histoire de l'angéologie des temps apostolique á la fin du Ve siècle." *Revue d'histoire et de littérature religieuses* 3, 1898.

Turner, D. H. *The Missal of the New Minster, Winchester.* HBS 93. London: Harrison and Sons, 1960.

Van Dam, Raymond. *Saints and their Miracles in Late Antique Gaul.* Princeton: Princeton University Press, 1993.

van Esbroeck, Michel. "Les Textes Littéraires sur l'Assomption avant le Xe Siècle." In

Les Actes Apocryphes des Apôtres: Christianisme et Monde Païen. Ed. François Bovon *et al.* Publications de la Faculté de Théologie de l'Université de Genève. Geneva: Labor et Fies, 1981, 265–85.

Vauchez, André. *La Sainteté en Occident aux derniers siècles du moyen âge: D'après les procès du canonisation et les documents hagiographiques.* Palais Farnèse: École Française de Rome, 1981.

Vermeule, Emily. *Aspects of Death in Early Greek Art and Poetry.* Berkeley: University of California Press, 1979.

Vogel, Cyrille. *Medieval Liturgy: An Introduction to the Sources.* Revised and translated by William G. Story and Niels Krogh Rasmussen. Washington, D.C.: The Pastoral Press, 1986.

von Rintelen, Wolfgang. *Kultgeographische Studien in der Italia byzantine.* Archiv für Vergleichende Kulturwissenschaft 3 (Meisenheim am Glan: Anton Hain, 1968).

Waitz, G. ed. "Liber de apparitione Sancti Michaelis in Monte Gargano." *MGH SRL.* Hanover, 1878: 541–43.

Wallace-Hadrill, J. M. *Bede's Ecclesiastical History of the English People: A Historical Commentary.* Oxford: Clarendon Press, 1988.

Ward, Benedicta. *Miracles and the Medieval Mind: Theory, Record, and Event, 1000–1215.* Philadelphia, 1982.

Warner, Rubie D.-N. *Early Enlgish Homilies from the Twelfth Century Manuscript Vespasian D xiv.* EETS OS 152. London: Oxford University Press, 1917.

Warren, F. E. *The Leofric Missal.* Oxford: Clarendon Press, 1883.

———. *The Antiphonary of Bangor.* HBS 10. London: Harrison and Sons, 1910.

Weatherly, Edward. *Speculum Sacerdotale.* EETS OS 200. London: 1936; repr. 1988.

Webber, Teresa. *Scribes and Scholars at Salisbury Cathedral c. 1075–c. 1175.* Oxford: Clarendon Press, 1992.

Wenger, Antoine. *L'Assomption de la Trés Sainte Vierge dans la Tradition Byzantine du VIe au Xe Siècle.* Paris: Institut Français d'Études Byzantines, 1955.

West, M. L. *Iambi et Elegi Graeci.* Oxford: Oxford University Press, 1992.

Wiegand, F. *Der Erzengel Michael in der bilden Kunst.* 1886.

Wieland, Gernot. *The Canterbury Hymnal.* Toronto Medieval Latin Texts 12. Toronto: Pontifical Institute of Mediaeval Studies, 1982.

Willard, Rudolph. "The Vercelli Homilies: An Edition of Seven Homilies from the Old English Vercelli Codex." Unpublished Ph.D. dissertation, Yale University, 1925.

———. *Two Apocrypha in Old English Homilies.* Beiträge zur englischen Philologie 30. Leipzig, 1935.

———. "On Blickling Homily XIII: 'The Assumption of the Virgin'." *The Review of English Studies* 12, no. 45 (1936): 1–17.

———. "The Two Accounts of the Assumption in Blickling Homily XIII." *The Review of English Studies* 14, no. 53 (1938): 1–19.

———, ed. *The Blickling Homilies.* EEMF 10. Copenhagen: Roskilde and Bagger, 1960.

Williams, A. L. "The Cult of the Angels at Colossæ." *JTS* 10 (1909): 413–38.

Williamson, G.A., trans. *Eusebius. The History of the Church from Christ to Constantine.* New York: Dorset, 1984.

Wilmart, André. *Analecta Reginensia: Extraits des Manuscrits Latins de la Reine Christine conservés au Vatican.* Rome: Vatican Library, 1933.

———. "Un témoin anglo-saxon du calendrier métrique d'York." *RB* 46 (1954): 41–69.

———. *Auteurs Spirituels et Textes Dévots du Moyen Age Latin.* Paris, 1971.

Wilson, David. *Anglo-Saxon Art.* Woodstock, New York: The Overlook Press, 1984.

Wilson, H. A. *The Missal of Robert of Jumièges.* HBS 11. London: Harrison and Sons, 1896.

———. *The Benedictional of Archbishop Robert.* HBS 24. London: Harrison and Sons, 1903.

———. *The Calendar of St. Willibrord.* HBS 55. London: Harrison and Sons, 1918.

Wilson, Peter Lambron. *Angels.* London: Thames and Hudson, 1980.

Wilson, Stephen. *Saints and their Cults: Studies in Religious Sociology, Folklore, and History.* Cambridge: Cambridge University Press, 1983.

Woodward, Kenneth L. "Angels: The Latest Search for Spiritual Meaning." *Newsweek* December 27, 1993.

Wormald, Francis. *English Kalendars before A.D. 1100.* HBS 72. London: Harrison and Sons, 1934.

———. "An English Eleventh-Century Psalter." *Walpole Society* 38 (1960–62): 1–13.

Wright, Charles D. "Some Evidence for an Irish Origin of Redaction XI of the *Visio Pauli.*" *Manuscripta* 34 (1990): 34–44.

———. "The Three 'Victories' of the Wind: A Hibernicism in the *Hisperica Famina, Collectanea Bedae,* and the Old English Prose *Solomon and Saturn* Pater Noster Dialogue." *Ériu* 41 (1990): 13–25.

———. *The Irish Tradition in Old English Literature.* CSASE 6. Cambridge: Cambridge University Press, 1993.

Wright, W. *Contributions to the Apocryphal Literature of the New Testament.* London: Williams and Norgate, 1865.

Yadin, Yigael. *The Scroll of the War of the Sons of Light Against the Sons of Darkness.* Oxford: Oxford University Press, 1962.

Zettel, Patrick H. "Ælfric's Hagiographic Sources and the Legendary Preserved in B. L. MS Cotton Nero E i + CCCC MS 9 and other Manuscripts." Unpublished doctoral thesis, University of Oxford, 1979.

———. "Saints' Lives in Old English: Latin Manuscripts and Vernacular Accounts: Ælfric." *Peritia* 1 (1982): 17–37.

Zupitza, J. *Ælfrics Grammatik und Glossar.* Sammlung englischer Denkmäler 1. Berlin, 1880; repr. with introduction by H. Gneuss, 1966.

Index